© 2025 J.I. Roe

All rights reserved. No part of this book may be reproduced, stored in a retrieval system, or transmitted in any form or by any means—electronic, mechanical, photocopying, recording, or otherwise—without the prior written permission of the publisher, except in the case of brief quotations used in reviews, articles, or scholarly works.
Copyright registration pending.
Scripture quotations are taken from the Hebrew Bible and Greek New Testament, translated and harmonized by the author with reference to various ancient manuscripts and commentaries.
ISBN (Hardback): 979-8-9996142-6-1
ISBN (Paperback): 979-8-9996142-9-2
ISBN (eBook/Kindle): 979-8-9996142-0-9
First Edition
Cover design by J.I. Roe
Published by Ha'Derekh Publishing
www.derekhtzar.com
Printed in the United States of America
Library of Congress Control Number: [Pending]
Publisher's Cataloging-in-Publication Data:
Roe, J.I., author.
The Biography of the Son of God: A Gospel Harmony / J.I. Roe
Includes Scripture references and commentary.
1. Gospels—Harmonies. 2. Bible—Study and teaching. 3. Yeshua (Jesus)—Biography. 4. Messianic Judaism. 5. New Testament Commentary.

Table of Contents

Preface

Introduction

Prologue

Ch. 1: The Birth of John the Baptist

Ch. 2: The Birth of Jesus

Ch. 3: Jesus Prepares for his Ministry

Ch. 4: Jesus Begin His Ministry

Ch. 5: Jesus Meets with Nicodemus

Ch. 6: Jesus Becomes More Popular

Ch. 7: Jesus Starts His Galilean Ministry

Ch. 8: The Sermon on the Mount

Ch. 9: The Controversy Begins

Ch. 10: Yeshua Returns to Galilee

Ch. 11: The Spread of the Gospel

Ch. 12: Second Year Ministry Begins

Ch. 13: Jesus Begins His Judean Ministry

Ch. 14: Jesus Begins His Perean Ministry

Ch. 15: The Countdown to the Final Passover

Ch. 16: The Final Hours Spent with His Disciples

Ch. 17: The Trial and Crucifixion

Ch. 18: The Resurrection and Ascension

Preface

In every generation, people have sought to know the life of Yeshua, the Son of God — to see His story not as fragments or separate accounts, but as one harmonious whole. The Gospels of Matthew, Mark, Luke, and John each bear unique witness to His birth, ministry, death, and resurrection. Together, they form a tapestry of divine purpose, fulfillment, and light shining in the darkness.

This work, The Biography of the Son of God: A Gospel Harmony, is my humble attempt to weave those sacred threads into a single, continuous narrative — one that remains faithful to the Word of God, yet draws the reader into the living world of the Gospels. I have sought not only to harmonize the events of Yeshua's life, but also to capture what the people of His day may have seen, felt, and experienced. For this reason, you will find certain embellishments woven through these pages — not to add to Scripture, but to help the reader walk beside those who heard His voice, witnessed His wonders, and pondered His words.

Hebrew names and divine titles are preserved out of reverence for the culture and covenant in which Yeshua lived and taught. The Torah, the Prophets, and the Psalms echo through this harmony, pointing always to the Messiah, the Light that shines in the darkness, the One whom the darkness has not overcome.

My prayer is that this biography helps you behold His life as those who first followed Him did — with awe, wonder, and longing for the Kingdom of GOD. May it stir your heart to seek His face and delight in His ways.

All glory to GOD Most High, who in His mercy sent us His Anointed One.

Introduction

The story of Yeshua of Nazaret is not merely a spiritual biography — it is a Jewish story. It is deeply rooted in the land, language, culture, and faith of first-century Israel. This book presents a chronological harmony of the four Gospels, crafted to restore their original Hebraic flavor and historical setting.

Rather than approaching the life of Yeshua as a detached theological abstraction, this harmony traces each step of his journey through a Jewish lens. The names of people and places have been rendered in transliterated Hebrew to reflect the authentic sounds of the time. The teachings and actions of Yeshua are shown not in isolation, but alongside the rich background of the Torah, the Prophets, and the Writings — as well as the insights preserved in Chassidic thought, the Oral Torah, and Talmudic tradition.

Throughout this book, you will find charts and side-by-side comparisons designed to bring context and clarity. These include historical timelines and events, Gospel harmonies, and tables of parallel teachings — all intended to illuminate how Yeshua's words and deeds aligned with and revived the spirit of Torah-faithful Judaism.

This work is not written to promote theological dogma, but to help both Jew and Gentile see the man from Galilee within his rightful context: as a Torah-observant sage, filled with the Ruach of Elohim, calling Israel back to covenant faithfulness.

Whether you are a scholar, a seeker, or a student of Scripture, may this book help you walk the ancient paths and rediscover the Jewish Messiah in his true light.

Prologue:

In the beginning was the Word—the Logos, the Memra—and the Word was with GOD, and the Word was Divine. GOD possessed the Torah from the very beginning, before His works of old. From eternity it was established; before the earth began, the Word was formed.

When there was no deep, the Word was brought forth. When there were no springs abounding with water, before the mountains were settled, before the hills were shaped, the Word stood beside Him. Before Adonai made the earth, the fields, or even the first dust of the world, the Torah was with Him as the master craftsman.

When He established the heavens, the Torah was there. When He inscribed the horizon upon the face of the deep, when He made firm the skies above, when the springs of the deep burst forth, when He set boundaries for the sea so that the waters would not transgress His command, when He marked out the foundations of the earth—then the Torah was His delight, rejoicing always before Him, rejoicing in His inhabited world, and delighting in the children of men.

All things were created through it; without it nothing came into being. In the Word was life, and that life was the light of men. The light shines in the darkness, and the darkness has not overcome it. From the beginning this light was destined to reveal the glory of GOD to all creation.

This prologue merges Yochanan's (John's) opening verses with Mishlei (Proverbs) 8 and Jewish mystical tradition, affirming that the Torah is the eternal blueprint through which Elohim created the world. The Memra or Logos—the Word—is not a separate being, but the living Torah, the will and wisdom of Elohim expressed. This aligns with Jewish thought and brings new understanding to the gospel of John.

CHAPTER 1 — The Birth of John the Baptist

The Angel Visits Zechariah　　　　　　　　　　　　　　　　　　　　　　　Luke 1:5–25

In those days, when King Herod ruled over Judea with an iron fist, the land lay beneath the shadow of Rome, and the hearts of the people were weary. The priests carried out their sacred duties in the Temple, offering incense and prayers on behalf of a nation longing for redemption. Among these priests was a man named Zechariah, of the division of Abijah—a man of quiet devotion, known for his steady service at the altar of Adonai.

Zechariah's wife, Elizabeth, shared his priestly heritage, for she was descended from the daughters of Aaron. Together, they lived uprightly, keeping the commandments and statutes of the Torah, blameless in the eyes of GOD. Yet despite their faithfulness, a deep sorrow marked their lives: they had no child. The years had passed, and the hope of holding a son or daughter had withered like the grass of the field under the summer sun. Their home, though filled with prayer, remained silent of a child's laughter.

> In the Second Temple era, the priesthood was divided into 24 divisions, each serving one week in the Temple, with all divisions serving during the three pilgrimage festivals (Pesach, Shavuot, Sukkot). Zechariah, of the Aviyah division (8th in line), likely served in the second half of Sivan (June) of 8 BCE, delayed slightly due to Shavuot. During his service, an angel appeared, announcing that his wife Elisheva (Elizabeth) would bear a son—Yochanan (John). She likely conceived in late Sivan or early Tammuz (June/July). Six months later, Miriam (Mary) conceived Yeshua around Tevet (December/January), as recorded in Luke 1. This places Yochanan's birth in Nisan (March/April) and Yeshua's birth in Tishrei (September/October) of 7 BCE, aligning with the Feast of Sukkot. This timing reflects deep Messianic symbolism: "The Word dwelled (tabernacled) among us" (John 1:14), connecting his birth to the joy and presence of Elohim during Sukkot

---

It was during one of these appointed times for the division of Abijah to serve in the Temple that Zechariah's story took a wondrous turn. He was chosen by lot to enter the sanctuary of Adonai and burn incense upon the altar—a sacred duty performed in solitude. While the fragrant smoke rose and the assembly of people prayed outside, without warning, the veil between heaven and earth seemed to part. A radiant figure—the Angel of Adonai—appeared to the right of the altar of incense.

When Zechariah saw him, he jumped in shock, his heart seized with fear.

But the angel spoke to him with gentle authority: "Calm down, Zechariah; there is no need to fear. Your prayer has been heard. Your wife Elizabeth will bear you a son, and you shall name him John. There will be joy and happiness for you, and many will rejoice at his birth. For he will be great in the eyes of Adonai. He will never drink wine or strong liquor, and he will be filled with the Holy Spirit even in his mother's womb. He will turn many of the children of Israel to Adonai their GOD. He will go before Him in the spirit and power of Elijah, to turn the hearts of the fathers to their children, and the disobedient to the understanding of the righteous, to make ready for Adonai a prepared people."

Zechariah's heart pounded in his chest. Could it be true? Could hope, long buried, rise again? And yet doubt found its voice: "How can I know this? For I am an old man, and my wife is well along in years."

The angel straightened, his voice now filled with heavenly weight: "I am Gabriel, who stands in the presence of GOD. I was sent to speak to you and tell you this good news. Now listen! You will become mute and unable to speak until the day these things take place, because you did not believe my words, which will be fulfilled at their appointed time."

Zechariah, as a priest of Adonai, should not have doubted the angel's message, for Adonai had delivered a similar promise to Abraham and Sarah in their old age.

Outside, the people waited, concerned by Zechariah's delay. They murmured among themselves: "Why is Zechariah taking so long?" and another said, "Has something gone wrong?"

When at last he emerged, his face was pale, his hands trembling. He tried to speak, to explain, but no words came. Only frantic gestures. The people realized he must have seen a vision in the sanctuary.

Days passed. Zechariah completed his service in the Temple and returned home. And soon the impossible happened: Elizabeth conceived. The barren woman, now with child, kept herself in seclusion for five months, treasuring the miracle and whispering in her prayers:

"Adonai has done this for me. He has looked on me with favor to take away my shame among the people."

The Angel Visits the Virgin Miriam   Luke 1:26–38

In the sixth month, far from the Temple courts and priestly orders, in a humble village of Galilee called Nazareth, another wonder began. A young virgin named Miriam, betrothed to Joseph of the house of David, lived quietly, perhaps dreaming of her coming marriage, tending to her daily tasks. No one would have marked her among the crowds. Yet heaven had marked her from eternity.

As she went about her day, suddenly a visitor from beyond this world stood before her: Gabriel, sent by GOD. The angel said: "Rejoice, favored woman! Adonai is with you!"

Miriam froze, startled by the greeting, her mind racing. What could this mean? Why would an angel address her so?

Seeing her distress, the angel spoke in a calming tone: "Fear not, Miriam, for you have found favor with GOD. Now listen: You will conceive and bear a son, and you are to call him

Yeshua. He will be great and will be called the Son of El Elyon. Adonai GOD will give him the throne of his father David, and he will reign over the house of Jacob forever; his kingdom will be everlasting."

Miriam, filled with wonder but confused, asked: "How can this be, since I am still a virgin?"

The angel replied with the authority of heaven: "The Holy Spirit will come upon you, and the power of El Elyon will overshadow you. Therefore, the holy one to be born will be called the Son of GOD. Even now, your relative Elizabeth has conceived a son in her old age, and she who was called barren is in her sixth month. For nothing is impossible with GOD."

With trembling faith and deep humility, Miriam said: "I am the servant of Adonai. May it be done for me according to your word." Then the angel departed.

Miriam Visits Elizabeth Luke 1:39–56

Not long after, Miriam set out for the hill country of Judea, eager to see the sign given to her. The path was long, but hope lightened her steps. Upon arriving, she entered Zechariah's house and greeted Elizabeth. When Elizabeth heard Miriam's greeting, the baby leaped within her. Filled with the Holy Spirit, Elizabeth cried out:

> "Blessed are you among women, and blessed is the child you will bear! But why am I so favored, that the mother of my Lord should come to me? As soon as your greeting reached my ears, the baby in my womb leaped for joy. Blessed is she who has believed that what Adonai has said to her will be fulfilled!"

And Miriam, moved by the Spirit, lifted her voice in praise:

> "My soul magnifies Adonai, and my spirit rejoices in GOD my Savior, for He has looked upon the humble state of His servant. From now on all generations will call me blessed, for the Mighty One has done great things for me—holy is His name. His mercy extends to those who fear Him, from generation to generation. He has performed mighty deeds with His arm; He has scattered the proud in the imagination of their hearts. He has brought down rulers from their thrones but lifted up the humble. He has filled the hungry with good things but sent the rich away empty. He has helped His servant Israel, remembering to be merciful to Abraham and his descendants forever, just as He promised our ancestors."

Miriam stayed with Elizabeth for about three months before returning home.

The Birth of Yochanan the Immerser Luke 1:57–80

When Elizabeth's time came, her house was filled with joy. Friends, neighbors, and relatives gathered, praising GOD for His mercy. On the eighth day, at the boy's circumcision, they assumed he would be named Zechariah after his father. But Elizabeth spoke firmly:

"No. His name shall be John." She said resolutely.

"But none of your relatives bears that name." They said clearly confused.

They made signs to Zechariah to ask what he wanted to name the child. He asked for a tablet and wrote: "His name is John."

All were amazed. At that moment, Zechariah's mouth was opened, his tongue set free, and he began to praise GOD. Fear came upon all who lived nearby, and throughout the hill country of Judea, people spoke of these things. All who heard it pondered and said:

"What then will this child become?" For the hand of Adonai was with him.

Filled with the Holy Spirit, Zechariah prophesied:

> "Blessed be Adonai, the GOD of Israel, for He has visited and redeemed His people. He has raised up a horn of salvation for us in the house of His servant David, as He said through His holy prophets of long ago—salvation from our enemies and from the hand of all who hate us, to show mercy to our ancestors and to remember His holy covenant, the oath He swore to our father Abraham: to rescue us from the hand of our enemies, to enable us to serve Him without fear in holiness and righteousness before Him all our days.
> And you, my child, will be called a prophet of El Elyon; for you will go before Adonai to prepare His ways, to give His people the knowledge of salvation through the forgiveness of their sins, because of the tender mercy of our GOD, by which the dawn from on high will visit us, to shine on those who sit in darkness and in the shadow of death, to guide our feet into the way of peace."

And the child grew and became strong in spirit. He lived in the wilderness until the day of his public appearance to Israel.

Chapter 2 – The Birth of Yeshua of Nazareth

A Righteous Man's Dilemma Matthew 1:18–21

Now the birth of the Messiah Yeshua was suspected; when as his mother Miriam was espoused to Joseph before they came together, she was discovered to have been impregnated by the Holy Spirit. Though Joseph her husband was a righteous man and was unwilling to make her a public example, so he thought to divorce her privately. But while he was meditating on these things, suddenly, the Angel of Adonai appeared to him in a dream, saying, "Joseph, Son of David, do not fear to take Miriam for your wife for the baby conceived in her is of the Holy Spirit. She shall give birth to a son, and you are to name him Yeshua for he shall save his people from their sins."

Immanuel Foretold Matthew 1:22–25

Now all this was done that it might be fulfilled which was spoken by Adonai through the prophet saying, "Behold a virgin shall conceive, and shall give birth to a son and they shall call his name Immanuel", which being interpreted is GOD with us. Then Joseph being awakened from his sleep did as the Angel of Adonai commanded him and took unto him his wife: and he did not have intimate relations with her until after she gave birth to her firstborn son: and called his name Yeshua.

From Nazareth to Bethlehem 7 BCE Luke 2:1–7

In those days, a decree went out from Caesar Augustus that the entire Roman empire should be registered. It was a census requiring every man to return to the town of his ancestors. And so, all went to be registered, each to his own city.

Yosef also went up from the town of Natzeret in the Galil to the region of Yehudah, to the city of David, which is called Beit-Lechem (Bethlehem), because he was of the house and lineage of David. He journeyed there to be registered, taking with him Miryam, to whom he was betrothed, and who at that time was carrying a child within her womb.

While they were staying in Beit-Lechem, the days were completed for her to give birth. And she brought forth her firstborn son, wrapped him in swaddling clothes, and lovingly laid him in a manger—because there was no room for them in any of the inns.

A Midnight Revelation Luke 2:8–14

In the same region, shepherds were guarding their flocks in the fields at night, and the Angel of Adonai appeared before them and the Glory of Adonai illuminated the fields around them, and they were terrified. The Angel of Adonai calmed them saying; "Fear not, for behold I bring you good news of a great joy that will be for all people. For to you this day a Savior who is Messiah the Lord was born in the city of David. This will be the sign for you: You will find the baby wrapped in swaddling clothes and lying in a manger."

Suddenly there was a multitude of the heavenly host with the Angel, praising GOD and singing:
"Glory to GOD in the Highest heaven! And Peace on Earth to people He favors!"

The Shepherds Witness the Sign   Luke 2:15–20

When the Angels had left them and returned to heaven, the Shepherds said to each other, "Let us hurry to Bethlehem and see what has happened, which Adonai has revealed to us!" Their hearts were pounding with awe, their breaths quick in the crisp night air as they gathered their cloaks and ran. The scent of sheep still clung to them as they moved through the fields toward the village, the sky above still echoing with a distant hush of glory. They hurried off and found both Miriam and Joseph, and the baby who was lying in the manger. The flickering lantern light revealed the quiet scene—Miriam's tired yet glowing face, Joseph's protective presence beside her, and the newborn sleeping peacefully in the feeding trough lined with straw.

After seeing them, they reported the message they were told about this child, their voices full of urgency and wonder, and all who heard it were amazed at what the shepherds said to them. But Miriam was treasuring all these things in her heart and meditating upon them. Her eyes glistened as she held the infant close, the words of strangers only deepening the mystery she quietly pondered.

The shepherds returned glorifying and praising GOD for all they had seen and heard just as they had been told. Their joy erupted into song as they made their way back through the still dark fields, forever changed by what their eyes had witnessed.

The Presentation of the Firstborn   Luke 2:21–24

Eight days after his birth at his circumcision he was named Yeshua; the name given by the Angel before he was conceived. The moment was solemn and sacred, the air filled with the scent of incense and ancient oil, as the covenantal sign was placed upon the child's flesh, binding him to the nation and the promise.

When the days of their purification according to the Torah was complete they brought him up to Jerusalem to present him to Adonai. Just as it is written in the Torah of the LORD every firstborn male will be dedicated to Adonai. As well as to offer up a sacrifice according to what is stated in the Torah of Adonai a pair of turtledoves or two young pigeons. The cooing of birds and the murmured prayers of other worshippers filled the Temple courts as Joseph and

Miriam carried out their humble yet holy obligation, unnoticed by most—yet not by heaven.

Simeon's Prophetic Vision   Luke 2:25–35

There was a righteous and devout man in Jerusalem whose name was Simeon that was looking forward to Israel's consolation, and the Holy Spirit was upon him. Years of prayer had carved gentle lines into his face; his eyes scanned every child, every family, waiting. It had been revealed to him by the Holy Spirit that he would not die before he saw Adonai's Messiah. Guided by the Spirit, he entered the Temple complex. At that moment, his steps quickened.

When the parents brought in the child Yeshua to perform for him what was customary under the Torah, Simeon took him up in his arms, his hands trembling not from age but from awe, and praised GOD, and said, "Now Adonai, You can dismiss your slave in peace, as you promised. For my eyes have beheld Your yeshuah (salvation). You have prepared it in the presence of all people a light for revelation to the Nations and glory to Your people Israel." His father and mother were shocked at what was being said about him. Their hearts beat faster, overwhelmed by the unexpected words of this stranger.

Then Simeon blessed them. His voice grew softer as he looked directly into Miriam's eyes—the weight in his words that she would carry for the rest of her life: "Indeed, this child is destined to cause the fall and rise of men in Israel and to be a sign that will be opposed, and a sword will pierce your own soul that the thoughts of many hearts will be revealed."

Anna the Faithful Prophetess   Luke 2:36–38

There was also a prophetess, Anna, a daughter of Phanuel, of the tribe of Asher. She was very old, having lived with her husband seven years after her marriage, and was a widow for 84 years. The temple had become her home, its rhythms her heartbeat. She did not leave the Temple complex, serving GOD night and day with fasting and prayers. Her prayers, rising like incense daily, now received their answer. At that very moment she came up and began to thank GOD and speak about Him to all who were looking forward to the redemption of Jerusalem. Her voice rang with fire, her joy overflowing as she proclaimed the arrival of hope to every ear willing to hear.

The Magi from the East Seek the King   Matthew 2:1–6

After Yeshua's birth in Bethlehem of Judea in the days of Herod the king, Magi from the east arrived in Jerusalem, their robes dusted with the long miles of desert journey, saying; "Where is he who has been born king of the Jews? For we saw his star in the east and have come to worship him," When Herod the king heard this he was troubled and all Jerusalem with him. Fear whispered through the palace halls, and the streets hummed with rumors.

Gathering together all the chief priests and scribes of the people he inquired of them where the Messiah was to be born. They said to him, "In Bethlehem of Judea; for this is what has been written by the prophet: 'And you Bethlehem, Land of Judah are by no means least among the leaders of Judah, for out of you shall come forth a Ruler who will shepherd My people Israel.'"

The Magi Worship the Child 5 BCE   Matthew 2:7–12

Then Herod secretly called the magi and determined from them when exactly the star first appeared. He then sent them to Bethlehem and said, "Go and search carefully for the child; and when you have found him report to me, so that I too may come and worship him." His voice was honey, but his eyes held something colder. After hearing the king, they went on their way and the star which they had seen in the east went before them until it came and stood over the place where the child was. The night sky, a tapestry of wonder, now revealed its final sign.

When they saw the star they rejoiced exceedingly with great joy. After coming into the house, they spotted the child with Miriam his mother; and they bowed down to the ground in worship of him. Their eyes filled with tears, overcome by the weight of the moment. Then opening their treasures, they presented to him gifts of gold, frankincense, and myrrh—offerings fit for royalty, divinity, and sacrifice. After having been warned by GOD in a dream not to return to Herod, the magi left for their own country by another way.

Flight to Egypt   Matthew 2:13–15

Now when they had left, behold, the Angel of Adonai appeared to Joseph in a dream and said, "Get up! Take the child and his mother and flee to Egypt, remain there until I tell you; for Herod is going to search for the child to kill him."

Yosef awoke with a start, his chest tight with urgency. A heavenly warning had pierced his sleep, urging him to flee. So, Yosef awoke and took the child and his mother while it was still night and departed for Mitzrayim (Egypt). The road was long and uncertain, the night wind biting, but his grip on the reins was steadily driven by obedience and fierce, silent love.

Mindful of the Torah's command not to return by the derekh Mitzrayim—the way of Egypt through the wilderness—Yosef chose instead a different path. He led his small family westward toward the sea, avoiding the forbidden road. After days of cautious travel, they reached a coastal port—perhaps Yaffo (Joppa) or Ashkelon—where ships from the Jewish communities of Alexandria often came to dock. There, amid the bustle of merchants and sailors, Yosef secured passage aboard a vessel bound for the great city of exile.

With each gust of sea wind, Yosef held the child close, his thoughts fixed on both the promise of protection and the weight of prophecy. Across the waters they went, not as wanderers in rebellion, but as pilgrims obeying the word of Elohim.

They arrived in Alexandria; a city filled with the children of Avraham. In this foreign land, Yosef found refuge, and the boy grew under the watchful eyes of heaven. He remained there until the death of Herod. This was to fulfill what had been spoken by Adonai through the prophet: "Out of Mitzrayim I have called My son."

The Slaughter of the Innocents Matthew 2:16–18

Once Herod saw that he was fooled by the magi he became enraged. His fury was a wildfire—irrational, consuming, and vengeful. With the cold calculation of fear, he sent soldiers to slaughter all the male children who were in Bethlehem and its surrounding land from the age of two and under, according to the time which he had determined from the magi. Screams pierced the streets. Doors shattered. Mothers clung to infants. Fathers stood helpless as steel fell upon innocence. The small town, once quiet and holy, now echoed with the horror of grief. Then what had been spoken through the prophet Jeremiah was fulfilled: "A voice was heard in Ramah, crying and loud wailing, Rachel mourning for her children; and she refused to be comforted, because they were no more."

Return from Exile 4 BCE Matthew 2:19–23

But when Herod died, behold, the Angel of Adonai appeared in a dream to Joseph in Egypt, and said, "Awake! Take the child with his mother and go to the land of Israel; for those who sought to kill the child are dead." The wind stirred as Joseph opened his eyes, the weight of exile finally lifting. So, Joseph got up and brought the child and his mother and returned to the land of Israel. With every step northward, the horizon looked more like promise. However, once he heard that Archelaus was reigning over Judea in place of his father Herod, he was fearful of going there. Memories of blood still clung to Judea's soil.

Josephus (Antiquities 17.6.4) records that **a lunar eclipse** occurred shortly before Herod's death. Modern astronomy confirms:
- A **partial lunar eclipse occurred on March 13, 4 BCE**.
- This eclipse is the best match for the one Josephus references.

"But Herod deprived this Matthias of the high priesthood, and burnt the other Matthias, who had raised the sedition, with his companions alive. And on that very night there was an eclipse of the moon." (Antiquities 17.6.4)

Passover Shortly After His Death
Josephus also says that **Herod died shortly before Passover** (Antiquities 17.9.3).
- In 4 BCE, **Passover began on April 11** (evening), about **four weeks after the March 13 eclipse**.
- This gives ample time for the events Josephus describes between the eclipse and Herod's death—his decline, palace intrigue, executions, his funeral, and the transition to his successors.

Scholarly Consensus
Most modern scholars and historians—including **Emil Schürer, F.F. Bruce,** and **Harold Hoehner**—agree that **Herod the Great died in 4 BCE**, probably in **late March or early April**, based on:
- The **March 13, 4 BCE lunar eclipse**
- **Jewish Passover timing**
- Josephus's detailed narrative of Herod's final days

So, after being warned by GOD in a dream and completing everything according to the law of GOD, he left for the region of Galilee and came to live in a city called Nazareth. The hills were quiet, the streets humble, yet in them prophecy stirred. This was to fulfill what was spoken through the prophets: "He shall be called a Notzri." The boy grew up and became strong, filled with wisdom, and GOD's grace was upon him. Laughter returned to the household. The child who had fled kings now played in the dust of Nazareth's alleys, watched over with quiet reverence.

The Lost Child in the Holy City   Luke 2:41–50

Every year his parents traveled to Jerusalem for the Passover Festival. The pilgrimage was sacred, but also familiar—the roads bustling with music, families, and song. When he was twelve years old, they went up according to the custom of the festival. After those days were over, as they were returning, the boy Yeshua stayed behind in Jerusalem without his parents knowing. The city, holy and vast, swallowed his small figure among the thousands.

Assuming he was part of the traveling caravan, they traveled a day's journey. Then they began to search for him amongst their friends and family. Concern became worry and worry soon turned into panic. When they were not able to locate him they returned to Jerusalem to search for him. Each alley, each crowd, brought fresh dread. After three days they found him in the Temple complex sitting amongst the Rabbis listening to them and asking them questions. The sound of his voice carried weight; his words, wrapped in curiosity and clarity, stirred the hearts of even the learned. All those who heard him were astounded at his understanding and his answers. Scrolls were opened, heads nodded, and the young boy sat in the midst of them like a lamp in the center of darkness.

A Mother's Heart and a Father's House   Luke 2:48–52

When his parents spotted him they were flabbergasted, and his mother said to him, "Son, why have you treated us in this way? Your father and I have been anxiously searching for you." Her voice cracked with both relief and anguish; eyes filled with tears not yet dry.

"Why were you searching for me?" He asked them. "Didn't you know that I had to have been in my Father's house?" His voice was calm—earnest, not defiant. Yet they did not understand what he said to them. His words, meant to comfort, stirred even deeper questions. He then returned with them and arrived in Nazareth and was obedient to them. Life resumed. But still, His mother kept all these things in her heart. Yeshua increased in wisdom and stature, and in favor with GOD and with people. He walked among them unnoticed, the promised light growing quietly in the hills of Galilee.

Chapter 3 – Yeshua Prepares for His Ministry

Voice in the Wilderness Luke 3:1–2 | John 1:6–14

In the fifteenth year of the reign of Tiberius Caesar (27-28 CE), while Pontius Pilate was governor of Judea, Herod was Tetrarch of Galilee, his brother Phillip Tetrarch of the region of Iturea and Trachonitis, and Lysanias Tetrarch of Abilene, during the High Priesthood of Annas and Caiaphas, there was a man sent from GOD, whose name was John the son of Zechariah in the wilderness.

John came to bear witness of the Light, that all men through him might believe. He was not that Light but was sent to bear witness of that Light. That was the true Light which shines upon every man that comes into the world. He was in the world, and the world was made by him, and the world knew him not. He came unto his own, and his own didn't welcome him. As many as did receive him, to them he gave the power to become the sons of GOD, even to them that believe on his name, who were born, not of blood, nor of the will of the flesh, nor of the will of man, but of GOD. So, the Torah was made flesh, and dwelled amongst us, and we beheld his glory as of the only begotten of the Father, full of grace and truth

The Voice in the Desert 28 CE Luke 3:3–6 | Matthew 3:1–4 | Mark 1:2–6

John went into all the vicinity of the Jordan in the wilderness of Judea, preaching a baptism of repentance for the forgiveness of sins saying; "Repent, for the kingdom of heaven is at hand," The blazing sun beat down on the rocky terrain as the call echoed across the arid valleys. Those who heard it felt it in their bones—a call not only to action, but to awakening.

As it is written in the book of the words of the prophet Isaiah: "A voice of one crying out in the wilderness: Prepare the way; make Adonai's paths straight! Every valley will be filled, every mountain and hill will be made low; the crooked will become straight, the rough ways smoothed, and everyone will see the salvation of GOD." John himself wore a garment of camel's hair and a leather belt around his waist; and his food was locusts and honey. His appearance was rugged, his voice thunderous—yet something in his words cut deeper than the Jordan's flow.

Multitudes Drawn Matthew 3:5–10 | Mark 1:5 | Luke 3:7–9

Crowds of people came out from Jerusalem, and all Judea and all the district around the Jordan to be baptized by him. They were being baptized by him in the Jordan River as they confessed their sins. The riverbanks became a sacred space—sobbing mingled with songs, feet splashed in the cool water, and lives were turned toward righteousness.

But when he saw many of the Pharisees and Sadducees coming for baptism he turned and said to them; "Brood of vipers! Who warned you to run from the coming wrath? Therefore, bear fruit in keeping with repentance; and do not assume that you can say to yourselves, 'We have Abraham for our father'; for I say to you that from these very stones GOD is able to raise up children to Abraham. The axe is already laid at the root of the trees; therefore, every tree that does not bear good fruit is cut down and thrown into the fire." Gasps and murmurs rippled through the crowds as his words struck their hearts. He was not afraid of robes or rank—only the truth.

The People Ask What Must Be Done   Luke 3:10–14

"What should we do?" The crowds asked him. Their eyes were wide with urgency; their hearts longed to be clean.

He replied to them, "The one who has two shirts must share with someone who has none, and the one who has food must do the same."

Tax collectors also came to be baptized, and they asked him, "Rabbi, what should we do?"

He told them, "Don't collect any more than what you are authorized."

Some soldiers also questioned him: "What should we do?"

He told them; "Don't take money from anyone by force or false accusation; be satisfied with your wages." The river didn't just cleanse flesh—it stirred conscience. Men and women returned home with new hearts and a different walk.

The Interrogation: Who Are You, John?   John 1:19–24

And this is the record of John, when the Jews sent priests and Levites from Jerusalem to ask him, "Who are you?"

He confessed, and denied not, but confessed, "I am not the Messiah."

So, they asked him; "What then? Are you Elijah?"

"No, I am not," he said.

"Are you that prophet?"

"No," he answered.

Then they asked of him; "Who are you? That we may give an answer to them that sent us. What do you say of yourself?"

He said, "I am the voice of one crying in the wilderness, 'Make straight the way of Adonai' as said the prophet Isaiah."

Those which were sent were of the Pharisees. They asked him and said to him, "Why are you baptizing then if you are not the Messiah, nor Elijah and neither that prophet?"

Their sandals were clean, their scrolls memorized—but they could not hear the cry from the wilderness for what it truly was: a trumpet blast before the arrival of the King.

The Expectation of a Nation Luke 3:15–18 | Matthew 3:11–12

Now the people were waiting expectantly, and all of them were debating in their minds whether John might be the Messiah. Their voices murmured along the banks of the Jordan, eyes watching every gesture, hearts straining to believe—was this wild prophet the one they had waited for? John answered them all, "I baptize you with water for repentance, but one is coming who is more powerful than I. I am not even fit to bend down and untie his sandals. He will baptize you with the Holy Spirit and fire. His winnowing fork is in His hand, and He will thoroughly clear his threshing floor; and he will gather his wheat into the barn, but he will burn up the chaff with unquenchable fire."

His words rang with both warning and promise—fire for the fruitless, Spirit for the sincere. The sky above felt closer, as though the judgment and joy of heaven were approaching with haste. Then along with many other exhortations, he proclaimed the good news to the people. (But Herod the Tetrarch, being rebuked by him about Herodias, his brother's wife and about all the things Herod had done, added this to everything else so eventually he imprisoned John.

The Righteous One Matthew 3:13–17 | Mark 1:9–11 | Luke 3:21–22

It happened in those days that Yeshua came from Nazareth of Galilee. His steps were quiet but steady. The long years of waiting had passed in silence—now the moment had come. And once all the people were baptized, he came to be baptized by John, but John attempted to prevent him saying; "I have need to be baptized by you, and do you come to me?" His eyes, wide with recognition, held awe and reluctance.

But Yeshua answered him saying; "Permit it at this time for in this way it is fitting for us to fulfill all righteousness." Then he permitted him.

After being baptized, Yeshua arose immediately from the water; and behold the heavens were opened, and he saw the Spirit of GOD descending like a dove and lighting upon him, and behold, a voice out of the heavens said; "This is My beloved son, whom I take delight in." The river grew still. Heaven breathed. Those who stood nearby were struck silent, the veil between worlds momentarily drawn back.

The Wilderness Trial   Matthew 4:1–11 | Mark 1:12–13 | Luke 4:1–13

Immediately the Spirit led Yeshua into the wilderness to be tempted by the devil. The wind howled through canyons, the sun scorched the rocks, and no human voice was heard. After he had fasted for forty days and forty nights, He then became hungry. His body weakened, but his spirit remained alert. The tempter came and said to him; "If you are the son of GOD, command that these stones become bread."

But he answered saying; "It is written, 'Man shall not live by bread alone, but by every word that proceeds from the mouth of GOD.'"

Then the devil took him into the holy city and had him stand on the pinnacle of the Temple and said to him; "If you are the Son of GOD, throw yourself down; for it is written, 'He will command His Angels concerning you'; and 'On their hands they will bear you up, so that you will not strike your foot against a stone.'"

Yeshua said to him; "However it is written you shall not put Adonai your GOD to the test."

Again, the devil took him to a very high mountain and showed him all the kingdoms of the world and their glory; and he told him, "All these things I will give you, if you fall down and worship me."

Then Yeshua said to him; "Begone Satan! For it is written, 'You shall worship Adonai your GOD and serve only Him.'"

Then the devil fled him; and behold he was among the beasts of the wilderness and the Angels began to minister to him. Their presence brought light to the dry and desolate place, and the silence was no longer empty.

Resisting the Accuser with Torah
When Yeshua was led by the Ruach (Spirit) into the wilderness, he fasted for forty days—mirroring Mosheh (Moses) on Sinai and the forty years Yisrael wandered in the desert. There, the Satan (Accuser) approached him with subtle temptations, each cloaked in scriptural language.
The Accuser misquoted or misapplied verses from the Ketuvim (Writings), attempting to twist the Word of Elohim to justify self-indulgence, reckless faith, and power-grabbing. But Yeshua answered each time with Torah—specifically from Devarim (Deuteronomy), the book that summarizes Israel's covenantal calling.

- **"Turn these stones into bread."**
  Yeshua replied: "It is written Man does not live by bread alone, but by every word that comes from the mouth of Adonai" (Deut. 8:3).

- **"Throw yourself down, for it is written…"**
  Yeshua countered: "It is also written: Do not test Adonai your Elohim" (Deut. 6:16).

- **"Bow to me and I'll give you all the kingdoms."**
  Yeshua stood firm: "It is written: You shall worship Adonai your Elohim, and Him only shall you serve" (Deut. 6:13).

Conclusion
Yeshua didn't resist the Accuser with mystical formulas or personal willpower. He stood on the foundation of Torah—the very Word that had shaped Israel's identity. The devil used scripture out of context, but Yeshua rightly divided it, showing that true discernment flows from a heart rooted in covenant. In every temptation—whether physical, emotional, or spiritual—the answer is the same: return to Torah. Let the Word dwell in you richly, and like Yeshua, you will stand when tested.

The Testimony of the Forerunner   John 1:29–34 | John 1:16–18

John gave testimony regarding Yeshua, and cried out, "Behold the lamb of GOD, who takes away the sin of the world! He is the one whom I spoke of when I said, 'A man is coming after me who is far greater than I am, for he existed long before me.' I did not recognize him as the Messiah, but I have been baptized with water so that he might be revealed to Israel."

Then John testified, "I beheld the Holy Spirit descending as a dove from heaven and alighting upon him. I did not know he was the one, but when GOD sent me to baptize with water, He told me, 'The one on whom you see the Spirit descend and rest upon is the one who will baptize with the Holy Spirit.' I witnessed this happen to Yeshua, so I testify that he is the chosen one of GOD!"

The people leaned in, some trembling, others rejoicing, as John—never one to exalt himself—lifted up the Lamb before the eyes of Israel. Of his fullness we have all received and grace for grace. For the Torah was given by Moses, but grace and truth came by Yeshua the Messiah. No man has seen GOD at any time, the only begotten Son, which is in the bosom of the Father, he hath declared him.

The Interrogation Intensifies   John 1:19–28

This was John's testimony when Judeans from Jerusalem sent priests and Levites to ask John, "Who are you?" The delegation came clothed in prestige; eyes narrowed with suspicion. Dust clung to their robes as they approached the wild prophet standing waist-deep in the river of repentance.

John didn't refuse to confess but openly declared, "I am not the Messiah."

A ripple of surprise crossed their faces. "Then who are you?" They asked him. "Are you Elijah?" They questioned, searching for what kind of authority he may have as prophet.

"I am not."

"Are you the Prophet?"

"No." he answered.

Their brows furrowed. Whispers exchanged. Scrolls clenched in frustration. So, they asked more of him, becoming frustrated by his simple answers so they would be able to bring an adequate answer back to Jerusalem. "Who exactly are you then? We are required to bring back an answer about who you are for those who sent us. What can you tell us about who you are?"

John smiled, having finally heard the honest reason for their questioning, and replied in the words of the Prophet Isaiah, "I am the voice of him who cries in the wilderness, 'Make straight the way of Adonai.'"

Now Pharisees who were sent began to question him, a little flustered because his answers were insufficient for them, and they didn't believe he therefore had the authority to baptize people: "Why then do you baptize if you are not the Messiah, nor are you Elijah, and you are not even the Prophet?!" Their tone sharpened, the authority of Yerushalayim pressing down upon the solitary voice in the wilderness.

John, unbothered by their line of questioning, replies to them saying, "I baptize with water, however there is a man amongst your ranks—you Pharisees—that you do not recognize. He is the one who comes after me, whose sandal straps I am not even worthy to untie." A quiet settled over the scene as John's words hung in the air like thunder just beyond the hills. This all happened at Bethany on the other side of the Jordan where John was baptizing.

Chapter 4 – Yeshua Begins His Ministry

The Lineage of the Redeemer Luke 3:23–38

As He began his ministry Yeshua was about 30 years old and was believed to be the son of Joseph, son of Heli, son of Matthat, son of Levi, son of Melchi, son of Jannai, son of Joseph, son of Mattathias, son of Amos, son of Nahum, son of Esli, son of Naggai, son of Maath, son of Mattathias, son of Semein, son of Josech, son of Joda, son of Joanan, son of Rhesa, son of Zerubbabel, son of Shealtiel, son of Neri, son of Melchi, son of Addi, son of Cosam, son of Elmadam, son of Er, son of Joshua, son of Eliezer, son of Jorim, son of Matthat, son of Levi, son of Simeon, son of Judah, son of Joseph, son of Jonam, son of Eliakim, son of Melea, son of Menna, son of Mattatha, son of Nathan, son of David, son of Jesse, son of Obed, son of Boaz, son of Salmon, son of Nahshon, son of Amminadab, son of Ram, son of Hezron, son of Perez, son of Judah, son of Jacob, son of Isaac, son of Abraham, son of Terah, son of Nahor, son of Serug, son of Reu, son of Peleg, son of Eber, son of Shelah, son of Cainan, son of Arphaxad, son of Shem, son of Noah, son of Lamech, son of Methuselah, son of Enoch, son of Jared, son of Mahalaleel, son of Cainan, son of Enos, son of Seth, son of Adam, son of God.

This was no ordinary man stepping into ministry. Behind his quiet appearance stood a lineage soaked in covenant, kingship, and divine design. From dust to destiny, the son of Adam—the Son of Elohim—was now revealed.

The Lamb Revealed John 1:35–42

The day after, John was standing with two of his disciples, and Yeshua walked past. The desert wind carried the scent of the Jordan and the dust of wandering feet. John's gaze locked onto him with unwavering conviction. John looked at him and declared, "Behold! There is the Lamb of GOD!" His voice pierced the stillness like a shofar blast. The two disciples heard him speak, and they followed Yeshua.

Then Yeshua turned and saw them following and asked of them, "What is it you seek?" His tone was not just curious—it was piercing, discerning. He looked beyond their words, into the depths of their yearning.

They said to him, "Rabbi, where do you live?"

He replied to them, "Come and see." The invitation was simple, yet profound. It was about more than location—it was a call into a new life. The time was about four in the evening when they went with him to the place where he was residing, and they remained there with him for the rest of the day. They sat in silence and asked questions. They laughed and listened. Something sacred was beginning.

One of the two which heard John speak and followed him was Andrew, Simon Peter's brother. Andrew went to locate his brother, Simon, and told him, "We have discovered the Messiah." His voice trembled with excitement, the kind that grips the heart when destiny is within reach.

Then, Andrew brought Simon to meet Yeshua. Clearly discerning Simon, Yeshua said, "Your name is Simon, son of John, but I shall call you Kepha." (which means Rock/Peter). Yeshua's words were not mere introduction—they were prophecy. The path of the fisherman would never be the same.

The Calling of Philip and Nathaniel   John 1:43–51

The following day Yeshua decided to go to the region of Galilee. The air was fresh with possibility, the hills quiet under the morning sun. There he found Philip and told him, "Come, follow me." Philip was from Bethesda, which was also Andrew and Peter's hometown. Familiar voices, familiar faces—yet a new mission was stirring among them.

Philip went to search for Nathaniel and told him, "We have discovered the person Moses, and the prophets wrote about! His name is Yeshua, the son of Joseph from Nazareth."

"Nazareth?!" exclaimed Nathaniel, who was perplexed at the thought. "Can anything good come out of Nazareth?"

"Come and see." That was all Philip said in return. Curiosity enveloped Nathaniel and he went with Philip.

As they approached, Yeshua said, "Now here is a genuine son of Israel in whom there is no deceit."

"How could you know anything about me?" Nathaniel asked, his confusion over who this man could be growing.

Yeshua responded, "I saw you under the fig tree before even Philip knew where you were."

Awestruck, Nathaniel realized who Yeshua was and exclaimed; "Rabbi, You are the Son of GOD! The King of Israel!"

Yeshua asked him, "Do you have faith only because I told you that I saw you under the fig tree? You will witness even greater things than this!" Then he declared, "I tell you the absolute truth that you will see the heavens open and see the Angels of GOD ascending and descending on the Son of Man."

The Wedding in Cana   John 2:1–11

There was a wedding taking place on the third day (Tuesday) in Cana of Galilee that Yeshua, his mother, and his disciples were invited to attend. The celebration echoed with laughter, music, and the clinking of cups—yet a quiet urgency began to ripple among the servants. They ran out of wine during the celebration, so the mother of Yeshua informed him, "They have run out of wine."

> His mother, knowing he was the Messiah, was hoping he would supply the wine that has been prepared for the messianic kingdom since the creation of the world. (Isaiah 25:6–8)

Yeshua responded to her saying, "My lady, why are you coming to me about there being no wine? It isn't time to reveal myself."

His mother commanded the servants, "Do what he commands you."

Nearby there were six stone water jars, which were placed there for the Judean rite of purification. Each could hold twenty to thirty gallons. Yeshua commanded the servants, "Completely fill these stone jars with water." So, they filled the stone jars to the brim. Then he commanded them, "Now draw some out and bring it to the master of the banquet."

So, they did. When the master of the banquet tasted the water that Yeshua had caused to become wine, he did not know where it came from, but the servants who had drawn the water knew. Then he addressed the bridegroom and said, "Usually everyone serves the finest wine first, then once the guests are drunk you serve the inferior wine. You, however, have guarded the finest wine until now."

The guests marveled, unaware of the miracle, but the servants—those closest to obedience—had seen the mystery unfold. The miracle that Yeshua performed in Cana of Galilee was his first, doing so revealed his glory, and his disciples believed in him. The wedding feast ended, but wonder had only begun.

A Journey to Capernaum   John 2:12

After this he traveled down to Capernaum with his mother, his brothers, and his disciples. The road wound through green hills and rocky paths. The water of the Kinneret shimmered in the distance. The group moved together—family and followers alike—unaware that the world would never be the same again.

The First Passover of Yeshua's Ministry John 2:13–25

When the time for the Judean Passover was about to take place, Yeshua traveled up to Jerusalem.

Religious feasts are celebrated at specific times by the Jewish people. Some other groups such as the Samaritans kept a different calendar. This would explain why the Gospel of John specifies the Judean Passover. Yeshua kept with the tradition of the Jewish people over the Samaritans.

The streets swelled with pilgrims—men, women, and children ascending the holy city in caravans and song. The air buzzed with excitement, but also with tension. In the courts of the Temple, the sound of animals and commerce drowned out the quiet prayers of the nations. Inside the Temple, Yeshua found men selling cattle, sheep, and doves, and money changers all residing in the court of the Gentiles. The area meant to welcome the nations had become a noisy, profit-driven stockyard.

So, Yeshua fashioned a whip out of rope and used it to cast them outside of the Temple—both the cattle and sheep. The animals cried out as they scattered in all directions, the people shouting in confusion as coins clattered across the stone floor. He then poured out the coins of the money changers and overturned their tables. The metallic sound rang out like thunder. Panic turned to stunned silence. Then he said to those who sold doves, "Remove these birds from this place! Do not make my Father's house into a marketplace!"

After witnessing this, the disciples remembered what was written: "Zeal for Your House will consume me." His passion ignited old prophecies in their hearts—the Messiah would burn with holy fire for the sanctity of Elohim's dwelling place. The Judeans responded to this by asking him, "What sign will you show to us that you have the authority to do this?"

Yeshua answered them, "Destroy this temple and in three days I will raise it up."

The Judeans, perplexed by his answer, responded, "It took forty-six years to build this temple, and you will raise it in three days?" However, unbeknownst to the Judeans, Yeshua was speaking about his body as the Temple. The sacred presence was no longer housed only in stone—but walking among them in flesh. So, when the time came that Yeshua was raised from the dead, his disciples remembered that he had said this, and they believed the scripture and the words which Yeshua had spoken.

While Yeshua was in Jerusalem for the feast of Passover and Unleavened Bread, many people witnessed the miracles he was performing, and so his name grew in popularity. Rumors spread like fire through the city—healings, signs, words of wisdom unlike any heard before. Yet, Yeshua would not trust them. He did not need anyone to explain to him the nature of man, for he knew already the nature of man. Behind the crowds and acclaim, he saw the hearts. Some came for healing, others for power, but few understood the path he had begun to walk—one of fire, mercy, and sacrifice.

Chapter 5 – Yeshua Meets with Nachdimon Ben Gurion

A Meeting in the Shadows   John 3:1-2

There was a Pharisee named Nicodemus who was from Judea. He came to Yeshua under the cover of night and said to Yeshua, "Rabbi, we know that you are a teacher who has been sent from GOD, because no one else would have been able to perform the signs that you do if GOD were not with him." The wind whispered through the alleys of Yerushalayim.

<small>The man referred to in the Gospels as Nicodemus is widely identified in Talmudic literature as Nachdimon ben Gurion (נַקְדִּימוֹן בֶּן גּוּרְיוֹן)—a wealthy, influential, and pious man who lived in Yerushalayim during the late Second Temple period.

Sources in the Talmud:

Ta'anit 19b–20a tells the famous story of Nachdimon's miraculous prayer for rain. When a drought threatened Yerushalayim, he secured water from a Roman officer on the condition it would be repaid by a certain date. When the deadline came and rain had not fallen, he prayed—and miraculously, rain fell just in time. The sun even reappeared ("nakad haḥamah") so he could repay the debt—hence the name "Nachdimon", meaning "one before whom the sun burst forth."

Gittin 56a and Ketubot 66b describe him as one of the three richest men in Jerusalem, alongside Kalba Savua and Ben Tzizit Hakeset. These men supported the people during the Roman siege. Yet, despite their wealth, the Talmud laments how quickly it vanished during the destruction of the Temple.</small>

A Question of Rebirth   John 3:3–8

Yeshua replied, "I tell you the truth, no one can see the Kingdom of GOD unless he is first reborn from above."

Nachdimon, confused, asked, "How can a man be born when he has already aged? Can he enter his mother's womb a second time to be born?" His voice was sincere, trembling between logic and longing.

Yeshua answered him saying, "I tell you the truth, no one can enter the Kingdom of GOD unless he is born of water and the Spirit. Human nature is born out from among the flesh; however, the Spirit is born from the Spirit. You should not have been so amazed when I said that 'it was necessary to be reborn from above.' The wind blows wherever it wishes. You can hear the sound of it, yet you do not know where it comes from or to where it is going. This is the same with everyone who is born of the Spirit."

The Teacher Taught   John 3:9–15

Astounded, Nicodemus asks, "How can this be?!?"

Yeshua responded with the question, "You are Israel's teacher, and you do not comprehend these things?" The rebuke was gentle but firm—like a father correcting a son. There was no shame, only invitation to rise higher.

Yeshua went on to say, "I tell you the truth, we talk about things we know, and we give testimony to what we have seen, and still, you people do not accept our testimony. If I discuss worldly matters with you and you do not trust me, how will you be able to have faith in when I tell you about heavenly matters? No one has ascended into heaven except for the Son of Man who descended from heaven. Just as Moses erected on a pole the bronze serpent in the desert, so too the Son of Man must be raised, so that everyone who places their faith in him will possess a spiritual existence eternally.

For GOD So Loved the World   John 3:16-18

For GOD so loved the world, He gave His only begotten son, so everyone who believes in him will not fully die but will have an eternal spiritual existence. For GOD did not send His son into the world to condemn the world but to bring the world salvation through him. Whoever chooses to place their faith in him will not be condemned. However, whoever chooses not to believe has already been condemned, since he has chosen to not believe in the name of GOD's only begotten son.

The Final Verdict: Light or Darkness   John 3:19–21

Now, this is the final verdict: the Light has entered the world, but men loved the darkness more than the Light, because their deeds were wicked. Everyone who participates in wickedness despises the Light and avoids the Light out of a fear that their deeds will be exposed. Whosoever practices the Truth goes into the Light so that it may be clearly seen that what he does has been achieved by GOD.

> Notice the law language of "verdict"—this was the type of language used in the Greek. People then were judged according to Torah Law. We know what Yeshua is referencing here is the Torah, therefore. We have further proof of this from passages that refer to the Torah as Light such as Proverbs 6:23 and Psalm 119:105. Truth is mentioned as something practiced. Torah is also referenced as Truth in passages from Psalm 119. We are commanded to practice, to do, to obey Torah—and not to practice sin, which is lawlessness or breaking of Torah commandments in passages like 1 John 3:4 and Matthew 7:23. Yeshua teaches: let our works be seen by men, and we are taught to not boast in ourselves about it, but to boast in GOD for the works that we do.

Chapter 6 – Yeshua Increases in Fame

Rivalry and Revelation   John 3:22–24

After concluding his conversation with Nicodemus, Yeshua and his disciples traveled into the Judean countryside, and he made camp with his disciples and began baptizing them. The fresh air of the open hills carried the sounds of flowing water and the quiet murmurs of those seeking repentance. It was a time of growth—of truth rising like early morning mist. John was also baptizing at Aenon near Salim since there was plenty of water there, and people were continuously coming to him to be baptized. (This was before he was thrown into prison). Two streams of ministry now flowed in parallel—Yeshua and his disciples in one region, and John in another. The people flocked to both, thirsty for hope, but tension was beginning to stir beneath the surface.

Concerned Disciples, a Humble Prophet   John 3:25–36

One day, controversy erupted between John's disciples and a person from Judea over the issue of ceremonial washing. Voices rose, hands gestured, and questions stirred: who held greater authority? So, John's disciples came to him and said, "Listen to this Rabbi, the man who was with you beyond the Jordan—you know, the man whom you testified about—well now he is baptizing people, and everyone is going to him!" Their words were tinged with anxiety, almost offense. But John—calm, grounded, full of clarity—offered no panic in reply.

John replied in a calm voice, unbothered by the news, "A man can only receive what is provided to him from heaven. You yourselves can bear witness that I said, 'I am not the Messiah, but I am sent ahead of him.' The bride belongs to the bridegroom. The friend of the bridegroom stands in wait and listens for him, then is overjoyed to hear the voice of the bridegroom. That is the pleasure I have, knowing my job is now finished."

Theme	Adam in the Garden (Genesis 3:8)	Song of Songs (2:8; 5:2)	Yochanan the Immerser (John 3:29)
Setting	Gan Eden (The Garden)	Allegorical love poem (Israel and Elohim/Mashiach)	Jordan River region during Yeshua's early ministry
Hebrew Word for Voice	Kol (קוֹל) – "They heard the **voice** of Adonai…"	Kol dodi (קוֹל דּוֹדִי) – "The **voice** of my beloved…"	Phōnē (Greek) – "He hears the **voice** of the bridegroom"
Who hears the voice?	Adam and Chavah	The bride (symbolizing Israel)	Yochanan (the friend of the Bridegroom)
Emotional response	Fear and hiding	Longing, excitement, love	Joy and fulfillment
Symbolic meaning	Human separation from Elohim	Intimacy and longing for union with the Beloved	The arrival of Mashiach, the true Bridegroom
Role of listener	Guilty and afraid	Yearning and receptive	Joyfully announcing and stepping aside
Covenant theme	Broken intimacy	Anticipated marriage covenant (Sinai/Messiah)	Covenant being fulfilled with arrival of Mashiach
Result of voice heard	Hiding, exile	Awakening, pursuit	Rejoicing, mission fulfilled

This chart shows how **"the voice of the Bridegroom"** ties together the full arc of redemption:
>From **separation** (Adam),   > To **yearning** (Song of Songs),   >To **reunion** (John/Yeshua).

John's voice grew warm. There was no envy in him, only joy that the one he had prepared the way for was now stepping forward. "It is necessary for him to become more popular, and I must become less popular. The one who comes from above is above all. The one who is from the earth belongs to the earth and speaks as one from the earth. The one who comes from heaven is above all."

John lifted his eyes as he spoke, his tone shifting from explanation to prophetic urgency. "He gives testimony to what he has seen and heard, however, nobody believes his words. Whoever chooses to believe his testimony has proven that GOD is True. For the messenger whom GOD has sent speaks the words of GOD, for the Spirit that is given is limitless. The Father loves the son and has placed everything in his hands.

Whoever places their faith in the son possesses an eternal spiritual existence, and whoever rebels against the son will not see life. No, instead the wrath of GOD awaits him." John's words echoed over the water and into the hearts of those gathered. His mission was nearly complete—but the truth he spoke would endure long after his voice was silenced.

Avoiding the Pharisees   John 4:1–42

As Yeshua's fame grew, the Pharisees noticed that he was gaining and baptizing more disciples than John (even though it was not actually Yeshua who was baptizing people but his disciples who were baptizing people in the name of Yeshua as his agents). So, he departed from Judea and traveled to the region of Samaria, knowing he would not be pursued by the Pharisees in Samaria.

Yeshua and the Woman of Shomron   John 4:5–9

While traveling through Samaria, he came into a town called Sychar, which is near a plot of land which Jacob had given to his son Joseph. A well that was dug by Jacob was located there. Now, Yeshua was weary from his journey, so he sat down near the well to relax as it was about noon, and he instructed his disciples to go ahead of him into the town to buy supplies for their journey.

After some time, a Samaritan woman came out to the well to draw water, and Yeshua asked of her, "Will you give me a drink?"

The Samaritan woman, perplexed, asked him, "You are a Jew, so why do you ask me, a Samaritan woman, for a drink?" (For Jews did not associate with the Samaritans.)

The Gift of Living Water   John 4:10–19

Yeshua responded to her inquiry saying, "If only you knew the gift of GOD who is asking of you for a drink, you would have asked of me, and I would have freely given you the gift of living water."

Astounded by his answer yet curious by his meaning, she said to him, "Sir, you have nothing with which you may draw water from the well, and this particular well is very deep. How then will you be able to give me this living water? Are you greater than our father Jacob, who gave us this well and drank from it himself along with his sons and his livestock?"

Yeshua answered her saying, "Everyone who drinks the water from this well will go thirsty again. However, whoever drinks the living water which I give to them will never go thirsty. In fact, the living water which I give to them will become a fountain of living water within them pouring out to eternal life."

The woman, intrigued, said to him longingly, "Sir, give me this living water so that I will never go thirsty—so that I will no longer need to keep coming to this well to draw out water from it."

Yeshua commanded her, "Go, and summon your husband to come here."

She responded, half-honestly and a little worried, thinking it may affect her receiving the living water, "I do not have a husband."

Yeshua, perceiving her intentions, exposed her openly, stating, "You were correct when you said you do not have a husband. The truth is you have had five husbands, and the man whom you are currently with is not your husband. What you have stated was the truth."

Shocked by his knowledge of her, she realized he was a prophet and said to him, "Lord, I now acknowledge that you are a prophet."

Where Should We Worship? John 4:20–26

She is now more inquisitive to find out more truths from a man who receives knowledge from GOD, so she states something that has bothered her due to the tension between the Jews and the Samaritans: "Our ancestors worshipped on this mountain, and yet you Jews claim that the place where we must worship is in Jerusalem."

Yeshua responds to her kindly, "My lady, believe me, a time is coming when you will worship the Father neither on this mountain nor in Jerusalem. You worship what you do not remember. We worship what we do remember, for salvation comes from the Jews. A time is coming, however, and is now upon us, when the true worshippers will worship the Father in Spirit and in Truth—for they are the type of worshippers that the Father desires. GOD is Spirit, and those who worship Him must do so in Spirit and in Truth."

The woman, enthralled by his words of teaching that comes from heaven, says to him, "I know that the Messiah is coming. When he arrives, He will explain absolutely everything to us."

Then Yeshua, as if on cue, reveals himself, "I who am speaking to you am he."

The Woman's Witness — John 4:27–30

No sooner had the words left his mouth revealing himself as the Messiah did his disciples return. They were astonished that he was speaking with a woman, but no one asked him what he wanted from her or even why he was speaking with her. The woman, in awestruck wonder, leaves her water jug behind and rushes back to the town and said to the villagers, "Come meet this man who told me everything I have ever done. Could he be the Messiah?" So, their curiosity piqued, they left the town, and they went toward the direction where Yeshua was last seen by the woman.

Food from Another World — John 4:31–38

Meanwhile, his disciples, worried about him being exhausted and hungry, urged him, saying, "Rabbi, have something to eat."

Yeshua responded to them in a cryptic message stating, "I have food to eat that you don't know of."

Confused by this, his disciples said to one another, "Has someone already brought him food?"

Yeshua allows this opportunity to be a teaching moment and answers plainly, "My food is to do the will of Him who sent me and to finish His work. You know the saying, 'There are still four months until harvest'? Well, I tell you to open your eyes and behold—the fields are already ripe for harvest. The one who reaps is paid his wages and continues to gather a crop for an eternal spiritual existence, so that both the one who sowed and the one who reaps may rejoice together. So, the saying 'One sows and another reaps' is true. I sent you out to harvest crops that you didn't have to work hard for. Others did the work for you, and now you have taken upon yourselves their laboring's."

The Messiah Welcomed in Samaria — John 4:39–42

Many of the Samaritans from the village placed their faith in him because of the testimony of the woman's statement, "He told me everything I have ever done." So, once the Samaritans came to him, they requested that he dwell with them, so he stayed with them for two days. Many more came to believe because of his message, and they said to the woman, "We now believe—but not because of your chattering, but because we have heard for ourselves. So now we know that this man really is the Savior of the world."

Chapter 7 – Yeshua Begins His Galilean Ministry

The Prophet Silenced   Luke 3:19–20 | Mark 6:17–18 | John 3:24 | Matthew 4:12

It was about this time, after two days had passed, that John the Immerser was imprisoned by Herod. For John had rebuked Herod the tetrarch for taking his brother's wife, Herodias, and for all the other evil things Herod had done. And Herod, adding this to his evils, locked John away in prison. The wilderness grew quiet. The prophet who had thundered like Elijah was silenced behind cold walls, his voice echoing only in the memories of those who had repented at the Jordan.

Withdrawal into Galilee   Matthew 4:12 | Mark 1:14

When Yeshua heard that John had been imprisoned, he departed from Samaria and withdrew into Galilee. He returned not in fear, but in timing. The mantle was passing—John's preparation complete. Now the Light would shine in the north.

Return to Natzeret (Nazareth)   Luke 4:16–30

Yeshua came to Nazareth, where He was raised as child by Miriam and Yosef. He entered the synagogue on the Sabbath, as was his custom, and He stood up to read. The scroll of the prophet Isaiah was handed to Him. He unrolled the scroll and found the place where it was written:

"The Spirit of Adonai is upon me, because He has anointed me to proclaim good news to the poor.
He has sent me to heal the brokenhearted, to deliverance to the slaves, and recovery of sight to the blind,
to set free the oppressed, to proclaim the year of Adonai's favor."

Then He rolled up the scroll, gave it back to the attendant, and sat down. The eyes of everyone in the synagogue were fixed on Him.

A Prophet Without Honor   Luke 4:21-30

He looked at them all and with a calm voice filled with authority he said to them, "Today this Scripture is fulfilled in your hearing."

At first, all spoke well of Him and marveled at the gracious words that came from His lips. But they soon began to question: "Isn't this Yosef's son?"

Yeshua said to them, "Surely you will quote this proverb to Me: 'Physician, heal yourself! Do here in Your hometown what we heard was done in Capernaum.' Truly I tell you, no prophet is accepted in his hometown. But I tell you the truth—there were many widows in Israel in the days of Eliyahu, when the heavens were shut for three and a half years and a severe famine came over the whole land; yet Eliyahu was not sent to any of them except to a widow in Zarephath in Sidon. And there were many in Israel with leprosy in the time of Elisha the prophet, yet none of them was cleansed except Naaman the Syrian."

When they heard this, everyone in the synagogue was filled with rage. They got up, drove Him out of Nazareth, and escorted Him to the edge of the mountain which their town was built on, intending to throw Him off the cliff. But He passed through the crowd and went on His way.

The Galilean Awakening Luke 4:14–15 | Mark 1:14–15 | John 4:43–45

He returned with the power of the Holy Spirit, and news about Him spread through all the surrounding regions. He was teaching in their synagogues, and all spoke well of Him. And He began proclaiming the good news of Elohim, saying, "The time has come. The kingdom of Elohim has drawn near. Repent and believe the good news." The Galileans welcomed Him enthusiastically because they had witnessed all the miracles He had performed in Jerusalem while He was there for the Feast of Passover.

The Desperate Plea of a Royal Father John 4:46–54

Once again He visited the town of Cana in the Galilee region, where He had turned water to wine. There was a certain royal official whose son was bedridden from a sickness in Kfar Nachum (Capernaum). When this man received news that Yeshua had arrived in Galilee from Judea, he went to see Him, and he pleaded with Yeshua to come and heal his son who was so close to death.

Yeshua said to him, "You people will never have faith unless you witness signs and miracles!"

The royal official pleaded more urgently, a deep concern showing on his face as he was close to tears, "Please Lord, come down before my child dies."

Yeshua looked at him with compassion and authority and said, "Go. Your son will live."

The man believed the words of Yeshua and went home. While he was still traveling toward his home, some of his servants greeted him with radiant faces and joyful voices, bearing news: The child was alive and well. He asked them what time of day his son got better, and they informed him, "Yesterday, at one in the afternoon, the fever broke."

It was upon hearing this that the father realized it was at that exact moment when Yeshua had said, "Your son will live." So, he and his entire household placed their faith in Yeshua. This was the second sign which Yeshua had performed after leaving Judea and entering the Galilee.

The Light Rises Over Galilee   Matthew 4:13–17; Isaiah 9:1–2

After departing from Natzeret (Nazareth), Yeshua went and lived in Kfar Nachum (Capernaum), a fishing village by the sea in the region of Zevulun and Naftali. This quiet relocation fulfilled what was spoken long ago through the prophet Yeshayahu (Isaiah):

"Land of Zevulun and land of Naftali, the Way of the Sea, beyond the Yarden (Jordan), Galil of the Goyim (Galilee of the Nations)— the people dwelling in darkness have seen a great light, and for those dwelling in the region and shadow of death, a light has dawned."

From that moment on, Yeshua's voice began to echo through the Galilean hills: "Repent! For the Kingdom of Heaven has drawn near!"

The Rabbi Teaches from the Sea   Luke 5:1–3

One morning, as the early mist still hovered over the Lake of Gennesaret (Sea of Galilee), crowds surged around Yeshua, eager to hear the Torah of Elohim flow from his lips like fresh water. The shoreline buzzed with life, fishermen mending nets after a long, fruitless night. Two boats sat anchored nearby, abandoned temporarily by their owners. Yeshua stepped into one— the vessel belonging to Shim'on (Simon)—and asked him to push out slightly from the shore. There, afloat above the gently lapping water, Yeshua sat down and taught the people, his voice echoing softly across the water's surface.

A Miraculous Catch and a Humble Heart   Luke 5:4–11

When he had finished teaching, Yeshua turned to Shim'on and said, "Put out into the deep, and let down your nets for a catch."

Shim'on, weary and skeptical, replied, "Rabbi, we've toiled all night and caught nothing. But because You say so, I will let down the nets." No sooner had the net hit the water than it surged with movement—fish, in swarms, overwhelming the mesh. The cords tightened under the strain as astonished shouts rang out. They called to their partners in the other boat for help, and together they hauled in the bounty—so much that both boats nearly sank.

Overcome by wonder and a sudden awareness of his own unworthiness, Shim'on fell at Yeshua's knees and cried out, "Depart from me, Lord, for I am a sinful man!" Terror and awe filled the hearts of all who were with him—Ya'akov (James), Yochanan (John), and the sons of Zavdai (Zebedee)—for never had they seen such a catch.

But Yeshua looked at him calmly and said, "Don't be afraid. Come follow me and from now on, you will be catching men." So, they pulled their boats onto the shore, and left everything behind to follow him.

The Call of the Brothers Matthew 4:21–22 | Mark 1:19–20

Walking a little farther along the shoreline, Yeshua saw two more brothers—Ya'akov son of Zavdai and his brother Yochanan—working with their father in their fishing boat, preparing their nets. The scent of sea salt lingered in the air, the cries of gulls overhead. Without hesitation, Yeshua called to them. The moment stirred something deep in their hearts. Immediately, they left the boat—nets, father, and hired men alike—and followed after him, drawn by a voice that resonated with eternity.

Yeshua Teaches with Authority Mark 1:21–28 | Luke 4:31–37

Yeshua went down to Kfar Nachum (Capernaum), a city in Galil (Galilee). On Shabbat, he entered the synagogue, as was his custom, and began to teach. The people were astonished at his teaching, because his word was with authority—not as the Sofrim (scribes) who recited tradition, but as one who carried the ruach (spirit) of divine insight. Even among the Prushim (Pharisees), none had ever spoken with such piercing truth.

In the synagogue, there was a man possessed by a ruach tamei (unclean spirit) who suddenly cried out in a loud voice, his whole body trembled with inner torment: "AAaaah! What are you doing here, Yeshua of Natzeret?! Have you come to destroy us? I know who you are—the Kedosh of Elohim (Holy One of GOD)!"

A wave of fear swept through the room. But Yeshua, calm and undaunted, rebuked him, saying: "Be silent, and get out of him!"

The man convulsed violently, thrown down before the entire congregation. With a shriek that echoed through the stone walls, the unclean spirit came out of him, leaving the man unharmed, exhausted but free. All the people were amazed, and they said to one another: "What is this new teaching?! With authority and power, he commands even the unclean spirits—and they obey him!" The entire region stirred. News about him spread immediately throughout every place in Galil.

Healing Shim'on's Mother-in-Law Matthew 8:14–15 | Mark 1:29–31 | Luke 4:38–39

After Yeshua left the synagogue on Shabbat, he went to the house of Shim'on (Kefas) and Andrew, together with Ya'akov (James) and Yochanan (John). Inside, Shim'on's mother-in-law lay sick in bed, burning with a high fever. They immediately spoke to Yeshua about her; concern etched into their faces. He approached her, stood over her, took her gently by the hand, and rebuked the fever—and it left her at once. Her eyes opened with clarity, her strength returned, and she rose without hesitation and began to serve them joyfully.

Yeshua Heals the Multitudes After Shabbat   Matthew 8:16–17 | Mark 1:32–34 | Luke 4:40–41

That evening, as the sun set and Shabbat ended, the quiet of the town gave way to crowds pressing into the streets, all gathering at Shim'on's door. People from Kfar Nachum and beyond came bringing their sick, their demon possessed, the hopeless and desperate, those with wasting diseases, those writhing from pain or seizures, the paralyzed and crippled. Yeshua laid his hands on every one of them. He healed them all. No cry went unheard, no illness ignored.

Demons were cast out, screaming as they went:

"You are the Son of Elohim!"

"You are the Kedosh of Elohim!"

But Yeshua rebuked them, not allowing them to speak further, because they knew he was the Messiah—and the fullness of his mission had yet to be revealed. This moment fulfilled the prophecy of Yeshayahu (Isaiah):

"He took our illnesses and bore our diseases." (Isaiah 53:4)

Yeshua Preaches Throughout Galil   Mark 1:35–39 | Luke 4:42–44

Very early the next morning, while it was still dark, Yeshua got up quietly, left the house, and went out to a solitary place to pray. Alone, he poured out his spirit before Avinu (our Father) in the stillness of dawn. When daylight broke, the crowds began searching for him again. Shim'on and those with him found Yeshua and said with urgency: "Everyone is looking for you!" The people pleaded with him not to leave.

But Yeshua replied: "I must proclaim the good news of the kingdom of Elohim to the other towns also—for that is why I was sent." And so, Yeshua continued going throughout all Galil, teaching in their synagogues, proclaiming the good news of the Kingdom, and healing every disease and affliction among the people.

Chapter 8: The Sermon on the Mount

The Multitudes Gather Before the Mountain — Matthew 4:23–25

His fame spread throughout all Syria, and they brought to him all who were ill—those suffering with various diseases and severe pain, the demon-possessed, the epileptics, and the paralyzed—and he healed them. Large crowds began to follow him, coming from the Galil, the Decapolis, Jerusalem, all Judea, and from beyond the Yarden.

Yeshua Ascends the Mountain to Teach — Matthew 5:1–2

Seeing these great crowds gathering around him, Yeshua went up onto a mountainside and sat down. His disciples came to him, drawing close with quiet anticipation. The multitudes settled on the slopes, hearts stirred, and eyes fixed on him. The hush of expectation swept across the crowd as the wind rustled the hillside. Yeshua looked out over the sea of faces—men and women, elders and children, rich and poor—all drawn by the hope of something eternal. His voice rang clear and steady, echoing across the hills with words that pierced the soul and comforted the broken hearted.

The Beatitudes: Blessings Upon the Faithful — Matthew 5:3–12

Then, with the calm authority of a master teacher, he opened his mouth and began to teach them, saying:

"Blessed are the ones who are humble in spirit, the anavim, for they belong to the Kingdom of Heaven."

– "The humble also shall increase their joy in Adonai, and the poor among men shall rejoice in the Holy One of Israel." (Isaiah 29:19)
– "To this one I will look: to the poor and broken in spirit, who trembles at My word." (Isaiah 66:2)

"Blessed are they who feel guilt and mourn for their sins, for they will be drawn close to the Holy One of Israel."

– "The sacrifices of Elohim are a broken spirit; a broken and contrite heart, O Elohim, You will not despise." (Psalm 51:17)
– "Adonai is near to those who have a broken heart and saves those with a contrite spirit." (Psalm 34:18)

"Blessed are the Chassidim, those who act with kindness and faithfulness, for they will inherit the Earth."

– "The meek shall inherit the land and shall delight themselves in the abundance of peace." (Psalm 37:11)

"Blessed are they who hunger and thirst for righteousness, for they will be satisfied."

– "Justice, justice shall you pursue, so that you may live and possess the land." (Deuteronomy 16:20)
– "My soul thirsts for Elohim, for the living El." (Psalm 42:2)

"Blessed are they who practice rachamim (mercy and compassion), for they will receive mercy from the Merciful One."

– "As a father has compassion on his children, so Adonai has compassion on those who fear Him." (Psalm 103:13)
– "Whoever is merciful to others, Heaven is merciful to him." (Shabbat 151b)

"Blessed are they who are pure hearted for they will know Elohim."

– "Who may ascend the mountain of Adonai? … He who has clean hands and a pure heart." (Psalm 24:3–4)
– "The Holy One, blessed be He, dwells only with one who is pure and humble." (Taanit 7a)

"Blessed are the Oseh Shalom (peacemakers), for they will be called children of Elohim."

"Blessed are they who are persecuted because they cling to tzedek (righteousness and justice), for they belong to the Kingdom of Heaven."

– "The reward is according to the suffering." (Avot 5:23)

"Blessed are you when people revile you, pursue you with hatred, and speak all manner of slander against you falsely on account of me. Be joyful and exult, for great is your reward with the Holy One blessed be He, in the heavens! For in the same way did they persecute the nevi'im (prophets) who were before you."

– "One who is insulted and does not insult back… concerning them the verse says: 'They that love Him shall be as the sun when it comes out in its strength.'" (Shabbat 88b)

The Calling of Salt and Light Matthew 5:13–16

Yeshua lifted his gaze and met the eyes of his disciples—the ones who had left their nets, families, and certainties behind—and he spoke words meant to anchor their identity in covenantal purpose: "You are the salt of the land—set apart to preserve the covenant and uphold righteousness in the land of Elohim. But if the salt loses its flavor—if you turn from the commandments and forsake your calling—what purpose remains for you? You will be cast out, scattered among the nations, and trampled underfoot."

– "You shall season all your grain offerings with salt. You shall not let the salt of the covenant of your Elohim be lacking…" (Leviticus 2:13)
– "He gave them statutes and judgments… that if they obeyed, they would be a peculiar treasure to Me… a kingdom of priests and a holy nation." (Exodus 19:5–6)
– "You have forsaken Me and served other gods… therefore I will drive you out of this land into a land that you have not known." (Jeremiah 16:11–13)
– "Just as salt preserves meat from decay, so too the covenant preserves Israel from destruction—so long as it is kept." (cf. Sifra on Leviticus 2:13)
– "If Israel keeps the Torah, they will be elevated; if they abandon it, they will be trampled by the nations." (Sanhedrin 105a)

"You are sparks of divine light, sent into the world to awaken holiness, illuminate darkness, and draw creation back to Elohim. A city set on a hill cannot be hidden."

– "Israel is compared to a lamp: just as a lamp brings light to the world, so Israel brings light to the world." (Midrash Tanchuma, Behaalotecha 2)
– "Each soul is a spark from the Divine flame." (Tanya, Likkutei Amarim, Ch. 2)
– "Whoever teaches Torah in public is like one who builds a city on a hill." (cf. Avot d'Rabbi Natan 21)

"Just as no one lights a lamp only to place it beneath a bushel, neither should you conceal the flame of your soul beneath the coverings of ego, doubt, or fear."

– "A person should always consider himself as if the entire world depends on his deeds." (Kiddushin 40b)
– "There is a candle within every soul; ego and sin are like coverings that dim the flame." (Tanya, ch. 29)

"Each mitzvah you perform is a spark of divine fire—tikkun nefesh, repairing your soul, and tikkun olam, healing the world. So let your light shine—through obedience, through mercy, through truth, through joy—that all who behold it may be drawn upward, glorifying Avinu Shebashamayim (our Father in the heavens)."

- "The commandment is a lamp and the Torah is light; and reproofs of instruction are the way of life." (Proverbs 6:23)
- "Let all your deeds be done for the sake of Heaven." (Pirkei Avot 2:12)
- "Tikkun olam—repairing the world—is the purpose for which man was created." (Tosefta Berakhot 4:1; Zohar I:114a)

The Enduring Fire of Torah   Matthew 5:16–20

"Do not assume that I came to annul the Torah or the Prophets. I did not come to make them obsolete—but to reveal their true depth and restore faithful observance."

- "He will magnify the Torah and make it honorable." (Isaiah 42:21)

"Amen, I tell you: Until the heavens vanish and the earth is no more, not even the smallest yod or the slightest stroke will pass from the Torah until all is fulfilled."

- "Forever, O Adonai, Your word is settled in heaven." (Psalm 119:89)
- "The grass withers, the flower fades, but the word of our Elohim shall stand forever." (Isaiah 40:8)

"For I tell you: unless your righteousness surpasses that of the scribes and Prushim (Pharisees), you will by no means enter the kingdom of heaven."

- "One who is inwardly pure is greater than one who is only outwardly righteous." (Yoma 72b)
- "There are seven kinds of Pharisees, and not all are pleasing to Heaven." (Sotah 22b)

　　1. The "Shoulder Pharisee" (פרוש שְׁכֶם / Shekhem)
Description: Carries his good deeds on his shoulder for all to see. He performs mitzvot (good deeds) only for show, seeking public praise.

　　2. The "Wait-a-Little Pharisee" (פרוש וְכִי / Vekhi)
Description: Always says, "Wait a little; I must do another mitzvah." He avoids real responsibilities by pretending to be always preparing for good deeds. Delays true service behind excuses.

　　3. The "Bleeding Pharisee" (פרוש נִקְפִּי / Nikpi)
Description: Walks with head down to avoid seeing women, constantly bumping into walls and injuring himself. Modern meaning: Over-exaggerated modesty becomes ridiculous. Outward piety with no inward transformation; extreme and impractical.

　　4. The "Pestle Pharisee" (פרוש קִיזָאִי / Kizai)
Description: Walks bent over like a pestle in a mortar, showing exaggerated humility. Feigns meekness to appear righteous.

　　5. The "What's-the-Duty Pharisee" (פרוש מַה חוֹבָתִי / Mah Chovati)
Description: Always asks, "What is my duty that I may do it?" Obeys the Torah legalistically, without love or spirit.

　　6. The "Fearful Pharisee" (פרוש מֵאַהֲבָה / Me'Ahavah or MeYir'ah)

- Variant 1: Some versions say "from love" (אהבה / ahavah).
- Variant 2: Others say "from fear" (יראה / yir'ah).

Description: Motivated only by fear of punishment or desire for reward.

　　7. The "Elohim-Fearing Pharisee" (פרוש אַהֲבָה / Ahavah)
Description: Serves Elohim out of love, as Avraham did. This is the only Pharisee commended. This is the ideal: Inner devotion, outward faithfulness.

- "Do not be like servants who serve their master for reward..." (Avot 1:3)

The Mitzvah of Reconciliation   Matthew 5:21–26

Yeshua looked upon the gathered listeners eyes burning with compassion and warning. "You have heard it said to those of old: 'You shall not murder' (Exodus 20:13), and anyone who murders shall be liable to judgment. But I say to you: Even one who harbors anger against his

brother without cause is already liable before the Heavenly Court. If one calls his brother 'empty one,' he brings himself before the Sanhedrin.
If he says, 'wicked fool,' he risks the fires of Gehinnom.

- "Do not hate your brother in your heart; rebuke your neighbor and do not bear sin because of him." (Leviticus 19:17)
- "He who says to the wicked, 'You are righteous,' peoples will curse him…" (Proverbs 24:24)
- "Anyone who shames his fellow in public is as if he sheds blood." (Bava Metzia 58b)
- "He who calls his fellow 'rasha' (wicked) will be punished in Gehinnom." (Rosh Hashanah 17a)
- "Anger removes a person from the world." (Nedarim 22b)
- "One who harbors hatred in the heart violates the prohibition, 'Do not hate your brother.'" (Yoma 23a)

So, if you are bringing your offering to the altar—if you are drawing near to Elohim in prayer, in study, or in sacrifice—and there you remember that your brother has a grievance against you, leave your gift there before the altar. First, go and seek shalom—make peace with your brother—and only then return to bring your gift. As it is written: 'If a man sin… he shall confess the sin… and he shall make restitution in full… then bring his offering' (Numbers 5:6–8).

- "When you spread out your hands in prayer, I will hide My eyes from you… wash yourselves, make yourselves clean
- "Offerings of the wicked are an abomination to YHWH." (Proverbs 15:8)… cease to do evil, learn to do good; seek justice." (Isaiah 1:15–17)
- "If one has wronged his fellow, even if he brings all the offerings in the world, he is not forgiven until he appeases him." (Bava Kama 92a)
- "Making peace between man and his fellow is greater than bringing offerings." (Midrash Tanchuma, Tzav 3)

Reconcile with your accuser quickly while you are still with him on the way, lest the case be brought before the judge, the judge hands you over to the officer, and you are thrown into prison. I assure you—you will not get out until you have paid the last penny."

- "Agree with your adversary quickly…" (Proverbs 25:8–9: "Do not go hastily to court… debate your case with your neighbor privately")
- "He who digs a pit will fall into it, and he who rolls a stone, it will return upon him." (Proverbs 26:27)
- "If your opponent has a case against you, make peace with him before it reaches judgment." (Avot d'Rabbi Natan 28)

- Anger as a Spiritual Defect (Tikkun HaMiddot) "Whoever loses his temper is like one who worships idols." (Nedarim 22b) The Chassidic masters taught that anger clouds the divine image within man. The Baal Shem Tov explained that anger disconnects one from the tzelem Elohim—thus violating not only the dignity of others, but one's connection to Elohim Himself.
- Offerings Require Integrity (Leviticus 6:2–7; Numbers 5:6–8 Before a guilt offering could be accepted, confession and restitution were required. The same is true of prayer and spiritual ascent. The Alter Rebbe of Lubavitch taught that one cannot draw close to Elohim (korban) if there remains sinat chinam (baseless hatred) between brethren.
- The Blemished Priest Cannot Serve (Leviticus 21:17–23) Just as a priest with a physical blemish could not serve at the altar, so too one with a spiritual blemish of resentment or unresolved strife is temporarily unfit for sacred service. One must cleanse the heart first—tahara hanefesh—before ascending to the altar.
- "Leave Your Gift" as a Profound Spiritual Lesson Rabbeinu Yonah writes (Shaarei Teshuvah 1:12) that Teshuvah is incomplete unless a person makes amends with those they've wronged. Yeshua teaches a living halakha: Reconciliation is not optional—it is prerequisite to divine connection.

The Covenant of the Heart: Guarding the Eyes Matthew 5:27–28 | Exodus 20:14 | Job 31:1

You have heard it said: 'Do not commit adultery.' But I tell you: the covenant of holiness is broken not only with the body, but with the eyes and the heart. He who gazes with lust kindles strange fire upon the altar of his soul. He has already transgressed the inner sanctum. Make a covenant with your eyes. Purify your thoughts. For the Shechinah does not dwell in a heart that burns with unholy fire."

TaNaKh Foundations	Talmudic and Rabbinic Insights	Chassidic Interpretation
Exodus 20:14 – The seventh commandment: "You shall not commit adultery."	Berakhot 61a: "The eye sees, the heart desires, and the body commits the sin."	Chassidut emphasizes that thoughts are spiritual garments of the soul. Rav Tzadok HaKohen of Lublin taught that sinful thoughts darken the nefesh, making it harder to connect with the Shechinah. The Ba'al Shem Tov taught that guarding one's eyes is the first step toward devekut (cleaving to Elohim).

"When the eyes are defiled, the soul is drawn downward. But when one sanctifies the eyes, the heart becomes a sanctuary." |
Job 31:1 – "I have made a covenant with my eyes; how then could I gaze upon a maiden?"	Yoma 29a: "Thoughts of sin are worse than the act itself."	
Proverbs 6:25 – "Do not lust in your heart after her beauty or let her captivate you with her eyes."	Avot 4:2: "A mitzvah draws another mitzvah, and a sin draws another sin." – Thus, even inner lust can draw one into greater spiritual danger.	
Genesis 6:5 – "Every inclination of the thoughts of his heart was only evil all the time."		
Yeshua, in the tradition of the prophets, elevates the mitzvah from an outer prohibition to an inner transformation—guarding not just the body but the lev (heart), the ayin (eye), and the machshavah (thought).	The sages understood that yetzer hara (the evil impulse) begins in the eyes and the mind. Yeshua's teaching mirrors this rabbinic logic: to truly fulfill the Torah, one must guard not only the act, but the impulse that precedes it.	

Guarding the Gates: The Discipline of the Soul   Matthew 5:29–30

"If your eye—the gateway of desire—leads you toward transgression, it is better to tear your gaze away than let your whole being descend into destruction. If your hand—the instrument of your will—causes you to stumble, bind it in restraint. For it is better to lose a limb of indulgence than lose the soul to Gehinnom. Guard your gates: the eye, the hand, the heart. It's better to prune the branch than to lose the tree.

TaNaKh Parallels	Talmudic Commentary & Midrash	Chassidic Interpretation
Proverbs 4:25–27 "Let your eyes look straight ahead… Do not swerve to the right or the left; turn your foot away from evil."	Berakhot 61a "The eye sees, the heart desires, and the body acts." This teaching shows the spiritual chain reaction of sin — starting from the gaze. Yeshua isolates the "eye" and the "hand" as gateways or agents of the yetzer hara.	The Ba'al Shem Tov taught that body parts correspond to spiritual vessels. The eye represents vision and desire; the hand represents action and control.
Psalm 101:3 "I will set no wicked thing before my eyes; I hate the work of those who turn aside; it shall not cling to me."	Sanhedrin 92a "Every part of the body is a witness for or against the soul in the World to Come." Talmud affirms that body parts are not morally neutral—they're spiritually accountable.	The "right eye" symbolizes chesed (lovingkindness) — when corrupted, even love can become indulgence.
Deuteronomy 13:7–10 If a loved one entices you to idolatry, you must not pity or spare them—even to the point of removal from the community. A very hard command but reflects the concept of cutting off the source of sin to preserve holiness.	Niddah 13b Discusses the need to "cut off" sinful behavior at its root. There is a rabbinic phrase used here: "Better that his belly be split than he bring evil into the world." Though extreme, it affirms that radical self-restraint may be better than sin's consequences.	The "right hand" symbolizes power, strength, agency — when misused, it becomes destructive.

Yeshua's words, in this context, are not advocating physical mutilation, but calling for inner circumcision — radical teshuvah (repentance), turning the heart back to Elohim by cutting off access points of sin. |
| Yeshua's teaching fits squarely within the prophetic and Deuteronomic tradition: radical separation from sin to preserve the community and soul. | Midrash Tanchuma, Vayikra 8
"If your right hand offends, tie it behind your back."
Precedent for metaphoric restraint to prevent habitual sin. | |
| Yeshua teaches in line with Torah and wisdom literature: sin must be cut off at its source—even if it is as close to you as your own eye or hand. Just as Deuteronomy commands Israel not to spare even the closest loved one if they lead others into idolatry, so too must one not spare their own faculties if they entice the soul to rebel against Elohim. This is not about self-mutilation but about radical self-discipline. The "eye" represents desire and intention, and the "hand" represents action. To "cast them off" means to separate oneself from sources of temptation, even when they feel like part of one's identity. Yeshua is calling for a kind of inner korban (sacrifice)—a willingness to lose comfort, pride, or habit for the sake of fidelity to Torah. This is the path of teshuvah (repentance) and tikkun (repair). | | |

On Divorce and Faithfulness to Covenant Matthew 5:31–32

You have heard it said: 'Whoever sends away his wife, let him give her a get (bill of divorce).' But I say to you: Whoever sends his wife away apart from a cause of sexual immorality or serious defilement causes her to become as one who commits adultery, for if she remarries, she is forbidden to return. And whoever marries a woman who has been sent away unjustly also shares in this defilement. For the Torah permits divorce only when a true ervat davar (matter of shame or indecency) has occurred (Deuteronomy 24:1–4)—and even then, the bond is not severed lightly, for Adonai hates divorce and regards it as betrayal (Malachi 2:14–16).

TaNaKh Parallel	Talmudic Commentary
Deuteronomy 24:1–4 1 "When a man takes a wife and marries her, and it happens that she does not find favor in his eyes because he has found some 'ervat davar' – a matter of indecency or immorality), he shall write her a get (bill of divorce), hand it to her, and send her out of his house. 2 If, after leaving his house, she goes and becomes another man's wife, 3 and the second man dislikes her and writes her a get, hands it to her, and sends her away—or if he dies— 4 then her first husband who sent her away may not take her again to be his wife after she has been defiled, for that is an abomination before Adonai, and you shall not bring sin upon the land that Adonai your Elohim is giving you as an inheritance." Implication: If the woman remarries and consummates that marriage, she is considered defiled to the first husband and cannot return to him. However, if she did not marry or lie with another man, the text does not prohibit return. Malachi 2:14–16 "Adonai has been witnessing between you and the wife of your youth, to whom you have been faithless… She is your companion and your wife by covenant. Did He not make them one? … So, guard yourselves in your spirit, and do not be faithless to the wife of your youth. For I hate divorce," says Adonai the Elohim of Israel. Leviticus 21:7 (Priestly Standard) "A kohen shall not marry a woman who is defiled by harlotry, nor shall they take a woman divorced from her husband; for he is holy to his Elohim." Connection: Yeshua, teaching within the Pharisaic worldview, elevates all of Israel to a priestly status (cf. Exodus 19:6: "a kingdom of priests"), implying that marriage must reflect priestly sanctity—not merely civil legality.	Talmud Bavli – Gittin 90a–90b Beit Shammai: A man may divorce his wife only for a matter of adultery or serious sexual sin (ervat davar). Beit Hillel: Permits divorce even for trivial reasons (e.g. if she burned his food). Rabbi Akiva: Permits divorce even if the man finds another woman more desirable. However, the ethical conclusion in Gittin 90b: "He who divorces his first wife, even the altar sheds tears." Midrash – Sifre on Deuteronomy 24:1 The Midrash focuses on the phrase ervat davar and argues that it refers not to mere dislike or triviality, but to something shameful that violates the covenant of marriage. It further implies the original purpose of divorce law was to protect the dignity and legal clarity for the woman—not to create a culture of casual divorce.
Chassidic-Mystical View on Divorce and Covenant Love (Matthew 5:31–32) 1. Marriage as a Reflection of Divine Union "The union between husband and wife mirrors the union between the Shechinah and Knesset Yisrael." Tanya, Iggeret HaKodesh In Chassidic thought, marriage is not merely a social contract—it is a sacred reflection of the bond between Elohim and His people. To sever that bond through divorce is to tear a cosmic thread, disrupting the harmony of the divine presence (Shechinah) in this world. The relationship between man and wife is seen as a miniature Mikdash (sanctuary) through which holiness enters the world. 2. Even in Betrayal, There Is Mercy "I will betroth you to Me forever. I will betroth you to Me with righteousness and justice, with lovingkindness and mercy." Hoshea 2:19–20 Despite Israel's betrayal through idolatry and spiritual infidelity, Elohim speaks not with finality, but with mercy and reconciliation. Chassidic teachings draw from this prophetic imagery to argue that even after great sin, the bond between the Divine and His people remains restorable. Teshuvah (repentance) reopens the gates of union.	
Tanakh Foundations Jeremiah 3:1–14 "If a man divorces his wife and she goes from him and becomes another man's; may he return to her again? Wouldn't the land be greatly defiled? But you have played the harlot with many lovers—yet return to Me, declares Adonai!" Though Elohim quotes Deuteronomy 24:4, He transcends its legal boundaries. In the face of Israel's defilement, He does not shut the door. The Chassidic interpretation here is profound: Elohim chooses restorative love over strict legality, teaching that divine compassion reaches where human law cannot.	

"Return, O backsliding children... for I am married to you." — Jeremiah 3:14. This declaration transforms the halachic framework into one of eternal covenants. Though unfaithful, Israel is still called "My wife." Chassidic Integration with Yeshua's Teaching in Matthew 5:31–32: Yeshua, speaking not as a messianic figure but as a Torah sage within a Pharisaic-priestly framework, emphasizes the spiritual gravity of divorce. His words align closely with Beit Shammai's narrow halachic stance: divorce is permitted only for ervat davar—serious moral failure. However, his deeper ethic goes beyond halachic boundaries: Do not use Torah's permission as a legal loophole. View marriage through the lens of divine oneness. Understand that unjust divorce causes spiritual harm, not only to individuals, but to the nation and the world. "Each marriage is a covenant; each divorce a tear in the fabric of holiness." — Zohar I:232a
Ethical-Mystical Summary Talmud (Gittin 90b) records both lenient and strict views but notes: "Even the altar weeps for a man who divorces his first wife." Chassidic Thought cautions: Even when permitted, divorce is a spiritual rupture. Elohim models restoration—taking back Israel even after deep betrayal.
Final Reflection Divorce, while not forbidden in Torah, is never ideal. Yeshua's words, the voice of the sages, and the whisper of the Shechinah all point in the same direction: If Elohim takes back an unfaithful bride—should not we also seek to heal, to forgive, to restore? Teshuvah is the lifeblood of Israel. So long as repentance is genuine, Chassidut teaches, even what seems defiled may become holy again.

On Oaths and Truthful Speech   Matthew 5:33–37

You have heard that it was said to the ancients: 'Do not swear falsely but fulfill your vows to Adonai' (Leviticus 19:12; Numbers 30:2; Deuteronomy 23:21–23). But I tell you: Do not swear at all—not by the heavens, for they are Elohim's throne (Isaiah 66:1), nor by the earth, for it is His footstool, nor by Jerusalem, for it is the city of the Great King (Psalm 48:2), nor by your head, for you cannot make a single hair white or black. Instead, let your words be trustworthy: When you mean 'yes,' say 'yes.' When you mean 'no,' say 'no.' Anything more than this arises from the yetzer hara (the Evil Inclination).

TaNaKh Parallels
. Zechariah 8:16–17 "These are the things you shall do: Speak truth each to his neighbor; judge with truth and the judgment of peace in your gates. Let none of you devise evil in your heart against his neighbor and love no false oath—for all these are what I hate," declares Adonai. Connection: Condemns false oaths and aligns with Yeshua's command to avoid invoking sacred words deceptively or manipulatively. 2. Jeremiah 5:2 "Though they say, 'As Adonai lives,' surely they swear falsely." Connection: Critiques false religious swearing, showing how invoking Adonai's Name doesn't sanctify dishonesty — it profanes it. 3. Psalm 15:1–4 "Who may dwell on Your holy hill? ... He who speaks truth in his heart... who swears to his own hurt and does not change." Connection: Upholds the integrity of one's word as a hallmark of righteousness. Even when difficult, a righteous person keeps their word — no need for extra oaths. 4. Ecclesiastes 5:4–6 "When you make a vow to Elohim, do not delay in fulfilling it... Better not to vow than to vow and not fulfill... Do not let your mouth cause your flesh to sin." Connection: Cautions against careless vows. Yeshua's teaching to avoid oaths entirely is consistent with the wisdom tradition that values restraint over risk. 6. Psalm 34:13–14 "Keep your tongue from evil, and your lips from speaking deceit. Depart from evil and do good; seek peace and pursue it." Connection: A foundation for the Chassidic concept of tikkun ha'dibur (repair of speech). Yeshua is pointing toward this elevated ethical path.

Talmudic Commentary	Chassidic Commentary on Matthew 5:33–37 Yeshua and the Mystical Path of Speech and Soul Refinement

Nedarim 9b
"Even one who vows and fulfills it is called wicked."
 	
Insight: The ideal in rabbinic piety is to avoid vows entirely, even if kept — to prevent potential sin and spiritual harm. Yeshua reflects this stringency in ethics.
 	
Bava Metzia 49a
"Let your 'yes' be yes and your 'no' be no."
 	
Insight: This phrase is used to enforce verbal honesty in financial matters and interpersonal trust. Yeshua uses the same idiom for spiritual integrity.
 	
Rambam – Mishneh Torah, Hilkhot Shevuot 12:1
"It is proper for a person to be careful not to swear at all... even to speak the truth. A person should be trustworthy and speak truth without oaths."
 	
Insight: Rambam's legal conclusion matches Yeshua's ethical teaching: a truly righteous person has no need to swear because their word is as strong as a vow.
 	
Pirkei Avot 1:17
"All my days I grew up among the sages, and I have found nothing better for the body than silence."
 	
Insight: Silence and restrained speech are seen as signs of wisdom. Yeshua's emphasis on minimal, honest speech fits squarely within this Chazal tradition.
	1. The Power of Speech – Dibur as a Creative Force
	In Chassidic and Kabbalistic thought, dibur (speech) is not merely communication — it is a vessel of divine power, part of the Ten Utterances through which the world was created (cf. Genesis 1).
	
	Zohar I:60b says: "The word is the garment of the soul. As garments reveal or conceal the body, so words reveal or conceal the soul." (Out of the heart the mouth speaks- Yeshua)
	
	Tanya, Sha'ar HaYichud Ve'haEmunah explains: Speech originates in the heart (emotion) and mind (thought), but it exits the lips — and once it exits, it becomes a force in the world.
	   ♦ Application to Yeshua's Teaching: Yeshua warns his disciples not to wrap deceit, manipulation, or vanity in sacred language. Every word, especially one that invokes Heaven or Jerusalem, affects not only those who hear, but the speaker's own soul. False or careless speech distorts the divine image (tzelem Elohim) within.
	
	2. Tikkun Ha'dibur – Repair of the Tongue
	Baal Shem Tov taught that the mouth is a gateway of holiness, and misuse of speech damages the spiritual structure of the self and the world.
	
	From Sichot HaRan (Rabbi Nachman of Breslov):
	"The greatest tikkun is to sanctify one's mouth. If the mouth is pure, the whole body is elevated."
	
	The Tanya (Iggeret HaKodesh 22) warns that even truthful oaths draw down spiritual energy from higher worlds. If spoken without reverence, this can bring judgment upon the soul, as the vessel is too fragile for such light.
	
	   ♦ Yeshua's "Do not swear at all" is thus not legalism — it is mystical caution. He urges his followers to abstain from oaths not because vows are unlawful, but because every spoken word is spiritual architecture. A twisted oath is a collapsed bridge between worlds.
	
	3. Inner–Outer Alignment: Yes Means Yes, No Means No
	Chassidic thought emphasizes achdut ha'nefesh — unity within the soul. When the heart, mind, and mouth are aligned, one's words carry the light of divine truth.
	
	Shem MiShmuel teaches:
	"The double affirmation ('yes, yes') reflects the inner 'yes' of the soul agreeing with the outer 'yes' of the lips. This is emunah (faithfulness) in action."
	
	The Baal Shem Tov added:
	"The one who speaks simply, with no ornament, brings healing to the world. The one who must swear, reveals a world that does not trust."
	
	   ♦ Yeshua's command to say only "yes, yes" or "no, no" is a call to this Chassidic wholeness of speech. It reflects a soul that needs no oath to be believed — because its inner light shines through its words.
	
	4. Swearing and the Illusion of Control
	When Yeshua says, "Do not swear by your head, for you cannot make one hair white or black," he touches a Chassidic principle of humility: Man is not the master. Elohim alone governs the world.
	
	Me'or Einayim (Chernobyler Rebbe) interprets this type of teaching as a mussar on false mastery — those who swear by created things imagine control they do not possess.
	
	To invoke Heaven or the body in an oath is to misuse divine gifts in the service of ego.
	
	   ♦ Chassidic humility teaches the opposite: recognize the Creator in all things — and speak accordingly.
	
	5. The Yetzer Hara and Exaggerated Speech
	Yeshua ends the teaching with: "Anything beyond this comes from the yetzer hara (evil inclination)."
	
	This is deeply consistent with: Zohar III:55a, which says that excessive speech opens the gates to the Sitra Achra (the Other Side), giving spiritual nourishment to forces of impurity.
	Rebbe Nachman, who said: "Exaggeration is the clothing of falsehood. It covers the lie in a garment of beauty and causes the soul to stumble."
	
	   ♦ Chassidic masters taught that speech should be measured, gentle, clean, and true. When it becomes manipulative or theatrical — even in pious-sounding ways — it becomes the tool of the yetzer hara.

On Mercy Over Retaliation Matthew 5:38–39

You have heard that it was said, "An eye for an eye, and a tooth for a tooth" (Exodus 21:24; Leviticus 24:20; Deuteronomy 19:21) — and rightly so, for Torah teaches justice through equal compensation, not vengeance. But I tell you: do not repay insult with force, nor injury with rage. If someone strikes you on the right cheek, offer him the other as well — not out of weakness, but to conquer evil with mercy. The one who masters' his impulse is greater than the one who executes judgment (Proverbs 16:32). Let your restraint become a tikkun — a repair — in this world of broken hearts.

TaNaKh Parallels	Talmudic Commentary	Chassidic Insight
Exodus 21:24 "An eye for an eye, a tooth for a tooth, a hand for a hand, a foot for a foot…" This appears within the context of judicial restitution — not personal revenge. The Oral Torah (Talmud Bavli, Bava Kamma 83b–84a) unanimously interprets this as monetary compensation, not literal mutilation. "An eye for an eye" means: the value of the eye must be paid. Leviticus 19:18 "Do not take vengeance or bear a grudge… but you shall love your neighbor as yourself." Yeshua's teaching in verse 39 grows out of this — it is not a contradiction of Torah, but a Chassidic intensification: go beyond the minimum requirement of avoiding vengeance — embrace peace in the face of insult. Proverbs 20:22 "Do not say, 'I will repay evil.' Wait for Adonai, and He will save you." This is a clear wisdom precedent for withholding retaliation. Lamentations 3:30 "Let him offer his cheek to the one who strikes him; let him be filled with reproach." Yeshua's language about "turning the other cheek" may echo this very verse — calling the righteous to bear insult in humility as an act of spiritual trust.	Bava Kamma 8:6 / 84a The Sages unanimously state that "eye for eye" is not literal but refers to financial restitution. They derive this from legal principles like: The need for a consistent, non-mutilating legal system. The Torah's use of "under the judges" in context Retaliation in person is strictly forbidden in halacha. ♦ Yeshua is not abrogating Torah law, but teaching that even when legal justice is available, the higher path is restraint and mercy — especially in non-criminal matters like insult or humiliation. Avot 4:1 "Who is mighty? One who conquers his impulse." This teaching supports Yeshua's ethic: strength lies not in revenge but in restraint. Sanhedrin 88b The shaming of others (especially public striking) is likened to shedding blood. Responding to such humiliation with calm is praised in rabbinic ethics.	♦ A. Going Beyond Justice – Chessed over Din In Chassidut, Din (judgment) is true, but incomplete without Chessed (lovingkindness). The Baal Shem Tov taught that truth without mercy is a sword, while mercy transforms reality. Yeshua calls his disciples to transcend strict justice. Not by denying Torah, but by mirroring the divine balance — as Elohim "slow to anger" and "abundant in mercy." ♦ B. Turning the Other Cheek – A Path of Tikun Shem MiShmuel teaches: "The one who accepts insult without responding builds a crown for the Shechinah." Zohar II:110b – one who restrains from revenge draws down light from the highest worlds and repairs damaged spiritual channels. Yeshua's teaching to "turn the other cheek" is an act of cosmic repair (tikkun) — a refusal to feed the kelipot (husks) with reactive energy. ♦ C. Mastery of the Yetzer Hara The yetzer hara thrives on ego, especially when insulted. The righteous person turns away from vengeance not out of weakness but out of inner mastery. As in Tanya Chapter 12, the beinoni (intermediate soul) does not destroy the yetzer hara but channels its energy upward — responding to provocation with spiritual calm.

On Reconciliation and Generosity Matthew 5:40 | Luke 12:58

If someone seeks to bring you before the Sanhedrin to sue you for your tunic, do not wait for judgment. Settle the matter quickly while you are still on the way with him (Luke 12:58).

Reconcile with your brother not through resistance, but through mercy and kindness, and give him not only your tunic, but your cloak as well (Exodus 22:26–27). For when you give beyond what is required, you are not diminished—you are multiplied. Mercy is never wasted; it becomes a fire that melts even the hardest heart and leaves behind the fragrance of peace.

TaNaKh Parallels	Talmud Parallels
Proverbs 17:14 "The beginning of strife is like releasing water; therefore, stop contention before a quarrel breaks out." Encourages early resolution — before the court process begins. Proverbs 25:8–10 "Do not go hastily to court, lest you be put to shame… Discuss your case with your neighbor himself, and do not reveal another's secret." Avoid litigation by working out your issues privately — exactly what your verse emphasizes. Psalm 34:14 "Seek peace and pursue it." Peace (shalom) is not passive — it must be pursued, as your version urges. Micah 6:8 "He has told you, O man, what is good: to do justice, love mercy, and walk humbly with your Elohim." All three elements of your wording — justice, mercy, humility — are in perfect harmony with this verse.	Sanhedrin 6b: It is a mitzvah to pursue peace and resolve disputes even when one is legally right. Avot 1:12: "Be like the disciples of Aharon: love peace, pursue peace…" Bava Kamma 92a: "One who yields even what is rightfully his, for the sake of shalom, is blessed.

Chassidic Insight
Baal Shem Tov (Tzava'at HaRivash §8) "To forgo your rights is to create a garment for the Shechinah in this world." Clothing in Chassidut symbolizes spiritual vessels. To give your cloak (simlah) is to say: "I give up this vessel of my self-concern to clothe the Divine Presence instead." The Baal Shem Tov taught: When someone tries to take from you unjustly, respond with expansive kindness, and you disarm the spiritual root of their aggression. Me'or Einayim: The one who gives beyond what is demanded transforms a moment of conflict into an act of divine generosity (hashpa'ah), turning judgment into chessed. Tanya, Chapter 12 – describes the beinoni (intermediate one) as one who masters inner impulses through divine awareness and self-restraint, even though the urge to react remains. Giving up your cloak when only the tunic is demanded is an act of emotional avodah (divine service). It reveals that the person is not ruled by pride or justice, but by chesed shel emet — true kindness. Shem MiShmuel (Vayigash, 5670): "When two forces oppose one another, and one yields with grace, the energy of opposition becomes a vessel for peace." The verse models transformative peacemaking. It turns potential resentment into tikkun ha-lev (repair of the heart). According to Zohar II:215a and Likkutei Torah (BaMidbar): The tunic represents the levush hanefesh — the outer emotions. The cloak represents the makifim — the surrounding light, or one's public dignity and status. To give both is to say: "I surrender both my inner feelings and my outer image in order to establish peace." This is a mystical form of self-nullification (bitul) — a key step in divine union. Etz Chaim, Shaar 5 "When the lower worlds generate chessed in response to gevurah, the upper worlds are sweetened, and harsh decrees are lifted." Giving to one who sues you unjustly sweetens judgment at its root — both in the soul and in the heavens.

Going the Second Mile: Turning Burden into Offering — Matthew 5:41

If a Roman soldier compels you to carry his pack for him for one mile, walk with him for two. For the first mile is for him, but the second mile is for Heaven. What he forces from you, let it become your offering. In this way, you will not be ruled by the hand that burdens you, but by the heart that rises above. You reclaim your dignity not by resisting service but by transforming it. As the Torah teaches: "If you see your enemy's donkey collapsing under its load… you must help him" (Exodus 23:5). Conquer evil not with defiance, but with chesed (lovingkindness), and your burden will become a blessing.

HISTORICAL CONTEXT

In first-century Judea, a Roman soldier could compel a civilian to carry equipment for one Roman mile under the practice of angareia (Latin: angarium), a form of state-mandated conscription for brief labor.
This is referenced in Matthew 27:32, where Simon of Cyrene is compelled to carry Yeshua's stake.
Most Jews resented this deeply, and it was seen as humiliating — especially by Zealots.

TaNaKh Parallels	Talmudic Commentary	Chassidic Insights
Exodus 23:4–5 – Help your enemy's animal if it is struggling, even if the owner hates you.	Bava Metzia 32b "If the animal of your enemy collapses under its burden, and your friend's animal also collapses, help your enemy first — to subdue your evil inclination."	A. Transforming the Act of Oppression Baal Shem Tov taught when hardship comes from others, it is an opportunity to elevate fallen sparks (nitzotzot). Zohar I:224a: "When din (judgment) is met with chesed (kindness), the din is sweetened, and peace is drawn into the world."
Deuteronomy 22:1–4 – You must return a lost item, even to an enemy, and help him lift his burden. ♦ The principle: Even if the person is your oppressor or enemy, respond with righteousness — not rebellion.	Directly parallels this verse: serve even the one who imposes upon you — it is a form of inner conquest. Avot 4:1 "Who is strong? One who conquers his yetzer (inclination)." Yeshua's instruction to go the second mile is an act of voluntary self-conquest and moral victory.	The first mile is imposed by external power (gevurah). The second mile is self-chosen (chesed), which sweetens the first and transforms the act into an offering. If someone compels you to walk a mile — that's din (judgment). If you go two, you're adding chesed (mercy) — you've transformed the act from imposition to mitzvah. Tanya, Chapter 12: A beinoni turns every situation — even one driven by injustice — into a moment of avodah (divine service).
Micah 6:8 "What does Adonai require of you? To act justly, love mercy, and walk humbly with your Elohim." The idea of walking an extra mile as a humble offering of mercy is drawn straight from here.	Avot 5:23 "According to the effort is the reward." Turning what is forced upon you into a spiritual avodah — your "offering" — reflects the core of rabbinic ethics: effort matters more than outcome. Pesachim 113b "Three are among those whom Elohim loves: one who does not get angry easily, one who does not take revenge, and one who yields in conflict."	♦ B. Two Miles = Din + Chessed In Kabbalistic symbolism: The first mile is gevurah (severity) — the imposed. The second mile is chesed (lovingkindness) — the voluntary. When you do both, you unite the two attributes — sweetening judgment through action. ♦ C. Walking = Spiritual Elevation (Halichah) In Chassidut, the word halachah (law) and halichah (walking) are linked. "Going the extra mile" is a form of halichah ruchanit — spiritual movement forward. The one who walks beyond what is required is the one who is truly growing. As Rebbe Nachman said: "Where I am going is not where I came from."

Give with an Open Hand   Matthew 5:42

When a beggar asks of you, give with an open hand. For what you give in kindness becomes a vessel for Heaven. Give not because you must, but because your Father gives without measure. As it is written: "You shall surely open your hand to your brother, to your poor and to your needy in your land" (Deuteronomy 15:8). And again: "He who is generous to the poor lends to Adonai, and He will repay him" (Proverbs 19:17). Give with joy, not reluctance, for Elohim loves a cheerful giver—one whose heart mirrors the generosity of Heaven.

TaNaKh Parallels	Talmudic Commentary	Chassidic Insight
Deuteronomy 15:7–8 "If there is a poor person among you... you shall not harden your heart or shut your hand, but you shall surely open your hand to him and lend him sufficient for his need."	Bava Metzia 71a "If you have money to lend to both a Jew and a non-Jew, lend to the Jew first. If to a poor person and a rich person, lend to the poor first."	Tanya, Iggeret HaKodesh 9 "Charity is the vessel for all blessing... it brings life and light from the highest worlds into the lowest."
Psalm 37:26 "All day long he is gracious and lends, and his seed is blessed."	Ketubot 67b "Even if a person is accustomed to riding a horse and has servants, you are obligated to provide according to his former dignity."	Zohar III:113a "One who withholds compassion closes the upper gates. Judgment awakens from above and below."
Proverbs 19:17 "One who is gracious to the poor lends to Adonai, and He will repay him for his good deed."	Rosh Hashanah 16b "Three things annul the harsh decree: prayer, repentance, and charity."	Sefat Emet (Va'era, 5637): "To give without condition is to walk in the path of the Blessed One, who gives to all, even those undeserving."

Love Your Enemies   Matthew 5:43–48 | Luke 6:27–36

You have heard it said: "Love your neighbor," and you have also heard, "Hate your enemy." But I say to you: Love even those who oppose you. Bless those who curse you. Do good to those who hate you. Pray for those who persecute you and slander you. In doing so, you become true children of Avinu Shebashamayim (our Father in Heaven), for He causes His sun to rise on both the evil and the good and sends rain on the righteous and the unrighteous alike. If you love only those who love you, what reward is there in that? Do not even the mochei ha'misim (tax collectors) do the same? And if you greet only your brothers, what are you doing more than others? Do not even the goyim (Gentiles) do the same? You must become tamim (whole, complete, blameless)—just as Avinu Shebashamayim is tamim. For in loving those who do not love you, you imitate the unceasing kindness of El Elyon.

TaNaKh Parallels	Talmudic Commentary	Chassidic Insights
Genesis 17:1: "Walk before Me and be tamim (complete)."	Berakhot 10a – On Rabbi Meir: When people persecuted him, his wife Bruriah said: "Do not pray for their death, pray for their repentance."	Zohar II:67b: "The one who resembles his Master in kindness draws the Shechinah to dwell upon him."
Leviticus 19:18 "You shall love your neighbor as yourself: I am Adonai."		Zohar I:66a – The sun is a metaphor for divine light; when you imitate Elohim's universal benevolence, you draw Shechinah into the world.
Core command of Torah. However, nowhere does Torah command "hate your enemy." Yeshua contrasts the written Torah with a popular but un-Torahic attitude — possibly from Essene or Zealot circles.	Avot 5:22: "Whoever brings peace between people, it is as though he becomes a son of Avraham."	Tanya, Ch. 15 – "The 'perfect one' is one whose acts, thoughts, and heart are aligned in divine service."
Deut. 18:13 – "You shall be wholehearted (tamim) with Adonai your Elohim."		Final Chassidic Reflection You become like Elohim not by miracles, but by mercy. Not by power, but by peace.
Proverbs 25:21–22	Berakhot 17a:	

"If your enemy is hungry, give him bread to eat; if he is thirsty, give him water to drink…" Psalm 145:9 "Adonai is good to all, and His mercy is over all His works." Job 31:29–32 "I did not rejoice at the ruin of my enemy… I did not withhold hospitality from the stranger."	"The students of the wise greet everyone with peace, even a non-Jew in the marketplace." Talmud Sanhedrin 103b: Even wicked kings showed love to their friends.	When you love not only the beloved, but also the bitter — then your heart becomes a vessel for the Shechinah. Be complete in kindness, as your Father in Heaven is complete in giving. This is the hidden fire that turns enemies into brothers and hatred into healing.

Give, Pray, and Fast in Secret Matthew 6:1–8

Be careful not to perform your tzedakah (acts of righteousness) before others merely to be seen by them. For if you do, there is no reward awaiting you from Avichem Shebashamayim (your Father in the heavens). When you give to the poor, do not blow a trumpet before you like the chanafim (hypocrites) do in the synagogues and in the streets, seeking praise from men. Amen, I tell you—they have already received their reward.

But when you give it, do it secretly so silently that your left hand does not even know what your right hand is doing. Let your act of chesed (loving-kindness) be hidden in humility. And Avichem, who sees what is done in secret, will reward you openly.

When you fast, do not disfigure your face with sorrow like the hypocrites do, putting on a mask of suffering to appear pious before men. I tell you the truth—they too have received their reward. But when you fast, wash your face and anoint your head with oil, so that your fasting will not be seen by others, but by Avichem who is hidden. And Avichem, who sees the secret hunger of your soul, will reward you in the open.

And when you pray, do not be like the hypocrites. They love to stand in synagogues and on street corners to be seen by others. Amen, I tell you—they have received their reward. But when you pray, enter your cheder (inner room), close the door, and pray to Avichem who is hidden. And Avichem, who sees what is done in the hidden place, will reward you. When you pray, do not babble on with vain repetitions like the pagans do. They think they will be heard because of their many words. Do not be like them, for Avichem knows what you need even before you ask.

TaNaKh Parallels	Talmudic Commentary		Chassidic Insights
Micah 6:8 "What does Adonai require of you? To do justice, love mercy, and walk humbly with your Elohim." Proverbs 21:14 "A secret gift pacifies anger." 1 Samuel 1:13 "Only her lips moved, but her	Talmud, Bava Batra 9b "Greater is the one who gives charity in secret than even Moshe our teacher." Berakhot 31a Channah's whispered prayer became the halachic model for silent prayer Yeshua echoes this when instructing prayer in the inner chamber — the chesed she-b'gevurah of quiet inward devotion. Avot 1:3 "Do not be like servants who serve the Master for the sake of reward…" Chullin 133a "Just as He is gracious and compassionate, so must you be."		Tzimtzum (Kabbalistic contraction): The hidden chamber represents the sacred void in which true relationship with Elohim occurs. Tanya, Chapter 41 "A person should meditate that the great King is watching even in secret — and this awe leads to genuine service." Zohar I:115a "All that is hidden before men is revealed before the Throne."

voice was not heard."	The intention behind a mitzvah is as important as the action. Seeking honor nullifies reward. Sanhedrin 106b "Whoever seeks his own honor through Torah — his Torah becomes meaningless." The hypocrite gets what they wanted — public honor — but forfeits divine intimacy.	Shem MiShmuel, Bo 5670 "Even one word spoken with pure heart lifts all the worlds, while ten thousand uttered mindlessly fall flat."

The Prayer of the Disciples   Matthew 6:9–13

"This then is how you should pray:

Avinu Shebashamayim, Yitkadesh Shimcha
Our Father in Heaven, sanctified be Your Name.
— [Isaiah 29:23, "They will sanctify My name…"]
Tavo Malchutcha bimherah
May Your Kingdom come soon.
— [Daniel 2:44, "In the days of those kings the God of Heaven will set up a Kingdom…"]
Ye'aseh Retzoncha ba'aretz k'mo bashamayim
Fulfill Your will upon this earth in our lives as it is done in Heaven.
— [Psalm 103:20–21, "His angels, mighty in strength, doing His word… His hosts, ministers of His will."]
Ten lanu hayom et lechem shel machar
Give us today the bread of tomorrow.
— [Proverbs 30:8, "Provide me with my allotted portion of bread."]
U'selach lanu al chata'einu k'mo shemesolchim la'acherim
Forgive us of our sins as we forgive those who sin against us.
— [Psalm 32:1, "Blessed is the one whose transgression is forgiven…"]
Al tevi'einu lidei nisayon
Lead us away from temptation
— [Psalm 141:4, "Do not incline my heart to any evil thing…"]
Ve'hatzileinu min haYetzer haRa
And deliver us from our evil inclinations.
— [Genesis 8:21, "The inclination of man's heart is evil from youth…"]
Ki lecha haMalchut, vehaGevurah, vehaShelitah le'olam va'ed
For to You belongs the Kingdom, and the Power, and Authority — forever and ever.
— [1 Chronicles 29:11, "Yours, Adonai, is the greatness and the power and the glory…"]

Forgiveness & Heavenly Treasure   Matthew 6:14–21   Matthew 18:21–35

Yeshua paused to let the words of the prayer settle deeply into the hearts of his disciples, and then he added with piercing clarity: "For if you forgive others for their offenses, Avichem Shebashamayim (your Father in the heavens) will also forgive you. But if you do not forgive others, Avichem Shebashamayim will not forgive you."

A hush lingered as his listeners reflected on these weighty words. "Do not store up treasures for yourselves here on earth, where moth and rust consume, and where thieves break in and steal. Rather, store up treasures in the heavens, where neither moth nor rust devours, and no thief can break in or steal. For where your treasure is, there your heart will also be." The listeners glanced at one another—some with shame, others with longing—realizing that earthly riches are passing shadows, but heavenly treasure endures.

TaNaKh Parallels	Talmudic Commentary	Chassidic Insights
Proverbs 23:4–5 "Do not weary yourself to gain wealth… when you set your eyes on it, it is gone, for it makes wings and flies away like an eagle." Ecclesiastes 5:10–14 "He who loves silver will not be satisfied… riches perish through misfortune." Psalm 49:16–18 "Do not fear when a man becomes rich… when he dies, he will take nothing with him."	Avot 4:1 "Who is rich? He who is content with what he has." Avot 2:8 "If you have acquired Torah, what do you lack? And if you lack Torah, what have you acquired?" Bava Batra 11a "Charity saves from death and stores merit in the world to come." This speaks directly to Yeshua's distinction between earthly accumulation and heavenly investment through righteousness (tzedakah, mitzvot).	Tanya – Chapters 6 & 37 Every mitzvah is a garment of light for the soul in the World to Come. Material obsession empowers the kelipot (husks) and diminishes one's spiritual clarity. Me'or Einayim (R. Menachem Nachum of Chernobyl) "That which is hidden in the heart shapes the form of one's service to God. If the treasure is Heaven, then the soul is drawn upward with it." Zohar III:276a "When a man clings to the lower world, he binds his soul to the dust; but when he longs for the upper world, the soul ascends."

The Eye: Gateway of the Soul Matthew 6:22–23 | Luke 11:34–36

Yeshua continued, raising his voice slightly as he turned toward the crowd: "The eye is the lamp of the body. If your eye is tovah—generous and whole—your entire body will be filled with light. But if your eye is rah—stingy, wicked, or corrupted—then your whole body will be filled with darkness. And if the light within you has become obscured—how great that corruption is!" He spoke not merely of vision, but of perspective, of desire, and of focus. A generous eye sees the good in others and gives freely, while a corrupt eye hoards, judges, and distorts. And so, Yeshua warned them: the quality of one's vision shapes the destiny of one's soul.

TaNaKh Parallels	Talmudic Commentary	Chassidic Insight
◆ Proverbs 22:9 "A good eye (ayin tovah) will be blessed, for he gives of his bread to the poor." The concept of a "good eye" in Jewish thought represents generosity and compassion. ◆ Deuteronomy 15:9 "Beware that there not be a base thought in your heart… and your eye be evil (ayin ra'ah) against your needy brother." ◆ Isaiah 5:20 "Woe to those who call evil good and good evil… who put darkness for light and light for darkness."	◆ Avot 5:19 "Whoever possesses a good eye, a humble spirit, and a lowly soul is a disciple of Abraham." This is key. The ayin tovah defines a righteous disciple. ◆ Sotah 38b The generous one is called a "wholehearted person" (shalem)—his eye is aligned with divine light. ◆ Bava Batra 9a "Tzedakah is equivalent to all the other mitzvot." The eye is metaphorical for the intent behind action — the da'at (conscious awareness) that either elevates or corrupts the soul's direction.	◆ Zohar II:148b "The eye is the mirror of the soul. When it seeks righteousness, the whole soul shines; when it seeks self, darkness rests upon it." ◆ Rabbi Nachman of Breslov "A person's eyes are the gates through which the heart is drawn. Guard your gaze and your gaze will guard you."

Trusting in Avichem Shebashamayim　　　　　　　　　　　　　　　　　　　Matthew 6:24–34

"No one can serve two masters," Yeshua declared, his voice now both gentle and firm. "He will either hate one and love the other, or cling to one and ignore the other. You cannot serve both Elohim and materialism."

He paused, letting the words settle into the crowd's hearts. "Therefore, I will tell you: Do not be anxious about your life—what you will eat or drink, or about your body—what you wear. Is the soul not more than food, and the body more than clothing? Look at the birds of the heavens. They neither sow nor reap nor gather into barns, yet Avichem Shebashamayim (your Father in the heavens) feeds them. Are you not worth more than they? Who among you, by worrying, can add even one moment to his life?

And why are you anxious about clothing? Consider the lilies of the field, how they grow. They do not toil or spin. Yet I tell you: even Shlomo (Solomon) in all his glory was not clothed like one of these. If this is how Elohim clothes the grass of the field—which is here today and tomorrow is thrown into the fire—will He not much more clothe you, you of little emunah (faith)?

So do not say anxiously: 'What shall we eat?' or 'What shall we drink?' or 'What shall we wear?' These are the things that the nations seek after, but Avichem Shebashamayim knows that you need them. Instead, seek first the Kingdom of Elohim and His righteousness, and all these things will be added to you. Therefore, do not worry about tomorrow. Tomorrow is not promised. Sufficient for each day is its own trouble."

TaNaKh Parallels	Talmudic Commentary	Chassidic Insights
Exodus 20:3 – "You shall have no other gods (elohim) before Me."	Berakhot 61b – "A man cannot serve two kings at once."	Baal Shem Tov: "Where your desire lies, there your soul is anchored." One cannot cling to both the upper and lower worlds with the same heart.
1 Kings 18:21 – Elijah: "How long will you waver between two opinions? If Adonai is Elohim, follow Him."	Avodah Zarah 2b – "One who serves money distances himself from Heaven."	
Psalm 55:23 – "Cast your burden upon Adonai and He will sustain you."	Sotah 48b – "When one relies on Heaven, Heaven sustains him."	Tanya, Chapter 26 – "Sorrow for material lack weakens one's service of Elohim; joy in emunah strengthens the soul."
Proverbs 3:5–6 – "Trust in Adonai with all your heart... and He will direct your path."	Berakhot 33b – "Everything is in the hands of Heaven except the fear of Heaven."	Rebbe Nachman of Breslov – "The world pursues livelihood. But the tzaddik knows: the moment you chase Elohim's Kingdom, livelihood chases you."
Psalm 147:9 – "He gives to the beast its food and to the young ravens that cry."		
Job 38:41 – "Who prepares for the raven its nourishment when its young cry to Elohim?"	Yoma 75a – "The righteous are sustained daily like the manna: enough for each day."	Zohar I:193a – "Man has two inclinations pulling at his soul... One pulls toward the dust, the other toward the heavens."
Isaiah 33:6 – "The fear of Adonai is His treasure."	Shabbat 151b – "Each day has its own troubles; worry not for tomorrow's bread."	Etz Chayim (Arizal) – Worry contracts the vessel (kli) that holds divine flow (shefa). Emunah expands the vessel.
Micah 6:8 – "What does Adonai require of you? To act justly, love mercy, and walk humbly with your Elohim."		

Judge with Righteous Judgment   Matthew 7:1–5 | John 7:24

"Do not judge rashly," Yeshua continued, his eyes sweeping across the crowd, "so that you will not be judged. For with the same measure of judgment you use for others, you will be equally judged." He paused, letting the weight of justice settle upon the hearts of those who prided themselves on piety.

"Why do you look at the speck in your brother's eye, but ignore the beam in your own eye? How can you say to your brother, 'Let me take the speck out of your eye,' while the beam is still in your own? Hypocrite! First remove the beam from your own eye, then you will see clearly to remove the speck from your brother's."

TaNaKh Parallels	Talmudic Commentary	Chassidic Insight
Leviticus 19:15 – "Do not pervert justice... judge your neighbor fairly. Leviticus 19:35–36 "You shall not commit injustice in judgment, in measuring length, weight, or volume. You shall have honest balances, honest weights, an honest ephah, and an honest hin. I am Adonai your Elohim, who brought you out of the land of Egypt." Proverbs 20:10 "Differing weights and differing measures—both are an abomination to Adonai."	Pirkei Avot 2:4 – "Do not judge your fellow until you have stood in his place." Sanhedrin 100a – "One who judges another harshly brings judgment upon himself." Sotah 8b – "With the measure a man uses, he is measured." Bava Metzia 59b – A rebuke without self-clarity is likened to one pointing with unwashed hands.	Baal Shem Tov taught: What you see in your fellow may reflect what you must correct in yourself. Reb Zusha: "If I see a fault in my friend, it is only because I have not yet cleansed it in myself."

Guard the Sanctity of the Sacred   Matthew 7:6

"Do not teach the Torah to those outside the covenant, nor cast sacred wisdom before idolaters, lest they desecrate what is holy and turn against you."

TaNaKh Parallels	Talmudic Commentary	Chassidic Insight
♦ Proverbs 23:9 "Do not speak in the ears of a fool, for he will despise the wisdom of your words." ♦ Psalm 50:16–17 "But to the wicked Elohim says: 'What right have you to declare My statutes or take My covenant in your mouth, since you hate instruction and cast My words behind you?'" Exodus 22:31 – "You shall not eat flesh that is torn by beasts in the field; throw it to the dogs." Deuteronomy 23:18 – Prohibits bringing the wages of a "dog" (understood by sages as a male prostitute or base person) into the Temple. 1 Samuel 17:43 – Goliath says to David: "Am I a dog?"—symbolizing spiritual opposition.	♦ Chagigah 13a "The mysteries of Torah are not to be handed over to every student, unless he is wise and understands of his own accord." ♦ Avodah Zarah 3a "One should not teach Torah to an idolater." ♦ Pesachim 49b "One who teaches Torah to an unworthy student is like	♦ The "pearl" = da'at haEloki (divine knowledge) The Baal Shem Tov warned against premature rebuke or revealing mystical truths to those unready, lest it harden their hearts or provoke resistance. Rebbe Nachman said: "When the heart is closed, even light becomes a sword." ♦ Zohar II: 95b "One who reveals the secrets of Torah to the unworthy removes the crown from the King's head." The "holy" here refers to sod (secret wisdom), and the "dogs" or "swine" symbolize unrefined vessels (kelim) incapable of receiving light without distortion. To give them "pearls" (wisdom) causes the light to collapse into judgment (din), and the teacher suffers spiritual backlash.

• Job 28:18 – "Wisdom is more precious than pearls." • Proverbs 3:15 – "She (Wisdom) is more precious than rubies, and all things you may desire are not to be compared to her."	one who throws a stone at a statue of Mercury"—i.e., empowering false worship.	Baal Shem Tov: "To speak words of Torah to a coarse soul is to enrobe light in mud." Zohar: Pearls = the secrets of the Torah (sod), and one who reveals these to the unworthy is judged from above (Zohar II:95b). Tikkun HaDibbur (Rectification of Speech): Only speech given in the right context uplifts. Else, it can create klipot (spiritual husks).
Yeshua is not condemning Gentiles universally (he ultimately praises the Canaanite woman's faith), but issuing a warning not to offer holy teaching to those who are hostile or unready: -The dogs = those outside the covenant who reject or profane sacred things -The swine = those whose nature is to trample truth, twisting it into attack -The pearls = Torah, wisdom, righteousness, the Kingdom teachings -The warning = Discern who is ready to receive, and who will weaponize or desecrate.		

Persistent Prayer and the Open Gate   Matthew 7:7–8

"Keep asking, and it will be given to you. Keep looking, and you will find. Keep knocking, and the door will open for you. For everyone who keeps asking receives, everyone who keeps seeking finds, and to the one who keeps knocking, the door will be opened. In the quiet of the soul, in the persistence of longing, the gates of Heaven begin to creak open. Just as a child tugs at the hem of their father's garment, not once but again and again, so too must the seeker press onward—with trust, with fervor, with hope. For Avichem Shebashamayim (your Father in Heaven) hears not just the loud cry, but the whispered knock of the heart.

Greek Grammar: The verbs in the Greek text — aiteite (ask), zēteite (seek), krouete (knock) — are in the present active imperative, which in Hebraic thinking implies continuous, ongoing action. It's not "ask once," but "keep on asking."		
TaNaKh Parallels	**Talmudic Commentary**	**Chassidic Insights**
Jeremiah 33:3 – "Call to Me and I will answer you, and I will tell you great and hidden things that you have not known." Psalm 145:18–19 – "Adonai is near to all who call upon Him… He fulfills the desire of those who fear Him; He also hears their cry and saves them." Deuteronomy 4:29 – "You will seek Adonai your Elohim and you will find Him, if you search after Him with all your heart and with all your soul." Isaiah 55:6 – "Seek Adonai while He may be found; call upon Him while He is near." Psalm 27:4 – "One thing I ask of Adonai, that I will seek after…" (Hebrew parallelism again reflects asking and seeking as ongoing.)	Berakhot 5b – "If a person takes one step toward sanctity, Heaven takes two toward him." Yoma 38b – "He who comes to purify himself is helped from above." Avodah Zarah 17a – "Even if a sword is placed on a person's neck, he should not stop praying for mercy." Talmud, Berakhot 32b: "Why were the righteous called those who knock? Because they do not cease from prayer until the gates of Heaven open." Pirkei Avot 2:13: "Do not say, 'When I have free time I will study,' for perhaps you will never have free time." (The implication: Seek always, with urgency.)	From the Baal Shem Tov and Rebbe Nachman: Ask (Bakashah) – Simple prayer from the heart — yearning for connection. Seek (Drishah) – Seeking through study, action, teshuvah. Knock (Dafak) – Pounding on the gates of Heaven with tears, silence, or surrender. Each verb implies increasing levels of soul effort and inner refinement. "Even the one far from Torah, if he knocks long enough with humility, the gates will open." — Rebbe Nachman

The Heart of the Father and the Heart of the Torah　　　　　　　　　　　　Matthew 7:9–12

"Who among you, if his son asks for bread, will give him a stone? Or if he asks for a fish, you give him a serpent? If you, though inclined toward selfishness, know how to give good gifts to your children, how much more will Avichem Shebashamayim (your Father in Heaven) give good things to those who keep asking Him?"

The crowd was hushed, hanging on every word, as Yeshua unfolded a vision of a Father whose goodness far surpasses even the purest intentions of earthly parents. Each metaphor painted a picture of the Holy One's overflowing kindness: bread in place of stone, nourishment instead of harm, love unshaken by fear.

He continued: "Therefore, whatever you would want others to do for you—do the same for them. This is the essence of the Torah and the Nevi'im (Prophets)." The people stirred. It was as if the entire weight of revelation—the scrolls, the commandments, the oracles of the prophets—had been brought into a single blazing line: treat others as you wish to be treated. In that moment, the Mount trembled not with thunder, but with the echo of divine mercy.

TaNaKh Parallels	Talmudic Commentary	Chassidic Insights
Psalm 103:13 – "As a father has compassion on his children, so does Adonai have compassion on those who fear Him." Isaiah 49:15 – "Can a mother forget her nursing child?... Even if she could forget, I will not forget you." Leviticus 19:18 – "Love your neighbor as yourself. I am Adonai." Proverbs 3:27 – "Do not withhold good from those to whom it is due, when it is in your power to act."	Shabbat 31a – "What is hateful to you, do not do to your fellow. This is the entire Torah; the rest is commentary. Go and learn it." Midrash Tehillim 18:2 – "Just as a father lifts his son over a puddle, so does the Holy One lift Israel over judgment when they cry out to Him." Taanit 23a – A man asked Choni the Circle-Maker for rain. Choni responded with a prayer, and rain came quickly. The sages said, "This one is like a beloved child before the King — what he asks is granted." Berakhot 5a – "If even earthly kings know how to honor their children, how much more the King of Kings will do for those who serve Him."	The Baal Shem Tov taught that the love of Elohim exceeds that of all fathers combined, and He gives even when we are not fully worthy — to arouse our teshuvah. Rebbe Elimelech of Lizhensk: "The true chassid anticipates the needs of others as though they were his own, for the soul sees no division." Zohar I: 105a – "As a person awakens below, so is it awakened above." Those who give freely on earth open the upper channels of kindness.

The Two Paths Before You　　　　　　　　　　　　Matthew 7:13–14

"Seek out and enter through the narrow gate. For wide is the gate and broad is the road that leads to destruction, and many enter through it. But narrow is the gate and difficult is the path that leads to life, and only a few are able to find it." Yeshua's voice carried solemn weight, echoing across the hillside. His listeners felt the urgency in his tone—a crossroads stood before each of them. One path was wide and welcoming, filled with the comfort of the crowd, but paved in self-indulgence and spiritual slumber.

The other was a narrow trail—rocky, steep, often lonely—yet lit with the fire of obedience and truth. He spoke not merely of destinations, but of choices. The gate to life was not obvious, not easy, not popular. It was the path of Torah, humility, teshuvah (repentance), and discipline. Few would have the courage to walk it, but to those who did, it led to the presence of Elohim Himself.

TaNaKh Parallels	Talmudic Commentary	Chassidic Insights
Deuteronomy 30:19 – "I have set before you life and death, blessing and curse. Therefore, choose life, that you and your offspring may live." Psalm 1:6 – "For Adonai knows the way of the righteous, but the way of the wicked will perish." Proverbs 14:12 – "There is a way that seems right to a man, but its end is the way of death."	Berakhot 28b – Rabbi Elazar ben Azariah: "The road to the World to Come is narrow, like the eye of a needle." Sotah 37b – On crossing the Sea: "Only those who walked straight through the parted sea were saved; others hesitated and perished."	Rebbe Nachman of Breslov: "The path to truth is very narrow — so narrow that you cannot carry your arrogance with you." The Baal Shem Tov: "Most of the world runs after what is easy and wide. The soul must labor through fire and water to reach the gate of Eden."

Discern the Wolves Among the Flock   Matthew 7:15–20

"Beware of false prophets who come to you in sheep's clothing, but inwardly they are ravenous wolves. They cloak themselves in piety—gentle words, sacred language, the garments of Torah—but within burns ambition, pride, and deceit." Yeshua's words were not a warning for distant generations, but for that very moment, for that very crowd. He urged his disciples not to judge by appearance, but to test the fruits. The Torah had long warned of such deceivers—those who might perform signs, but whose teachings led hearts away from the covenant.

"Can grapes be gathered from thornbushes, or figs from thistles? Every good tree bears good fruit, but a rotten tree bears bad fruit. A good tree cannot produce bad fruit, and a rotten tree cannot produce good fruit. Yeshua's imagery summoned the Galilean hills—vines and fig trees, thorns and brambles. Just as the land itself bore evidence of its health, so too a teacher's character, humility, and obedience revealed his root. Every tree that does not bear good fruit is cut down and thrown into the fire. So then, you will know them by their fruits. The righteous are known not by their claims, but by their consistency: love, justice, mercy, and awe of Elohim. The false, though skilled in speech, cannot hide the rot of their intentions forever."

TaNaKh Parallels	Talmudic Commentary	Chassidic Insights
Deuteronomy 13:1–5 – Warns against prophets who perform signs yet lead the people away from Torah: "You shall not listen to the words of that prophet... for Adonai your Elohim is testing you." Jeremiah 23:16–17, 21–22 – "Do not listen to the words of the prophets who prophesy to you... I did not send them, yet they ran; I did not speak to them, yet they prophesied."	Eruvin 100b – "A person is known by three things: his cup (behavior when drinking), his purse (how he spends), and his anger — and some say by his laughter." Avot 4:1 – "Who is wise? One who learns from every person... Who is honorable? One who honors others." Avodah Zarah 19a – "He who learns from an unworthy teacher is like one who eats unripe grapes or drinks wine straight from the press."	Baal Shem Tov: "A tree is judged not by its trunk or its bark, but by the sweetness of its fruit — and the sweetness of fruit is drawn from hidden roots." Rebbe Nachman: "The greatest danger is not the sinner who knows he is sinful, but the righteous who cloak their pride in humility. This is the wolf in wool." Zohar I: 3b "The Torah is the Tree of Life; its branches are mitzvot, its fruit is the Shechinah that dwells among those who study it."

Ezekiel 13:2–3 – "Woe to the foolish prophets who follow their own spirit and have seen nothing!" Proverbs 8:19 "My fruit is better than gold, even fine gold, and my yield than choice silver."	Taanit 7a "Just as rain gives life to the earth, so words of Torah give life to the soul... Torah is compared to wine, oil, honey, and milk — and fruit." Taanit 7a "Just as rain gives life to the earth, so words of Torah give life to the soul... Torah is compared to wine, oil, honey, and milk — and fruit	Tanya, Likkutei Amarim, Ch. 5 "Torah study is like digesting the fruit of the tree of life; it becomes part of the soul, uniting the mind with the Divine Will." Sefer HaBahir (early Kabbalistic text) – Par. 98 "The righteous are like trees... their fruit is the Torah made manifest in the world."

Who Enters Heaven Matthew 7:21–23 | Matthew 15:8–9

"Not everyone who says to me, 'Master, Master,' will enter the Kingdom of Heaven, but only the one who does the will of Avichem Shebashamayim—which is to walk in His Torah." Yeshua's voice carried a tone of gravity. The crowd, filled with emotion and admiration, leaned in.

"Many will say to me on that day, 'Master, Master, did we not prophesy in your name, and drive out demons in your name, and do many mighty works?' Then I will say to them plainly: 'I never knew you. Depart from me, you who willfully reject the Torah.'" Yeshua, as judge, declared not ignorance but estrangement. "I never knew you"—not in intimacy, not in covenant, not in obedience. To reject the Torah, to live lawlessly while claiming his name, is to walk in contradiction. "These people honor Me with their lips, but their hearts are far from Me" (Isaiah 29:13, cf. Matthew 15:8–9).

TaNaKh Parallels	Talmudic Commentary	Chassidic Insights
Deuteronomy 10:12–13 "What does Adonai your Elohim require of you? Only to fear Adonai... to walk in all His ways, and to love Him, and to serve Him... to keep the commandments..." Psalm 40:8 "I delight to do Your will, O my Elohim — Your Torah is within my heart." Ecclesiastes 12:13 "Fear Elohim and keep His commandments, for this is the whole duty of man." Isaiah 29:13 "This people draw near with their mouths and honor Me with their lips, but their hearts are far from Me." Jeremiah 7:9–10 "Will you steal, murder... and then come and stand before Me in this house and say, 'We are delivered'—only to go on doing these abominations?" Psalm 50:16–17 "To the wicked, Elohim says: What right have you to recite My statutes or take My covenant on your lips? You hate discipline and cast My words behind you."	Sotah 22b – "One who is outwardly righteous but inwardly corrupt is like a carcass smeared with spices." "A scholar whose inside is not like his outside is not a true sage." Berakhot 17a – "The world is judged by its deeds, not its noise. Not one who shouts 'Torah!' the loudest enters the World to Come, but one who lives it." Avot 1:17 – "Not study [alone] is the main thing, but action." Avot 3:17 – "If there is no Torah, there is no proper conduct. And if there is no proper conduct, there is no Torah." Pirkei Avot 2:4 – "Make His will your will, so that He may make your will His." Sanhedrin 99b "Whoever denies the Torah has no share in the World to Come." Nedarim 81a "Why were the sages of earlier generations remembered with favor? Because they would make their Torah learning part of their deeds."	Baal Shem Tov: "One may study Torah for 70 years and remain unknown in Heaven, if pride and self-serve as the motivation." "A person may perform miracles yet still be far from the Holy One if his heart is full of ego. Only one whose soul cleaves to heaven is known Above." Rebbe Nachman – "A tzaddik who is full of pride is worse than a rasha who knows he is a sinner, for the tzaddik deceives others with holiness." Zohar I:265a "Whoever turns from Torah turns from the Tree of Life and cleaves to the Sitra Achra (the Other Side)."

The Rock or the Sand: Foundations of a Life   Matthew 7:24–27

"Everyone who hears these words of mine and does them is like a wise man who built his house upon the rock. The rain fell, the floods came, and the wind blew and beat upon that house — but it did not fall, for the foundation was upon the rock. But everyone who hears these words of mine and does not do them is like a foolish man who built his house on sand. The rain fell, the floods came, and the wind blew and beat upon that house — and it collapsed. And great was its fall.

TaNaKh Parallels	Talmudic Commentary	Chassidic Insight
Deuteronomy 32:1–4 "Give ear, O heavens, and I will speak... May my teaching drop as the rain... He is the Rock; His work is perfect..." Psalm 18:2 "Adonai is my Rock, my Fortress, and my Deliverer." Isaiah 28:16 "Behold, I lay in Zion a stone, a tested stone, a precious cornerstone, a sure foundation; whoever believes shall not panic."	Avot 1:17 – "Not learning is the main thing but doing." Sotah 21a – "A pious fool is among those who destroy the world." Taanit 7a – "Words of Torah are compared to water... just as water erodes rock, so Torah shapes the soul."	Tanya, Chapter 41: "True fear of Heaven is the foundation upon which all structures of service to G-d are built." Baal Shem Tov teaches: One who builds a spiritual life on "borrowed garments" (external rituals without heart) will collapse when tested.

The Awe of the Crowds   Matthew 7:28–29; 8:1 | Mark 1:22 | Luke 4:32

And it came to pass, when Yeshua finished speaking these words, the crowds were left in stunned silence, their hearts pierced with both wonder and conviction. His words had not merely instructed—they had reached into their very souls. They were astonished at his teaching—not because it was eloquent, but because it was true. Because he taught as one who had reshut—true authority from Heaven. Not with the rehearsed formula of the scribes, who recited traditions without the fire of experience, but as one who knew the Torah intimately, lived it deeply, and spoke it as though it flowed from the Source.

Every word felt like thunder wrapped in light, familiar yet weighty, old yet alive. This was not a commentary on the Torah. It was the Torah alive, walking, breathing, revealing itself. When Yeshua finished his sermon, he descended from the mountain—the same way Moshe had descended from Sinai, having delivered words of covenant and life. And large crowds followed him. Not out of curiosity alone, but because something had been awakened within them. A thirst. A hunger. A hope. They followed the voice that stirred their spirits and the footsteps of the one who had spoken like no other.

Chapter 9: The Beginning of Controversy

Cleansing the Tzaru'a Matthew 8:2–4 | Mark 1:40–45 | Luke 5:12–16

While Yeshua was traveling through one of the towns, a man who was afflicted with tzara'at (a spiritual skin affliction) came to him. His body bore the shame of exile, and his soul carried the weight of rejection. When the man saw Yeshua, he fell with his face to the ground in an act of both humility and desperation, and pleaded with him, saying, "Master, if you are willing, you can make me clean."

Filled with compassion that surged like a river overflowing its banks—Yeshua did the unthinkable. He reached out and touched him. Flesh to flesh. Spirit to spirit. Restoring dignity before healing the disease. "I am willing," he said. "Be cleansed."

Immediately, like shadows retreating from the sunrise, the tzara'at left the man, and he was made clean. Yeshua gave him a stern warning and sent him away at once, saying, "See that you tell no one. But go, show yourself to the kohen (priest), and offer the gift that Moshe commanded, as a testimony to them." His instructions were precise—not just to obey the Torah, but to present a witness that a greater restoration was now at work in Israel.

But the man, overwhelmed with joy and unable to contain his gratitude, went out and began to proclaim it freely, spreading the news everywhere. As a result, Yeshua could no longer enter towns openly but stayed outside in the desolate places—lonely places, like those the lepers themselves once inhabited. Yet people kept coming to him from every direction. The wilderness became a sanctuary. And controversy had begun to stir.

The Healing of the Paralyzed Man Matthew 9:1–8 | Mark 2:1–12 | Luke 5:17–26

After some days, Yeshua entered Kfar Nachum (Capernaum) again, and when the people heard that he had returned home, a great crowd gathered—so many that there was no longer room, not even outside the door. Word had spread like wildfire: the Healer had returned. Eager souls pressed in from every direction, filling the house and spilling out into the streets, just to hear him teach the Torah of Elohim. Among those present were some Prushim (Pharisees) and Torah teachers who had come from every village of Galil and Judea, and even from Yerushalayim (Jerusalem). These were men trained in the scrolls of Moshe and the traditions of the fathers—now observing Yeshua with cautious curiosity. The power of Adonai was present for him to heal.

Then came a commotion—a stirring at the edge of the crowd. Some men had arrived, carrying a paralyzed man on a mat. There were four of them, bearing their friend with urgency and hope. But the crowd was dense, impenetrable. They could not find a way through. Undeterred, they climbed to the rooftop. Dust rained down as they began removing the roof tiles with trembling hands. The people inside looked up in wonder. Then, slowly, they lowered the mat through the hole they had made—right in front of Yeshua.

The silence in the room was heavy with awe. When Yeshua saw their faith—not just the desperation, but the trust behind it—he said to the paralyzed man, "Friend, your sins are forgiven you."

Gasps echoed across the room. The Torah teachers and Prushim began whispering among themselves, their faces tightening: "Who is this man who speaks blasphemies? Who can forgive sins except Elohim alone?"

But Yeshua knew their thoughts. He turned to them and said, "Why are you thinking these things in your hearts? Which is easier to say, 'Your sins are forgiven,' or to say, 'Get up and walk'? But so that you may know that the Son of Man has authority on earth to forgive sins..." —he turned to the paralyzed man—"I say to you, get up, take your mat, and go home." The words, like thunder from Heaven, shook the hearts of all.

Immediately, the man stood up before them, his legs once lifeless now full of strength. He bent down, lifted his mat, and walked out in full view of them all—his eyes wet with wonder, his voice lifted in praise, glorifying Elohim. Everyone was amazed and filled with awe. Many stood frozen in silence. They praised Elohim, saying: "We have seen remarkable things today!" and "We have never seen anything like this!"

The Calling of Levi Matthew 9:9–13 | Mark 2:13–17 | Luke 5:27–32

The day after these events, Yeshua went out again beside the sea—the breeze curling off the waters, the murmurs of the crowd growing louder. The people came to him from every direction, eager and restless, and he taught them as he walked along the shoreline, the waves lapping gently at his feet.

As he passed through a town, his gaze fell upon a man seated at a tax booth—Levi, also called Mattityahu (Matthew). The man sat behind a table scattered with scrolls and coins. A tax collector—viewed by many as a traitor and collaborator with Rome—yet Yeshua's eyes saw beyond what others saw.

Yeshua walked up to him and looked directly into his eyes and with a smile said, "Follow me." Without hesitation, Levi rose. He left everything behind—the ledgers, the coins, the safety of his post—and followed him. Something in the voice of the Teacher awakened his soul. Later, Levi prepared a great banquet for Yeshua at his house. Laughter and conversation filled the air. A large crowd of tax collectors and others who were considered sinners reclined at the table with them, basking in the acceptance they rarely felt from religious society.

When the Prushim (Pharisees) and some of the Torah teachers saw Yeshua eating with tax collectors and sinners, they looked on in disapproval. They pulled aside his disciples and asked, "Why does your master eat and drink with tax collectors and sinners?"

But Yeshua heard them. He turned and responded with sharp clarity: "It is not the healthy who need a physician, but those who are sick. Go and learn what this means: 'I desire mercy and not sacrifice.' For I did not come to call the righteous, but sinners to repentance."

Fasting and the Bridegroom Matthew 9:14–17 | Mark 2:18–22 | Luke 5:33–39

Then the disciples of Yochanan (John the Immerser) came to Yeshua, accompanied by some of the Prushim (Pharisees). The atmosphere was charged with curiosity and tension. They observed Yeshua and his disciples eating and enjoying fellowship, while others observed a fast day—eyes narrowing, questions forming. They approached him and asked, "Rabbi, why is it that Yochanan's disciples and the disciples of the Prushim fast and offer prayers, but your disciples do not fast?"

Yeshua answered them with a presence both joyful and prophetic: "Can you make the friends of the bridegroom fast while the bridegroom is still with them? The room grew still as the imagery began to settle into their hearts. The days will come when the bridegroom will be taken away from them; in those days they will fast."

He then shared with them a parable that stirred the minds of the learned and simple alike: "No one tears off a piece from a new garment to repair an old one. The fabric of his voice wove deeper truths: If he does, he will ruin the new garment, and the patch from the new will not match the old. And no one pours new wine into old wineskins. If he does, the new wine will burst the skin and the wine will spill out, and so the skin will be ruined. No, new wine must be put into fresh wineskins. And no one after drinking the old wine wants the new, for he says, 'The old is better.'"

Controversy in the Grainfields Matthew 12:1–8 | Mark 2:23–28 | Luke 6:1–5

One Shabbat, as Yeshua was passing through the grainfields, his disciples were hungry and began to pluck heads of grain, rubbing them in their hands and eating them as they walked. The sound of stalks breaking and the peaceful quiet of the countryside were interrupted by voices of accusation. Some of the Prushim (Pharisees) saw this and said to him, "Look! Why are they doing what is not permitted on Shabbat?"

Yeshua turned to them and replied, not with anger but with authority: "Have you never read what David did when he and his companions were hungry and in need? How he entered the House of Elohim — in the days of Aviathar the Kohen Gadol — and ate the lechem ha-panim (Bread of the Presence), which was not lawful for anyone to eat except the kohanim, and even gave some to those who were with him?" The Pharisees fell silent, the weight of Scripture pressing on their hearts. Then Yeshua said to them, "Shabbat was made for man, not man for Shabbat. So then, the Son of Man is Master even over the Shabbat."

TaNaKh Parallel	Talmudic Commentary
Exodus 34:21 – "Even during plowing and harvest, you must rest." Deuteronomy 23:25 – "When you enter your neighbor's standing grain, you may pluck heads with your hand, but you shall not put a sickle to it." According to Torah, the disciples did not violate Shabbat. They plucked grain by hand, not with a sickle, and for immediate consumption — aligning with Deut. 23:25.	Yoma 85b: "The Sabbath is handed over to you, not you to the Sabbath." Sanhedrin 74a: Only 3 commandments must never be violated (idolatry, sexual immorality, and murder). All others, including Shabbat, may be overridden to save life or preserve dignity. The Mishnah and Talmud define **39 categories of melachah** forbidden on Shabbat (Mishnah Shabbat 7:2). The disciples' actions touch on several **rabbinically prohibited labors:** | Action	Possible Melachah Violation
Plucking	Reaping (קוצר)
Rubbing grain	Threshing (דש)
Blowing away chaff	Winnowing (זורה)
Eating	No violation | But the Talmud itself recognizes that pikuach nefesh (preservation of life) and on-the-way eating may override these, especially if it is not a commercial or planned act. The definition of melachah on Shabbat includes not just the action, but the intent, scale, and outcome. ♦ Mishnah Shabbat 7:2 Lists the 39 melachot, including: • Kotzer (reaping) • Dash (threshing) • Zoreh (winnowing) BUT... ♦ Talmud Shabbat 73a–75b Clarifies that these melachot must be constructive, meant for collection or processing, and done in usual fashion to incur full liability. While plucking grain and rubbing it might seem to match "reaping and threshing," the Chachamim (sages) recognize degree and intent: Hand-plucking is not reaping (kotzer) in the full halachic sense. Casual rubbing is not threshing (dash) if done to eat immediately. Eating right away is not me'amer (gathering) or borer (selecting), because the action is direct consumption. These distinctions are found throughout: • Talmud Shabbat 95a – discusses rubbing heads of grain on Shabbat. • Talmud Beitzah 12b–13a – clarifies differences between preparation and consumption.

The Withered Hand Restored   Matthew 12:9–14 | Mark 3:1–6 | Luke 6:6–11

On another Shabbat, Yeshua entered the synagogue and was teaching. A man was there whose right hand was withered and paralyzed. The Torah scholars and some of the Prushim (Pharisees) were watching him closely, looking for a reason to accuse him. They wanted to see whether he would heal on the Shabbat. But Yeshua knew their thoughts. The tension in the synagogue was palpable, eyes shifting between the man in need and the teacher who might violate tradition. He said to the man with the withered hand, "Get up and stand here in front of everyone." So, the man rose and stood there—every gaze fixed upon him, waiting.

Then Yeshua said to them all, "I ask you: Is it permitted on Shabbat to do good or to do harm? To save life or to destroy it?" But they remained silent, hardened by fear, pride, and jealousy. Looking around at all of them with anger, grieved by the hardness of their hearts, he said to the man: "Stretch out your hand."
He stretched it out—and his hand was completely restored, healthy as the other. But the

Prushim and Torah scholars were filled with fury and began plotting with the Herodians how they might destroy him.

Healing at the Pool of Beit Chasda John 5:1–18

Sometime later, there was a pilgrimage festival of the Yehudim, and Yeshua went up to Yerushalayim. Within Yerushalayim, near the Sheep Gate, there is a pool called in Hebrew Beit Chasda (House of Mercy), surrounded by five porticos. Within them lay a great number of the sick, the blind, the lame, and the paralyzed, waiting for the stirring of the waters. For at certain times, The Angel of Adonai would descend and stir the waters, and the first to enter after the stirring would be healed of whatever affliction he had.

One man was there who had been disabled for thirty-eight years. Yeshua saw him lying there and, knowing he had already been in that condition a long time, said to him: "Do you want to be made whole?"

The sick man answered him, "Master, I have no one to help me into the pool when the water is stirred. While I am trying to get in, someone else steps down before me."

Yeshua said to him, "Rise, take up your mat, and walk." Immediately the man was made whole. He took up his mat and walked.

Now it was Shabbat on that day. So, the Sadducees said to the man who had been healed, "It is the Shabbat! It is not permitted for you to carry your mat!"

But he answered them, "The one who made me whole told me, 'Take up your mat and walk.'"

They asked him, "Who is the man who told you to do this—'Take it up and walk'?" But the man who was healed did not know who it was, for Yeshua had withdrawn into the crowd that was there.

Later, Yeshua found him in the Temple and said to him: "See, you have been made whole. Do not sin anymore, so that nothing worse may happen to you."

The man went and informed the Judeans that it was Yeshua who had made him whole. Because of this, the Sadducees began persecuting Yeshua—because he was doing these things on the Shabbat.

But Yeshua answered them: "Avi (My Father) is still working even now, and I too am working."

Because of this, the Sadducees were all the more eager to put him to death—not only because he was doing these things on the Shabbat, but also because he was calling Elohim his own Father, making himself appear as one entrusted with authority from Elohim.

So, Yeshua responded and said to them: "Amein, amein, I tell you: the Son is not able to do anything on his own, but only what he sees the Av doing. For whatever the Av does, these things the Son also does in like manner. For the Av loves the Son and shows him everything He is doing—and even greater work than these He will show him, so that you may be amazed.

For just as the Av raises the dead and gives them life, so also the Son gives life to whomever he is sent to. And the Av judges no one directly but has entrusted all judgment to the Son—so that all may give kavod (honor) to the Son as they give kavod to the Av. Whoever does not give kavod to the Son does not give kavod to the Av who sent him."

Important Turning Point
John 5:17–23 Is a Turning Point
1. Public Identification as a Shaliach (Divine Agent) Yeshua does not call himself Elohim or equal in essence but says: "The Son can do nothing by himself… only what he sees the Father doing."   This mirrors the halachic principle of שלוחו של אדם כמותו – "a man's agent is as himself" (Talmud, Kiddushin 41b). In other words, he is a divinely authorized prophet and legal representative — a Shaliach. This is his first public, theological self-description — not as Mashiach (yet), but as a prophet and divine agent acting with the Av's delegated authority.   2. Revealing the Inner Relationship Between Prophet and Elohim   Yeshua introduces language of: "The Av loves the Son…" "Shows him all He is doing…"   This reveals his prophetic intimacy with Elohim — not unlike how Moshe is described: "With him I speak mouth to mouth, clearly, and not in riddles" (Numbers 12:8). This frames Yeshua as a prophet in the line of Moshe — one who sees the inner workings of the Divine will.   3. Claim to Judicial and Eschatological Authority   "The Av has entrusted all judgment to the Son."   In Jewish eschatology, judgment belongs to Elohim alone — so entrusting judgment to a human figure implies divine appointment, not divinity. This mirrors Daniel 7's "Son of Man" imagery — a human figure exalted by Elohim to a judicial role on behalf of the righteous. This is the first moment Yeshua openly claims authority to give life, judge justly, and act as the Father's agent of tikkun (restoration)

The Authority of the Son and the Judgment to Come　　　　　　　　　　John 5:24–30

"Amein, amein, I tell you: Whoever hears my words and trusts in the One who sent me has eternal life and does not come into judgment but has passed over from death into life. Amein, amein, I say to you:
The hour is coming—and even now is here—when the dead will hear the voice of the Son of Man, and those who hear will live. For just as the Av (Father) has life in Himself, so also He has granted the Son to have life within himself. And He has given him authority to execute judgment, because he is the Son of Man.

Do not be amazed at this, for the hour is coming in which all who are in the graves will hear his voice and come out—those who have done good to a resurrection of life, and those who have practiced evil to a resurrection of judgment. I can do nothing on my own. As I hear, I judge. And my judgment is righteous, because I do not seek my own will, but the will of the One who sent me."

The Witnesses to the Son John 5:31–47

"If I alone testify about myself, my testimony is not valid. But there is another who testifies on my behalf, and I know that the testimony he gives concerning me is true. You yourselves sent to Yochanan (John), and he has testified to the truth. I do not receive testimony from man, but I say these things so that you might be saved. Yochanan was a burning and shining lamp, and for a time you were willing to rejoice in his light. But the testimony I have is greater than that of Yochanan.

For the work which the Av has given me to complete—the very deeds I am doing—bear witness about me that the Av has sent me. And the Av who sent me has Himself borne witness about me. You have never heard His voice nor seen His form, nor does His word abide in you—for you do not believe the one whom He sent."

The Testimony of the Scriptures John 5:39–47

"You search the Scriptures because you think that in them you have eternal life—and yet it is they that testify about me. But you are unwilling to come to me so that you may have life. I do not receive kavod (honor) from men, but I know you: you do not have the love of Elohim within you. I have come in the Name of my Av, and you do not receive me. If another comes in his own name, you will receive him. How can you trust, when you receive kavod from one another, but do not seek the kavod that comes from the only Elohim? Do not think that I will accuse you before the Av. Your accuser is Moshe, in whom you have placed your hope. For if you believed Moshe, you would believe me—for he wrote about me.
But if you do not believe his writings, how will you believe my words?"

Chapter 10 Yeshua Returns to the Galilee

Crowds Seek Healing and Deliverance   Mark 3:7–12 | Luke 6:17–19 | Matthew 12:15–16

Yeshua withdrew with his talmidim to the sea — to the northern shores of the Galil. Though the controversy in Yerushalayim had been growing, and tensions with the Prushim and Torah scholars were mounting, he did not cease his mission. The open waters and distant hills became his refuge.

Large multitudes followed him — not only from the Galil, but also from Yehudah, from Yerushalayim, from Idumea in the south, from the regions beyond the Yarden, and from around Tzor and Tzidon in the northwest. Word of his healings and teachings had spread like fire through dry grass, carried by travelers, merchants, and pilgrims. Mothers clung to the hope that their children might be healed. Fathers brought their lame sons. The broken and burdened came by the thousands.

Yeshua came down with his talmidim and stood on a level place. A large crowd of his disciples were there, along with the vast multitude of people from all over Judea and Yerushalayim, and from the coastal regions of Tzor and Tzidon. They had come to hear him and to be healed of their sicknesses, and those afflicted with unclean spirits were being delivered. The entire crowd was pressing in hoping to just have a chance to touch him, because power was going out from him, and he healed them all. His very presence stirred the ruach — the Spirit of Elohim flowed from him like light from a lamp. Those who touched even the tzitzits (fringes) of his garment were healed.

And whenever those possessed by unclean spirits saw him, they fell down before him and cried out, "You are the Son of Elohim!" Their shrieks tore through the crowd like storm winds through a field, but Yeshua rebuked them sharply and forbade them from revealing his identity — for it was not yet time for these things to be known. His mission was not driven by spectacle or acclaim, but by obedience to the will of Avinu Shebashamayim. To keep from being crushed by the crowd, he instructed his talmidim to prepare a small boat for him — so he could step back and teach without being overwhelmed.

Yeshua Appoints the Twelve Apostles   Mark 3:13–19 | Luke 6:12–16 | Matthew 10:1–4

After the multitudes had pressed in upon him, Yeshua withdrew once again — this time to a mountain to pray. The sun had set, but the mountain was bathed in divine stillness. Under the canopy of stars, Yeshua remained there throughout the night, devoting himself in heartfelt communion with Elohim. The cool mountain air, the rustling leaves, and the distant cries of nocturnal animals bore witness to a sacred moment. Each prayer rising from his lips was like incense offered in the Temple above. He sought not popularity, but discernment — that he might choose vessels fit to carry the burden of the Kingdom.

When the day came, the first rays of light broke through the horizon, and with them came the time to act. He called to himself those talmidim who had been faithfully following him — those who had walked dusty roads at his side, listened to his teachings, witnessed his healings, and felt their hearts burn as he spoke of the Kingdom. From among them, he chose twelve — appointing them to be his shlichim (apostles), those who are sent.

These twelve he appointed to be with him continually — to walk by his side, to be shaped by his words and his way of life, and to go forth as emissaries of the Kingdom. He conferred upon them the authority to proclaim the good news, to bring healing to the sick, and to drive out unclean spirits — all by the power of Elohim, not their own strength.

These are the twelve he appointed:

> **Shim'on**, whom he called **Kefa** ("Rock") — bold, impetuous, and destined to be a foundation stone among the twelve.
>
> **Ya'akov (James)** son of **Zavdai**, and **Yochanan (John)** his brother — to whom he gave the name **Bnei Regesh** ("Sons of Thunder") for their passionate spirits and unyielding zeal.
>
> **Andrei (Andrew)** — the brother of Shim'on, a humble seeker who had once followed Yochanan the Immerser.
>
> **Philippos (Philip)** — from **Beit-Tzaidah**, a man of inquiry and conviction, always searching for deeper truth.
>
> **Bar-Talmai (Bartholomew)** — likely the same as **Nathanel**, a man without guile, whose heart was pure before Elohim.
>
> **Mattityahu (Matthew)** — also called **Levi**, once a tax collector for Rome, now a meticulous scribe of righteousness.
>
> **T'oma (Thomas)** — also called **Didymus**, the twin, who would later wrestle with doubt, only to confess with clarity.
>
> **Ya'akov** son of **Halfai (Alphaeus)** — often called **"the Less."**
>
> **Taddai (Thaddaeus)** — also called **Yehudah ben Ya'akov**, known for his devotion and loyalty.
>
> **Shim'on the Zealot** — also called the **Cananaean**, whose fervor had once burned for political deliverance, now set aflame for heavenly redemption.
>
> **Yehudah Ish-Keriot (Judas Iscariot)** — who would later betray him, though at the time, none yet knew the shadow he carried.

They were twelve men of diverse backgrounds — fishermen, scribes, revolutionaries, seekers. But each was called by name, each chosen for a purpose in the unfolding drama of redemption. Through them, the light of Torah and the voice of the Messiah would reach to the ends of the earth.

The Sermon on the Plain — Blessings and Warnings Luke 6:17–23

Yeshua descended with the Twelve and stood upon a level place. A large crowd of his talmidim was there, along with a vast multitude of people from all across Yehudah and Yerushalayim, and from the coastal regions of Tzor (Tyre) and Tzidon (Sidon). They had come to hear him speak and to be healed of their afflictions — both physical and spiritual. Those tormented by unclean spirits were being restored, released from the shadows that bound them. The crowd surged toward him, seeking just to touch him, for a radiant power was going out from him — and he healed them all.

Then, lifting his eyes toward his talmidim, Yeshua began to speak words of blessing and hope — words that would turn the values of the world upside down and call forth a people purified in suffering and made rich in emunah (faith): "Blessed are you who are poor, for yours is the Kingdom of Elohim. Blessed are you who hunger now, for you shall be satisfied. Blessed are you who weep now, for you shall laugh with joy. Blessed are you when people hate you, and when they exclude you, revile you, and treat your name as shameful on account of the Son of Man. Rejoice in that day and leap for joy! For behold, your reward is great in the heavens —for this is how their ancestors treated the nevi'im (prophets)."

TaNaKh Parallels			
Blessed are the poor – Isaiah 61:1 "The Spirit of Adonai Elohim is upon me... He has anointed me to bring good news to the poor..."	Hunger → Satisfaction – Psalm 107:9 "For He satisfies the longing soul, and the hungry soul He fills with goodness."	Weeping → Laughter – Psalm 126:5 "Those who sow in tears shall reap with shouts of joy."	Persecution for righteousness 2 Chronicles 36:16 "They mocked the messengers of Elohim, despised His words, and scoffed at His prophets..."

Woes Against the Proud Luke 6:24–26

"But oy lachem — woe to you who are rich now, for you have already received your comfort. Woe to you who are full now, for you will hunger. Woe to you who laugh now, for you will mourn and weep. Woe to you when all people speak well of you, for that is how their ancestors spoke of the false prophets."

These words cut like a prophet's blade — not to destroy, but to pierce through delusion. The blessings are for those who cling to Elohim in their emptiness. The woes are for those who trust in their abundance, forgetting the poor, and ignoring the call to righteousness.

TaNaKh Parallels			
Woe to the rich – Amos 6:1, 4–7	Woe to the full – Deuteronomy 8:12–14	Woe to laughter now – Ecclesiastes 7:3–4	Woe to the praised – Jeremiah 5:31

"Woe to those who are at ease in Tzion... who lie on beds of ivory... but are not grieved for the affliction of Yosef."	"When you have eaten and are satisfied... beware lest your heart becomes proud and you forget Adonai your Elohim..."	"Sorrow is better than laughter, for by a sad face the heart is made better... The wise are in the house of mourning."	"The prophets prophesy falsely... and My people love to have it so. But what will you do in the end?"

The Way of Radical Mercy Luke 6:27–36

Yeshua lifted his eyes toward the crowd and spoke directly to the hearts of those willing to listen: "But I say to you who are truly listening — you who desire to walk in the ways of the Kingdom: Love your enemies. Not with words only, but in works and truth. Do good to those who hate you. Let your compassion silence their contempt. Bless those who curse you. Speak peace over the ones who spit venom at your name. Pray — not just for your friends — but for those who slander you, mistreat you, and plot against you. Stand in the heavenly courts on their behalf. If someone strikes you on one cheek, turn the other also — not to submit to abuse, but to rise above it. If someone takes your cloak, let him have your tunic as well. For your dignity is not in fabric, but in righteousness.

Give freely to everyone who asks of you. If someone takes what is yours, do not demand it back. Why? Because the treasures of this world are passing — but generosity stores up riches in the heavens. And this is the heart of Torah: As you want others to do to you, do that for them. If you love only those who love you, what merit is there in that? Even sinners who walk far from the covenant — do the same. And if you do good only to those who repay you with kindness, what heavenly reward awaits you? Even the wicked practice this kind of transaction. And if you lend only to those from whom you expect repayment, where is the righteousness in that? Even sinners lend to sinners hoping to gain back the same.

Instead, I say: Love your enemies. Do good to them. Lend without expecting anything in return. Release your grip on justice and take hold of mercy. Then your reward will be great — and you will be called true children of Elyon (the Most High), for He is kind even to the ungrateful and the wicked. Be merciful — as Avichem (your Father) in the heavens is merciful."

The Heart That Judges, and the Fruit It Bear Luke 6:37–45

Yeshua looked upon the gathered crowd and warned them with tender severity: "Do not judge hastily, and you will not be judged. Do not condemn others, and you will not be condemned. Forgive — and you will be forgiven. Give freely, and it will be given to you. A good measure — pressed down, shaken together, and overflowing — will be poured into your lap. For with the same measure you use, it will be measured back to you." Then he offered them a parable, vivid and piercing: "Can a blind man lead a blind man? Will they not both fall into a pit? A talmid (disciple) is not above his Rav (teacher), but when he is fully trained, he will be like his teacher."

Yeshua then turned to the deeper matter of the heart: "Why do you fixate on the splinter in your brother's eye, but fail to see the beam in your own? How can you say, 'Brother, let me remove the splinter from your eye,' when you yourself do not see the beam that blinds your own sight? Hypocrite! First remove the beam from your own eye. Only then will you see clearly enough to help your brother with his."

And again, he gave them a parable of nature, that the inner life is known by its outward fruit: "No healthy tree produces rotten fruit, nor does a rotten tree yield good fruit. Each tree is known by its fruit — people do not gather figs from thorn bushes, nor do they pick grapes from briars. The good person, out of the storehouse of his heart, brings forth what is good. But the evil person, out of the evil hidden within, brings forth evil — for the mouth speaks from the overflow of the heart."

TaNaKh Parallels	Talmudic Commentary
Heart as the source of behavior Proverbs 4:23 "Guard your heart with all diligence, for from it flow the issues of life."	The inner man is revealed by words Eruvin 65b "A person is known in three ways: by his cup (behavior under intoxication), by his purse (how he spends), and by his anger. Some add by his speech."
Speech reveals the soul Proverbs 10:11 "The mouth of the righteous is a fountain of life, but violence overwhelms the mouth of the wicked."	Righteous speech is stored like treasure Avot 3:13 "One whose deeds exceed his wisdom, his wisdom will endure. One whose wisdom exceeds his deeds, his wisdom will not endure."
Good storehouse vs. evil storehouse Jeremiah 17:9–10 "The heart is deceitful above all things... I, Adonai, search the heart and examine the mind, to reward each person according to their conduct."	→ A "good storehouse" means internal alignment of wisdom and action.
Speech as fruit Proverbs 12:14 "From the fruit of his mouth a man will be satisfied with good..."	The wicked twist the gift of speech Pesachim 113b "There are three whom the Holy One hates... one who speaks one thing with his mouth and another in his heart."

The Wise Builder and the Foolish Builder   Luke 6:46–49

Yeshua looked out over the multitude and raised his voice in warning: "Why do you call me 'Master, Master,' yet refuse to walk in the derech (way) I show you? If you truly seek to be my talmid (disciple), then heed not only my words but embody them.

Let me paint for you a picture: The one who comes to me, who listens with intention and then puts my words into practice — he is like a skilled builder. Before laying even one stone, he digs deep into the earth, carving out a foundation until he reaches solid rock. Upon this unshakable base, he builds his house. And when the torrent rises and the floodwaters beat against it, the house stands firm — unshaken, unmoved — because its foundation is secure. But the one who hears and ignores my words is like a foolish man who built a house quickly, laying no foundation at all. When the same storm comes and the river crashes against it, that house crumbles instantly. And its destruction is not small — it is a complete and utter ruin and a warning."

The Centurion's Faith Matthew 8:5–13 | Luke 7:1–10

After Yeshua had finished teaching the people, he made his way back to Kfar Nachum. Word had already spread through the town — not only about his teachings, but of his healings, his authority, and the miracles done through him. Now in that town lived a Roman centurion — a commander of a hundred soldiers — who was unlike most others. Though a man of rank and discipline, he had developed a deep respect for the Jewish people and even built a synagogue for them with his own wealth. This man had a servant who was dear to him — gravely ill, paralyzed and suffering, on the brink of death. The centurion, having heard many things about Yeshua, believed that help could come through him.

Out of reverence and humility, he did not approach Yeshua himself. Instead, he sent some respected Jewish elders to intercede. When they came to Yeshua, they pleaded earnestly: "He is worthy for this, Rabbi. He loves our people. He even built our synagogue."

So Yeshua went with them. But when Yeshua drew near the house, the centurion sent some of his own friends to intercept him, saying, "Master, do not trouble yourself to enter my home, for I am not worthy to have you under my roof. That is why I didn't come myself. Just say the word, and my servant will be healed. I too understand authority. I serve under superiors and have men under me. I say to this one, 'Go,' and he goes. To another, 'Come,' and he comes. I say to my servant, 'Do this,' and he does it. I know that you — under the authority of Elohim — have but to speak, and it shall be done."

Yeshua stopped in his tracks. Turning to the crowd that followed him, he marveled aloud, "I tell you the truth: I have not found such emunah — such faith — even in all Yisrael! Truly, I say to you: many will come from the east and the west and will recline at the banquet with Avraham, Yitzchak, and Yaakov in the Kingdom of Heaven. But the sons of the Kingdom will be cast out into outer darkness, where there will be weeping and grinding of teeth."

Then, turning to those who had been sent, Yeshua said, "Go. As you have believed, so let it be done for you." And when they returned to the house, they found the servant healed — completely restored — at that very hour.

The Widow's Son and the Conflict Luke 7:11–17; Mark 3:20–21

Soon after healing the centurion's servant, Yeshua traveled to a village called Na'im, nestled near the foothills of the Galil. His disciples were with him, along with a large crowd that followed from place to place, drawn by wonder, by hope, and by the words of life he spoke. As they approached the town's gate, the sounds of mourning broke through the air. A funeral procession was making its way out of the city. The body of a young man, wrapped for burial, was being carried on a wooden bier. His mother walked beside him — a widow now left without a child, without an heir, alone in her grief. A large crowd from the town was with her, sharing in her sorrow.

When Yeshua saw her, something within him stirred — not just pity, but the deep compassion of the Father for the broken-hearted. He stepped toward her and gently said, "Do not weep." Then, without hesitation, he approached the coffin and touched it. The men carrying it froze in place, astonished. And Yeshua spoke: "Young man, I say to you, arise."

At once, the breath of life returned. The dead man sat up and began to speak. Gasps turned into cries of joy. Lamentation turned into praise. And Yeshua took the young man and returned him to his mother — restoring not just a life, but a family, a future, a testimony of divine mercy. A holy awe gripped everyone there. Whispers turned to proclamations: "A great prophet has arisen among us!" and "Elohim has visited His people!" News of the miracle spread quickly throughout all Yehudah and the surrounding regions. But not all were rejoicing.

When Yeshua returned to the house where he was staying — likely back in the Galil — another crowd had gathered, pressing in so tightly that he and his disciples couldn't even eat. Word of his teachings and miracles had reached his own family. Concerned and confused by his growing fame and strange behavior, they came to seize him, whispering among themselves, "He's out of his mind…"

Yochanan's Question   Luke 7:18–35 | Matthew 11:2–19

While he sat confined in the fortress prison of Herod Antipas, Yochanan the Immerser — the fiery voice who once thundered repentance in the wilderness — began to hear whispers of the miracles and teachings of Yeshua. The stories stirred something in him, a longing for clarity. Was this the one whose sandals he had said he was unworthy to untie? Was this truly the promised one? Or was there yet another to come?

So Yochanan summoned two of his disciples and entrusted them with a message. They journeyed north, seeking out Yeshua in the Galil. When they found him, surrounded as always by crowds and healings, they delivered their master's question: "Yochanan the Immerser has sent us to ask you: Are you the one who is to come, or should we look for another?"

In that very hour, Yeshua was performing wonders. The lame walked. The blind opened their eyes. Those afflicted with tzara'at were made clean. The deaf heard. The dead were raised. The poor — those forgotten by the world — were receiving words of hope, of life, of the Kingdom of Elohim.

Yeshua turned to the messengers and answered with the language of the prophets, the signs of Mashiach: "Go and report to Yochanan what you have seen and heard: the blind see, the lame walk, those with tzara'at are cleansed, the deaf hear, the dead are raised, and the poor are told the good news. Blessed is the one who does not stumble over me."

After Yochanan's disciples departed, Yeshua turned to address the crowd that had gathered. Their eyes followed the departing messengers. "What did you go out into the wilderness to see?" Yeshua asked them. "A reed swaying in the wind? No? Then what did you go out to see — a man dressed in fine garments? Look, those who wear soft clothes live in the palaces of kings. Then what was it? A prophet? Yes. And I tell you, even more than a prophet. For it is written: 'Behold, I send my messenger ahead of you, Who will prepare your way before you.'"

Then, lifting his voice with solemnity, he declared: "Amein, I tell you: Among those born of women, no one has arisen greater than Yochanan the Immerser. And yet — the least in the Kingdom of Elohim is greater than he. From the days of Yochanan until now, the Kingdom of Heaven is advancing forcefully, and forceful ones seize hold of it. For all the prophets and the Torah spoke until Yochanan. And if you are willing to accept it — he is Eliyahu who was to come. Let the one who has ears, hear!"

Yeshua paused, his eyes scanning the crowd, then continued: "To what shall I compare this generation? They are like children sitting in the marketplace, calling to one another: 'We played the flute for you, but you did not dance. We sang a dirge, but you did not mourn.'"

He shook his head gently and said, "For Yochanan came neither eating bread nor drinking wine, and they say, 'He has a demon.' The Son of Man comes eating and drinking, and they say, 'Look! A glutton and a drunkard — a friend of tax collectors and sinners!' But wisdom is justified by all her children."

Sin Unforgivable Matthew 12:22–50 | Mark 3:20–35 | Luke 11:14–26

Then a man possessed by a demon — blind and mute — was brought to Yeshua. With a word of authority and compassion, he healed him, so that the man could both speak and see. The crowd was amazed and began to murmur among themselves, awe in their voices: "Could this be the Son of David?"

But some of the Prushim (Pharisees) and scribes who had come down from Yerushalayim, filled with suspicion and jealousy, said with contempt: "It is by Beelzebul, the prince of demons, that this man drives out demons." They could not deny the miracle, but they sought to discredit its source.

Others, hoping to trap him, tested him by demanding a sign from the heavens. But Yeshua, perceiving their thoughts as one who sees through to the heart, called them together and spoke to them in parables. "Every kingdom divided against itself is laid waste, and a house divided against itself will fall," he said solemnly. "If Satan casts out Satan, he is divided against himself — how then can his kingdom stand? And if I drive out demons by Beelzebul, by whom do your own sons drive them out? Therefore, they will be your judges. But if I drive out demons by the Spirit of Elohim — or by the finger of Elohim — then the Kingdom of Elohim has come upon you."

His voice grew firm as he warned them: "When a strong man, fully armed, guards his house, his possessions are secure. But when someone stronger attacks and overpowers him, he takes away the armor in which the man trusted and divides up his plunder."

Then, raising his voice so the crowd could hear, Yeshua declared: "Whoever is not with me is against me, and whoever does not gather with me scatters. I tell you the truth: People will be forgiven for every sin and blasphemy — but blasphemy against the Ruach HaKodesh will not be forgiven. Anyone who speaks a word against the Son of Man will be forgiven, but anyone who speaks against the Ruach HaKodesh will never be forgiven — neither in this age nor in the age to come. He is guilty of an eternal sin." (Yeshua said this because they were saying: "He has an impure spirit.")

Turning back to the gathered crowd, his words now sharpened with rebuke, Yeshua continued: "Either make the tree good and its fruit good or make the tree bad and its fruit bad — for the tree is known by its fruit. You brood of vipers! How can you, being evil, say what is good? For the mouth speaks from what fills the heart. A good person brings forth good from the treasure of his heart, and an evil person brings forth evil from the store of wickedness. And I tell you this: On the Day of Judgment, people will give an account for every careless word they have spoken. For by your words, you will be declared righteous, and by your words you will be condemned."

The Sign of Yonah Matthew 12:38–45 | Luke 11:29–32

Then some of the scribes and Prushim, still pressing him, said to him, "Rabbi, we want to see a sign from you."

But he answered them with a grave tone: "An evil and unfaithful generation seeks after a sign, but no sign will be given to it except the sign of Yonah the prophet. For just as Yonah was in the belly of the great fish for three days and three nights, so the Son of Man will be in the heart of the earth three days and three nights.

"The men of Nineveh will rise up at the judgment with this generation and condemn it, for they repented at the proclamation of Yonah, and behold — something greater than Yonah is here.

"The Queen of the South will rise at the judgment with this generation and condemn it, for she came from the ends of the earth to hear the wisdom of Shlomo and behold — something greater than Shlomo is here."

Yeshua then warned them of spiritual complacency: "When an unclean spirit goes out of a man, it passes through arid places seeking rest but finds none. Then it says, 'I will return to the house I left.' When it returns, it finds the house unoccupied, swept clean, and put in order. Then it goes and brings with it seven other spirits more wicked than itself, and they enter and dwell there, and the final state of that man is worse than the first. So it will be with this wicked generation.

True Family in the Kingdom Matthew 12:46–50| Mark 3:31–35 | Luke 8:19–21

While Yeshua was still teaching the people, his mother and his brothers came and stood outside. They could not reach him because of the crowd, so they sent word to him, calling him. A man in the crowd said to him, "Your mother and your brothers are outside, wanting to speak with you."

But Yeshua responded to the one who spoke, saying: "Who is my mother, and who are my brothers?" Looking around at those seated in a circle around him — his disciples and those listening to the word of Elohim — he stretched out his hand toward them and said: "Here are my mother and my brothers! For whoever does the will of Elohim — he is my brother, my sister, and my mother."

Parable of the Two Debtors Luke 7:36–50 |8:1–3

One of the Prushim (Pharisees), a man named Shimon, invited Yeshua to dine with him at his home. Yeshua accepted the invitation, entered his house, and reclined at the table in the customary fashion. Now in that city was a woman who was known by all as a sinner — a woman whose reputation bore the scars of her past. When she learned that Yeshua was eating in the house of the Pharisee, her heart stirred with boldness and reverence.

She came, carrying an alabaster jar filled with costly perfumed oil. Standing behind him at his feet, overcome with emotion, she began to weep. Her tears fell like rain upon his dusty feet. Kneeling, she let down her hair — something unheard of in public — and gently wiped his feet with it. She kissed them with devotion and then anointed them with the fragrant oil.

The scent filled the room, but the atmosphere was divided. Shimon the Pharisee, seeing what she was doing, whispered to himself in silent judgment: "If this man were truly a prophet, he would know who and what kind of woman is touching him — that she is a sinner."

But Yeshua, perceiving his thoughts, turned to him and said, "Shimon, I have something to say to you."

Shimon replied, "Say it, Rabbi."

Yeshua spoke in a parable: "A certain lender had two debtors. One owed five hundred denarii, and the other fifty. Neither could repay him, so he graciously forgave both. Now tell me — which of them will love him more?"

Shimon considered and answered, "I suppose the one whom he forgave more."

"You have judged rightly," Yeshua said.

Then he turned toward the woman but continued speaking to Shimon: "Do you see this woman? I entered your house — you gave me no water for my feet, yet she has washed my feet with her tears and wiped them with her hair. You gave me no kiss, yet from the moment I arrived, she has not stopped kissing my feet. You did not anoint my head with oil, yet she has anointed my feet with fragrant oil.

"Therefore, I tell you — her many sins have been forgiven, and that is why she has shown such great love. But whoever is forgiven little, loves little." Then, turning directly to the woman, he said: "Your sins have been forgiven."

Those reclining at the table began murmuring among themselves, scandalized: "Who is this who even forgives sins?"

But Yeshua, unmoved by their whispers, looked into her very soul and said gently, "Your emunah (faith) has saved you. Go in shalom (peace)."

The Women Who Followed   Luke 8:1-3

After this, Yeshua continued his journey throughout the towns and villages of the Galil, proclaiming and teaching the Good News of the Kingdom of Elohim. The Twelve were with him, and also certain women who had been healed of evil spirits and afflictions: Miryam called the Magdalene — from whom seven unclean spirits had been cast out; Yochanah (Joanna), the wife of Chuza, Herod's steward; Shoshanah (Susanna); and many other women. These devoted women ministered to him and his disciples, supporting them from their own resources, walking alongside them in the mission of the Kingdom.

Parable of the Sower   Matthew 13:1–17 | Mark 4:1–12 | Luke 8:4–10

Again, Yeshua began to teach by the sea — the Sea of Galil. A vast multitude gathered around him from every nearby town and village, so large that he stepped into a boat and sat down, casting off slightly from the shore. The whole crowd remained standing along the water's edge, leaning in to hear every word. He taught them many things in parables, veiling deep truths in the stories of daily life — truths hidden from the hardened, but revealed to the humble.

In this teaching, he began with a cry to awaken their attention: "Listen! A farmer went out to sow his seed. As he scattered the seed, some fell along the hardened path — exposed and unprotected. It was trampled underfoot, and the birds of the heavens came down and devoured it. Other seed fell on rocky ground, where the soil was thin and shallow. It sprang up quickly with enthusiasm, but because it lacked depth, when the sun rose and beat upon it, the plant withered and dried up — it had no root to endure.

"Still other seed fell among thorns. The thorns grew up alongside it and choked it, so that it could not bear fruit. But other seed — ah, the good seed — fell upon rich and receptive soil. It grew, flourished, and yielded a harvest — some a hundredfold, some sixty, and some thirty." Then Yeshua lifted his voice and called out across the lake, "The one who has ears to hear — let him understand!"

Later, when he was alone with his closest followers — the Twelve and a few others who remained — they approached him and asked about the parable. The talmidim said to him, "Rabbi, why do you speak to the people in parables?"

Yeshua answered, revealing the hidden wisdom behind the riddles: "To you it has been given to know the secrets of the Kingdom of Elohim — the mysteries of Heaven's reign — but to those on the outside, all things come in parables. For whoever has — whoever receives with an open heart — more will be given, and he will have abundance. But whoever does not have, even what he thinks he has will be taken away. That is why I speak to them in parables — because seeing, they do not truly see, and hear, they do not truly understand or perceive."

Then Yeshua quoted the prophet Yeshayahu (Isaiah), saying: "Hearing you will hear, but never understand; Seeing you will see, but never perceive. For the heart of this people has become dull.
Their ears are hard of hearing, Their eyes they have closed — Lest they should see with their eyes, Hear with their ears, Understand with their heart, Turn — and I would heal them."

Yeshua paused and looked upon his talmidim with compassion and blessing: "But blessed are your eyes, because they see — and your ears, because they hear. For truly I tell you, many prophets and righteous ones longed to see what you now see but did not see it; and to hear what you now hear but did not hear it."

Sower Explained Matthew 13:18–23 | Mark 4:13–20 | Luke 8:11–15

Then Yeshua turned to his disciples and asked, "Do you not understand this parable? And if you do not understand this one, how will you comprehend any of the parables?"

He explained to them plainly, saying: "The farmer — he sows the Torah of Elohim, casting it like seed upon the hearts of men. The seed sown beside the hardened path represents those who hear the word, but the accuser — the adversary — comes immediately and snatches away what was sown in their hearts, so that they cannot believe and be restored.

"The seed sown on rocky ground are those who, when they hear the Torah, receive it at once with joy. Yet, because they have no root in themselves — no depth, no endurance — they believe for a time, but in the heat of tribulation or persecution that arises on account of the word, they stumble and fall away.

"The seed that falls among thorns represents those who hear, but the worries of this age, the deceit of riches, and the cravings for other things creep in and choke the word. It is suffocated by distraction and never matures — it bears no fruit.

"But the seed sown on good soil — these are the pure-hearted ones. They hear the Torah, receive it, understand it, and hold fast to it with a good and faithful heart. In them, the word bears fruit — some thirtyfold, some sixtyfold, and some a hundredfold."

The Parable of the Wheat and the Tares   Matthew 13:24–30

Then, lifting their minds to the mystery of the world to come, Yeshua spoke another parable to them: "The Kingdom of the Heavens is like a man who went out and sowed good seed in his field. But while men slept, an enemy came and sowed tares — weeds that look like wheat — among the grain and then slipped away into the darkness. When the wheat sprouted and began to form grain, the tares also appeared, growing alongside them. So the servants of the master came to him and said, 'Master, did you not plant good seed in your field? Where then did these tares come from?'

He replied, 'An enemy has done this.'

The servants asked him, 'Do you want us to go and pull up the tares now?'

But the master said, 'No — for if you uproot the tares now, you may also tear up the wheat with them. Let's grow together until the time of the harvest. Then, at the appointed time, I will say to the harvesters: First gather the tares and bind them in bundles to be burned. Then gather the wheat and store it in my granary.'"

The Lamp and the Measure   Mark 4:21–25 | Luke 8:16–18

He said to them: "Is a lamp brought in to be placed under a basket or under a bed? Is it not to be placed on a lampstand? For nothing is hidden that will not be revealed, nor secret that will not be made known and come to light. Take heed how you hear: With the measure you use, it will be measured to you — and more will be added to you. For the one who has, more will be given; but from the one who does not have, even what he thinks he has will be taken away."

The Growing Seed   Mark 4:26–29

And he said: "The Kingdom of Elohim is like a man who casts seed upon the earth. He sleeps and rises night and day, and the seed sprouts and grows — how, he does not know. The earth yields fruit by itself: first the blade, then the head, then the full grain in the head. But when the grain is ripe, he immediately sends in the sickle, for the harvest has come."

Mustard Seed   Matthew 13:31–32 | Mark 4:30–32 | Luke 13:18–19

Then Yeshua continued with another parable: "The Kingdom of the Heavens is like a mustard seed, which a man took and sowed in his field. Though it is the smallest of all the seeds, when it has grown, it is larger than all garden plants and becomes a tree, so that the birds of the heavens come and nest in its branches."

The Leaven   Matthew 13:33 | Luke 13:20–21

Yeshua spoke another mashal to them, saying: "The reign of the heavens is like leaven that a woman took and concealed within three measures of fine flour, until it permeated all of it."

Fulfillment of Prophecy and Private Teaching   Matthew 13:34–36

Yeshua spoke all these things to the crowds in parables; he did not speak to them without a mashal (parable). This was to fulfill what was spoken through the prophet: "I will open my mouth in parables; I will speak forth hidden things from ancient days."

Then Yeshua left the multitude and entered a house. His disciples came close to him, eager to learn, and said, "Rabbeinu (our Teacher), explain to us the parable of the tares in the field."

The Explanation of the Tares   Matthew 13:37–43

He answered them with clarity and authority: "The one sowing the good seed is the Son of Man. The field is the world; the good seed—these are the sons of the Kingdom. But the tares are the sons of the wicked one, and the enemy who sowed them is the adversary himself. The harvest is the end of the age, and the harvesters are the malakhim (messengers).

At the end of the age, the tares will be gathered and burned. The Son of Man will send out his messengers, and they will remove from his Kingdom all those who cause stumbling and those who walk in lawlessness. They will be thrown into the fiery furnace. There will be weeping and grinding of teeth. Then the righteous will shine like the sun in the Kingdom of their Father. Whoever has ears to hear, let him hear!"

The Hidden Treasure   Matthew 13:44

Yeshua continued, saying: "The reign of the heavens is like a treasure hidden in a field, which a man found and then concealed. In his joy, he went and sold everything he had in order to purchase that field."

The Pearl of Great Price   Matthew 13:45–46

"Again, the reign of the heavens is like a merchant searching for fine pearls. When he found one of surpassing worth, he went and sold all that he possessed and bought it."

The Dragnet   Matthew 13:47–51

"Once more, the reign of the heavens is like a great dragnet cast into the sea, gathering all kinds of fish. When it was full, the fishermen drew it to shore, sat down, and sorted the catch — they gathered the good into containers but threw the spoiled away. So it will be at the end of the age. The messengers will go out and separate the wicked from among the righteous, and they will cast them into the fiery furnace, where there will be weeping and grinding of teeth."

Then Yeshua turned to his disciples and asked, "Have you understood all these things?"

They answered him, "Yes, Rabbi."

The Torah Scholar and the Householder   Matthew 13:52

Then Yeshua said to them, "Every sofer (Torah scholar) who has become a disciple of the reign of the heavens is like the master of a household, who brings forth from his treasury both the new and the ancient — drawing from both the revealed and the concealed, from the present wisdom and the foundations of old."

More Parables   Mark 4:33–34 | Matthew 13:31–32

With many such parables, he continued to speak the word to the crowds, as much as they were able to receive. He did not speak to them without a mashal (parable), for the mysteries of the Kingdom were veiled in symbols — but privately, he explained everything to his own talmidim (disciples), revealing the deeper truths to those who sought with understanding hearts.

Again he said, "To what shall we liken the reign of Elohim? With what parable shall we present it?"

"It is like a mustard seed, which, when it is sown upon the earth, is the smallest of all the seeds. But once sown, it grows and becomes the largest of the garden plants, spreading out great branches — so that even the birds of the heavens come and make their nests in its shade."

The Cost of Discipleship   Matthew 8:18–22 | Luke 9:57–60

When Yeshua saw a great crowd encircling him, pressing in with curiosity and hunger, he gave the command to cross to the other side of the sea, seeking a moment of quiet beyond the multitude.

Then a sofer (Torah scholar) stepped forward and said to him with zeal, "Rabbi, I will follow you wherever you go."

Yeshua turned to him and said: "The foxes have holes, and the birds of the heavens have nests — but the Son of Man has nowhere to lay his head."

Another man, already among the talmidim, came forward and said, "Master, permit me first to go and bury my father."

But Yeshua, seeing into his heart, replied: "Follow me — and let the dead bury their own dead."

When the prophet Eliyahu found Elisha plowing his field, he cast his mantle upon him — a silent yet powerful call. Elisha asked to return and kiss his parents goodbye. Eliyahu allowed it. But Elisha did not hesitate. He slaughtered his oxen, burned his plow, and left everything behind. He made sure there was nothing to return to.

But when Yeshua walked among the crowds, his call was even more urgent shown in what one disciple asked: to bury his father first. But Yeshua said, "Follow me — and let the dead bury their own dead." And to another who asked only to say farewell at home, Yeshua warned: "No one who puts his hand to the plow and looks back is fit for the Kingdom of Elohim."

This warning echoes the fate of Lot's wife, who was delivered from destruction — yet turned back toward what she had left behind. She became a pillar of salt, a symbol of hesitation when heaven demands urgency. Her story, too, reminds us: you cannot be delivered while clinging to what Elohim is calling you to leave.

Elisha looked forward. Lot's wife looked back. Yeshua calls us to abandon comfort, delay, and nostalgia — and to follow him with a whole heart, without pause.

The path of the Kingdom has no rearview mirror. To follow Yeshua is to forsake everything — and never look back.

Storm on the Sea Matthew 8:23–27 | Mark 4:35–41 | Luke 8:22–25

And it happened on that very day, when evening had come, that Yeshua said to his talmidim (disciples), "Let us cross over to the other side of the lake."

So, they left the crowd behind, and Yeshua entered the boat. His talmidim followed him, and they took him along just as he was. Other boats accompanied them across the water. As they sailed, Yeshua, weary from teaching, found rest, and fell asleep on a cushion in the stern of the boat. Suddenly, a fierce windstorm burst forth upon the lake. The skies darkened, the waters surged, and waves began to crash violently into the vessel — so that it was already filling with water. The small craft rocked and reeled, and they were in real danger of sinking. Yet Yeshua slept.

In desperation, they came to him their clothes drenched, shaking him awake with panic in their voices and yelling above the storm they said to him, "Rabbi, do you not care that we are perishing? Master, Save us!"

He awoke and stood calm amidst the chaos. With resolute authority, he rebuked the wind and the raging sea. He spoke to the storm: "Be silent. Be still." And instantly, the wind ceased. The waters were stilled. A great calm spread over the lake, like glass laid over the surface of the deep. Then Yeshua turned to them and said, "Why are you afraid, O you of little emunah (trust)? Where is your faith? Do you still have no trust?"

And awe fell upon them. They were gripped with holy fear and marveled among themselves, saying:
"Who then is this, that even the wind and the sea obey him?"

Yeshua & Legion Matthew 8:28–34 | Mark 5:1–20 | Luke 8:26–39

They came to the other side of the sea, to the region of the Gerasenes, which lies opposite the Galil. The land there was rugged, remote, and scattered with tombs — a place feared by many. As Yeshua stepped out of the boat onto the shore, a man emerged from among the burial caves to meet him — a man possessed by unclean spirits. He had not worn clothing for a long time, and he lived not in a house, but among the tombs, dwelling in the places of the dead. His appearance was wild, and his eyes haunted. He was a terror to the region, exceedingly violent and untamable. No one had the strength to subdue him, not even with chains. Though many had tried to bind him with shackles, he would break the bonds apart. The iron was no match for the fury that possessed him.

Day and night he wandered among the tombs and in the hills, crying out in agony and despair, gashing his own flesh with sharp stones. The spirit within him drove him into desolate and solitary places, separating him from the living. When he saw Yeshua from a distance, he ran — not to attack, but to fall at his feet. With a great cry, he shouted, "What have I to do with you, Yeshua, Son of El Elyon? I beg you by Elohim, do not torment me!"

For Yeshua had already spoken to the spirit, saying, "Come out of him, you unclean spirit!"

Then Yeshua asked, "What is your name?"

And the spirit answered, "Legion," for many demons had entered into the man, a multitude warring within his soul. The demons begged him continually not to send them out of the region, and not to cast them into the abyss — the place of confinement for the rebellious spirits. Now nearby, on the slope of a hillside, a large herd of pigs was feeding. The demons pleaded with him, saying, "Send us into the pigs, that we may enter them."

Yeshua gave them permission. Then the unclean spirits came out of the man and entered the pigs, and the entire herd — about two thousand — rushed down the steep bank into the sea and were drowned in the waters below. The herdsmen, overwhelmed and terrified, fled from the scene and reported everything in the town and throughout the surrounding countryside. The people came out in considerable numbers to see what had taken place. They approached Yeshua and saw the man who had once been filled with demons — now sitting calmly at Yeshua's feet, clothed, and in his right mind. And they were afraid.

Those who had witnessed the miracle recounted to them how the man had been delivered and what had happened to the pigs. Then all the people of the surrounding region, seized with great fear, begged Yeshua to leave their territory. As Yeshua prepared to depart and stepped into the boat, the man who had been set free clung to him and begged to go with him. But Yeshua did not permit him. Instead, he said: "Return to your home and declare how much Elohim has done for you." So the man went, obedient and overflowing with gratitude, proclaiming throughout the whole city how much Yeshua had done for him — and all who heard were amazed.

The Healing of the Woman and the Plea of Ya'ir   Matthew 9:18–22 | Mark 5:21–34 | Luke 8:40–48

Yeshua crossed again in the boat to the other side of the lake, and a great crowd gathered to meet him, pressing in on every side as he stood by the sea. Among them came a man named Ya'ir (Jairus), a leader of the local synagogue, a man of prominence and dignity. But dignity fled from him in his desperation. Falling at Yeshua's feet, he pleaded earnestly, tears in his eyes and fear trembling in his voice:

"My little daughter is dying! Come—please lay your hands upon her so that she may be healed and live."

Without hesitation, Yeshua arose and went with him. His talmidim followed closely, but so did the pressing crowd—thronging him, jostling for a touch, a word, a miracle. And behold—within that pressing crowd was a woman who had suffered for twelve long years from a discharge of blood. Her affliction had made her ritually impure, isolating her from the community and from the courts of worship. She had spent all she had on physicians, searching for relief—but no one could heal her. Her strength was drained, her dignity stripped, her hope worn thin—yet her emunah (faith) endured.

She came up behind Yeshua, silently, reverently, and reached out through the crowd. Her hand found the fringe of his cloak—tzitzit, a sign of covenant obedience—and in her heart she said, "If I can only touch his garment, I shall be healed." And in that very moment, her flow of blood stopped. The source of her affliction dried up. She felt it deep within her—restoration. Wholeness. Shalom.

Yeshua, immediately sensing that power had gone forth from him, stopped and turned in the crowd. "Who touched my garments?" he asked aloud.

His talmidim were puzzled and a bit overwhelmed. "Rabbi, the crowd is pressing all around you—and yet you ask, 'Who touched me?'" But Yeshua continued looking, searching with eyes that saw deeper than the surface.

Then the woman, trembling and knowing she had been healed, came forward. She fell at his feet, overcome with reverence, and in the presence of all the people she poured out her story—why she had touched him, and how in that instant, she was made whole. Yeshua looked upon her with compassion and said, "Daughter, your emunah has healed you. Go in shalom, and be whole from your affliction."

Torah Background	Talmudic Commentary
Leviticus 15:25–27 "If a woman has a discharge of blood for many days, not during the time of her niddah, or if it continues beyond her regular period, she shall be unclean all the days of her unclean discharge, as in the days of her niddah... Anyone who touches her shall be unclean..." ♦ Key points: A woman with an abnormal blood flow is a zavah gedolah (great flow), not a regular niddah She is ritually impure for as long as the blood flows (even indefinitely) Cannot enter the Temple (Beit HaMikdash) or touch sacred things Anyone she touches becomes tamei (ritually impure) Therefore, this woman in the Gospel narrative was: -Excluded from Temple worship -Considered perpetually impure -Likely socially isolated (anyone she touched was impure) Prophetic Parallel: Malachi 4:2 (Hebrew 3:20) וְזָרְחָה לָכֶם יִרְאֵי שְׁמִי שֶׁמֶשׁ צְדָקָה וּמַרְפֵּא בִּכְנָפֶיהָ "But for you who revere My Name, the sun of righteousness shall rise with healing in its wings (kanafav)..."Kanaf = "Wing", "Corner", or Hem In Numbers 15:38–40, Israel is commanded to attach tzitzit (fringes) to the kanaf (corner) of their garments Yeshua, as a Torah-observant Jew, wore a tallit with tzitzit The woman touches the "fringe" (Greek: κρασπέδου – kraspedon) of his garment, which is clearly the tzitzit. The act of touching the tzitzit (kanaf) directly fulfills Malachi's prophecy: "The sun of righteousness will arise with healing in his tzitzit." To the woman—and to any Torah-faithful Jew—this was not superstition, but faith in a prophetic promise.	Talmud Bavli, Berakhot 5b and Shabbat 110a Describes numerous folk remedies and medical procedures for a woman with a continual discharge of blood: Drinking various potions Carrying barley grain in a linen rag Burning ostrich eggs and drinking their ashes Even placing certain amulets or incantations This aligns exactly with the Gospel account: "She had spent all her livelihood on physicians and was not healed by anyone." (Luke 8:43) The Talmud confirms that such treatments were known and commonly used—and often ineffective. Halachic Risk She Took She entered a dense crowd, making all she touched tamei She touched a Torah teacher, rendering him ritually impure—unless he is the one whose tzitzit brings healing. This was a bold act of faith, not mere desperation. Her action was both halachically dangerous and theologically profound.

The Raising of the Daughter of Ya'ir   Matthew 9:23–26 | Mark 5:35–43 | Luke 8:49–56

While Yeshua was still speaking to the woman he had healed, a messenger came quickly from the house of Ya'ir, the synagogue ruler. With downcast eyes and a heavy heart, he delivered the sorrowful news:
"Your daughter has died. Do not trouble the teacher any longer."

But Yeshua, hearing this, turned at once to Ya'ir and said with quiet firmness, "Do not be afraid—only trust, and she will be healed."

Then Yeshua continued on toward the house, but he did not allow the crowd to follow. Only Kefa, Ya'akov, and Yochanan—the three closest talmidim—accompanied him. As they approached the home, the sound of mourning met their ears: a loud commotion, weeping, wailing, and the chaos of despair. The child's death had shaken the household to its core.

Yeshua entered and said to the mourners, "Why all this noise and lamentation? The child is not dead, but asleep." They scoffed and laughed at him, mocking such a statement in their grief and unbelief. But he sent them all outside. Then, taking with him the girl's father and mother and the three talmidim, he entered the room where the lifeless child lay. The air was still. The parents' faces were etched with grief. Yeshua approached the little girl, took her hand gently in his, and said to her with authority: "Talita kumi"—an Aramaic phrase meaning, "Little girl, arise."

And her spirit returned to her. Life surged back into her young body, and immediately she stood up and began to walk—full of strength and vitality. She was twelve years old. The parents and those with them stood in stunned silence, overtaken by amazement. Awe and joy intermingled in the room like incense. But Yeshua gave them strict instructions not to tell anyone what had happened. Then, with practical tenderness, he told them to give her something to eat.

The Blind See, and the Mute Speaks Matthew 9:27–34 | Mark 6:1–6a

As Yeshua departed from there, two blind men began to follow after him. Their voices rang out down the road: "Chonenu, Ben David!" ("Have mercy on us, Son of David!") Their plea echoed with desperation and hope. When Yeshua entered the house, the blind men came in after him, drawn by faith more than by sight.

Yeshua turned to them and asked, "Do you believe that I am able to do this?"

They said to him, "Ken, Adoni (yes, Master.)"

Then Yeshua reached out and touched their eyes and said, "Let it be done for you according to your emunah."

And at once, their eyes were opened. Sight flooded in where darkness had reigned. Yet Yeshua warned them sternly, "See that no one knows." But filled with joy and wonder, they went out and spread the news about him throughout all that region.

As they were going out, some brought to Yeshua a man who was mute and possessed by a shed (unclean spirit). When Yeshua cast the demon out, the mute man began to speak. The crowds stood in awe, marveling and saying, "Never has such a thing been seen in Yisrael!"

But the Prushim (Pharisees) dismissed the miracle, saying, "By the prince of demons he casts out demons."

Without Honor in His Hometown Mark 6:1–6a | Matthew 13:54–58

Then Yeshua journeyed to his hometown, and his talmidim went with him. When Shabbat came, he entered the synagogue and began to teach. Those who heard him were astonished, whispering among themselves: "Where did this man get these things? What is this wisdom given to him? How are such mighty works being done by his hands? Isn't this the builder, the craftsman? The son of Miryam? Brother of Yaakov, Yosef, Shimon, and Yehudah? And aren't his sisters here with us?" Their familiarity became a stumbling block. Rather than rejoicing, they took offense at him.

But Yeshua said, "A navi is not without honor—except in his hometown, among his own relatives, and in his own house." Because of their lack of emunah, he could do no mighty work there—only laying his hands on a few sick people and healing them. And he marveled at their unbelief.

Chapter 11: The Gospel Spreads Out

The Twelve Are Sent Out Matthew 10:1–23 | Mark 6:7 | Luke 9:1–6

Yeshua called the Twelve near to him and began to send them out two by two. He gave them samchut (authority) over unclean spirits, and to heal every disease and sickness. These are the names of the twelve shlichim (sent ones): First, Shim'on called Kefa, and Andrew his brother; Yaakov son of Zavdai, and Yochanan his brother; Philip and Bar-Talmai; T'oma and Mattityahu the tax collector; Yaakov son of Halfai, and Taddai; Shim'on the Kana'ani (Zealot), and Yehudah Ish-Kriot, who would later deliver him.

Yeshua instructed them, saying: "Do not go into the way of the nations (Goyim), and do not enter a city of the Shomronim (Samaritans). Rather, go to the lost sheep of Beit Yisrael. And as you go, proclaim, saying: 'The Kingdom of Heaven has drawn near.' Heal the sick, raise the dead, cleanse the metzora'im (those with skin afflictions), cast out demons. Freely you received, freely give. Do not take gold, silver, or copper in your belts, no traveling bag for the road, or two tunics, or sandals, or staff—for the worker is worthy of his food.

When you enter a town or village, inquire who is worthy, and stay there until you leave. And when you enter a house, greet it with shalom. If the house is worthy, let your shalom rest upon it; but if it is not worthy, let your shalom return to you. And if anyone will not receive you or hear your words, shake off the dust from your feet as you leave that house or that town. Truly I say to you: It will be more bearable for Sodom and Amora (Gomorrah) on the day of judgment than for that town."

"Behold, I am sending you out as sheep among wolves. Be wise as serpents and harmless as doves. Beware of men, for they will hand you over to the Sanhedrin and flog you in their synagogues. You will be brought before governors and kings because of me, as a witness to them and to the nations. But when they give you up, do not worry about how or what you will say—for it will be given to you in that hour what to say. For it is not you speaking, but the Ruach (Spirit) of your Heavenly Father speaking through you.

Brother will deliver brother to death, and a father his child. Children will rise against parents and put them to death. You will be hated by all because of my name. But the one who endures to the end will be delivered. When they persecute you in one town, flee to another. For truly I say to you: You will not finish going through all the towns of Yisrael before the Son of Man comes."

The Cost of Discipleship and the Mission of the Twelve Matthew 10:24–42 | Mark 6:12–13 | Luke 12:2–9

"A talmid (disciple) is not above his rabbi, nor a servant above his master. It is enough for the talmid to be like his rabbi, and the servant like his master. If they have called the master of the house Ba'al-Z'vuv (Beelzebul), how much more the members of his household! So do not fear them. For nothing is covered that will not be revealed or hidden that will not be made known. What I tell you in the dark, speak in the light; what you hear whispered, proclaim from the housetops."

"Do not fear those who kill the body but cannot kill the soul. Rather, fear Him who can destroy both soul and body in Gehinnom. Are not two sparrows sold for a penny? Yet not one of them falls to the ground apart from your Father. Even the hairs of your head are all numbered. Therefore, do not fear—you are more valuable than many sparrows."

"Everyone who acknowledges me before men, I also will acknowledge before my Father in the heavens. But whoever denies me before men, I will also deny before my Father."

"Do not think that I came to bring peace on the earth; I did not come to bring peace, but a sword. For I have come to set a man against his father, a daughter against her mother, and a daughter-in-law against her mother-in-law—and a man's enemies will be those of his own household. Whoever loves father or mother more than me is not worthy of me. And whoever loves son or daughter more than me is not worthy of me. And whoever does not take up his patibulum and follows after me is not worthy of me. Whoever finds his life will lose it, and whoever loses his life for my sake will find it."

A Patibulum is the Horizontal crossbeam carried by the criminal on his way to be executed on a cross. Often implied by "stauros" in Greek. The Greek word means stake which has lead some believers to believe that Yeshua was crucified on a single pole but by the time of the Romans it was a cross and not a single pole. Archeology has proven that it was a cross.

"Whoever receives you receives me, and whoever receives me receives the One who sent me. Whoever receives a prophet in the name of a prophet will receive a prophet's reward. Whoever receives a righteous one in the name of a righteous one will receive a tzaddik's (righteous one's) reward. And whoever gives one of these little ones even a cup of cold water to drink because he is a talmid—amen I say to you, he will surely not lose his reward." And the Twelve went out, proclaiming the Good News and calling the people to make teshuvah (repentance). They cast out many demons, anointed the sick with oil, and healed them everywhere.

The Death of Yochanan the Immerser   Matthew 14:1–12 | Mark 6:14–29 | Luke 9:7–9

Now Herod the tetrarch heard of all that was happening, for Yeshua's name had become well-known, and he was perplexed. Some were saying, "Yochanan the Immerser has risen from the dead! That is why these powers are working in him."

Others said, "It is Eliyahu," and others, "He is a prophet, like one of the prophets of old."

But when Herod heard it, he said, "This is Yochanan, whom I beheaded—he has been raised!" For Herod had arrested Yochanan and put him in prison on account of Herodias, the wife of his brother Philip, whom he had taken as his own wife. For Yochanan had been saying to him, "It is not permitted for you to have your brother's wife." Herod wanted to put him to death, but he feared the people, because they regarded Yochanan as a navi (prophet). But Herodias held a grudge against him and wanted to kill him. Yet she could not, because Herod was afraid of Yochanan, knowing him to be a righteous and set-apart man, and he kept him safe. He would listen to him often and was disturbed—yet he liked to listen to him.

But an opportunity came on Herod's birthday, when he gave a feast for his nobles, military commanders, and the leading men of the Galil. The daughter of Herodias came in and danced before them, and pleased Herod and his guests. And the king said to the girl, "Ask me whatever you desire, and I will give it to you." He swore to her, "Whatever you ask of me, I will give you, up to half of my kingdom."

And she went out and said to her mother, "What should I ask?"

She knew immediately what she wanted, and she instructed her daughter her voice dripping with venom her eyes cold and determined, "The head of Yochanan the Immerser."

Immediately she hurried back to the king and said, "I want you to give me right now the head of Yochanan the Immerser on a platter." The king immediately went pale eyes wide with horror and was deeply grieved, yet because of his oaths and his guests, he did not want to break his word to her. And immediately the king sent an executioner and commanded him to bring Yochanan's head. He went and beheaded Yochanan in prison. He brought his head on a platter and gave it to the girl, and the girl gave it to her mother. When Yochanan's talmidim (disciples) heard of it, they took his body and laid it in a tomb. They went and reported everything to Yeshua.

The Feeding of the Five Thousand Matthew 14:13–21, Mark 6:30–44, Luke 9:10–17 | John 6:1–13

The shlichim (sent ones) gathered together with Yeshua and reported to him all that they had done and taught. He said to them: "Come away by yourselves to a desolate place and rest a little." For many were coming and going, and they had no leisure even to eat. So, they went away in a boat to a solitary place by themselves. Now the time of the feast of Pesach (Passover), the festival of the Yehudim (Jews), was drawing near. But the crowds saw them leaving and recognized them. Many ran there on foot from all the surrounding towns and arrived ahead of them.

When Yeshua went ashore and saw the great multitude, he was filled with compassion for them, for they were like sheep without a shepherd. So, he welcomed them and began to teach them many things about the Kingdom of Elohim, and he healed their sick and those who needed restoration. When the day was drawing to a close, the talmidim came to him and said: "This is a desolate place, and the hour is late. Send the crowds away, so they can go into the surrounding villages and buy food for themselves."

But Yeshua answered them: "They do not need to go away. You give them something to eat."

They said to him: "Shall we go and spend our two hundred denarii on bread and give it to them? How are we to go and buy food for all these people?" For there were about five thousand men—besides women and children.

Yeshua said: "Can you go and see how many loaves you already have?"

They went and checked their supplies and said, "Five, and we have two fish as well, but what are they among so many?"

He said, "Bring them here to me." Then he commanded them to have the people sit down in groups on the green grass.

So, they sat down in groups of hundreds and fifties. Taking the five loaves and the two fish, Yeshua looked up toward the heavens, blessed them, broke the loaves, and gave them to the talmidim to set before the people. And he divided the two fish among them all. And all ate and were satisfied. Then they picked up twelve baskets full of broken pieces of bread and fish.

Commentary on the Five Loaves and Two Fish		
The Five Loaves : The Written Torah The five loaves unmistakably point to the Five Books of Moshe—the Torah Shebichtav (Written Torah): Bread is the recurring symbol of Torah in Scripture: "Man does not live by bread alone, but by every word that proceeds from the mouth of YHWH" (Deut. 8:3). Yeshua, as a Torah sage, is distributing spiritual nourishment from the very heart of the covenant. Just as Moshe gave the Torah in the wilderness, so too Yeshua feeds the people in the wilderness—mirroring the giving of manna and Sinai revelation.	The Two Fish — Layered Symbolism 1. The Two Houses of Israel: Judah and Ephraim The descendants of Yosef were blessed to multiply like fish (Gen. 48:16). The northern kingdom (Ephraim/Israel) was scattered among the nations (Hoshea 7:8), yet still part of the covenantal hope. The two fish represent the two divided kingdoms—Judah and Israel/Ephraim—both to be restored through the nourishment of Torah. 2. The Two Torot: Written and Oral Fish are silent and hidden beneath the surface, just as Oral Torah was transmitted secretly and humbly. The loaves are visible (Written Torah); the fish swim beneath the surface (Oral Torah), yet both come from the same waters of Divine Wisdom. Together they form a complete revelation: the foundational text and the interpretive tradition. 3. Moshe and Yeshua: The Two Redeemers Moshe: the first redeemer, who brought forth the Torah and manna. Yeshua: the final sage-redeemer, restoring the heart of the Torah to the people. Both are men of humility, signs, and wilderness leadership. In mystical thought (Zohar I:25b), Moshe and the future redeemer are two expressions of one essence—two fish, yet from the same waters of Elohim's chesed (lovingkindness)	The 12 Baskets Left Over — Restoration of the 12 Tribes The leftovers are not just scraps—they are the overflow of Torah. Twelve baskets (Greek: kophinoi) symbolize the twelve tribes of Israel—each one filled and sustained. The Torah and the words of the Redeemer are enough and more for all of Israel.

Those who ate were about five thousand men, besides women and children.

The Prophet, Prayer, and Rebuke John 6:14–15 | Matthew 11:20–30 | Mark 6:45–46 | Luke 10:13–15

When the people saw the sign he had done, they said: "This is truly the prophet who is to come into the world!" But Yeshua, knowing they were about to come and seize him to make him king by force, he immediately made his talmidim get into the boat and go ahead of him to the other side—to Beit Tzaidah—while he dismissed the crowd. After sending them away, he went up on the mountain by himself to pray.

Then Yeshua began to denounce the cities in which most of his miracles had been done, because they did not turn back in teshuvah. "Woe to you, Chorazin! Woe to you, Beit Tzaidah! For if the mighty deeds performed in you had been done in Tzor and Tzidon, they would have repented long ago in sackcloth and ashes. But I say to you: it will be more bearable for Tzor and Tzidon on the Day of Judgment than for you. And you, K'far Nachum (Capernaum)—will you be lifted up to the heavens? No, you will be brought down to She'ol. For if the mighty works done in you had been done in Sodom, it would have remained until this day. But I say to you: it will be more bearable for the land of Sodom on the Day of Judgment than for you."

At that time Yeshua lifted his eyes and said: "I thank You, Avi, Adon of Ha'Shamayim and Ha'Eretz, because You have hidden these things from the wise and learned, and revealed them to the infants—yes, Abba, for this was Your good pleasure. All things have been handed over to me by my Father. No one knows the Son except the Father, and no one knows the Father except the Son, and those to whom the Son chooses to reveal Him.

"Come to me, all you who labor and are burdened, and I will give you rest. Take my yoke upon you and learn from me, for I am gentle and lowly in heart, and you will find rest for your souls. For my yoke is pleasant, and my burden is light."

Yeshua Walks on Water and Heals the Multitudes Matthew 14:23–36 | Mark 6:47–56 | John 6:16–21

When evening came, he was there alone. But the boat was already far from land, many stadia away, being battered by the waves, for the wind was against them. It was the fourth watch of the night (between 3 and 6 a.m.). Yeshua came to them, walking on the tumultuous sea. When the talmidim saw him walking on the water, they were terrified, saying, "It is a ghost!" And they cried out in fear.

But immediately Yeshua spoke to them, saying: "Take heart—it is I, do not be afraid."

Then Kefa answered and said, "Master, if it is you, command me to come to you on the water."

And he said, "Come."

Kefa stepped out of the boat and walked on the water to go toward Yeshua. But when he saw the wind, he became afraid, and beginning to sink, he cried out: "Master, save me!"

Immediately Yeshua reached out his hand and took hold of him and said: "O you of little faith—why did you doubt?"

And when they got into the boat, the wind ceased. And those in the boat bowed down before him, saying, "Truly, you are a son of Elohim." Then they were willing to take him onto the boat, and immediately the boat reached the land to which they were going. They arrived at the region of Ginosar (Gennesaret) and came to shore.

When they had crossed over, they came to the land of Gennesaret and anchored there. As soon as they came out of the boat, the people recognized Yeshua. The men of that place sent word into all the surrounding regions. People began to bring to him all who were ill, carrying them on mats and stretchers wherever they heard he was. They laid the sick in the marketplaces, and they begged him that they might just touch the edge of his garment—his tzitzit. And as many as touched it were made whole. Wherever he went—villages, towns, or open countryside—they placed the sick in public places, and he healed them all.

The Crowds Seek Yeshua for Another Sign　　　　　　　　　　　　　　　　John 6:22–29

The crowd that had remained on the other side of the sea saw that there had only been one boat there, and that Yeshua had not entered it with his disciples, because his disciples had gone away alone. Then other boats from Tiveriyah (Tiberias) arrived near the place where the people had eaten the bread after giving thanks to Elohim. When the crowd saw that neither Yeshua nor his disciples were there, they themselves got into the boats and went to Kfar Nachum (Capernaum), seeking Yeshua.

When they found him across the sea, they said to him, "Rabbi, when did you arrive here?"

Yeshua answered and said to them, "Amen, amen I tell you: You are seeking me not because you saw the signs, but because you ate of the loaves and were satisfied."

"Do not labor for the food that perishes, but for the food that endures to life of the coming age, which the Son of Man will give to you. For upon him the Father—Elohim Himself—has set His seal."

Then they said to him, "What must we do to perform the works of Elohim?"

Yeshua answered them, "This is the work of Elohim: That you place your trust in the one whom He has sent."

Key Hebraic Nuances to Notice
Chayei Olam HaBa = life in the world to come (eternal life in Jewish thought)
Seal (חותם) = a sign of divine appointment or sanctification
Works of Elohim = phrase often used in Jewish teaching to refer to mitzvot
Sent one = a Torah shaliach (שליח), a messenger or emissary with divine authority, not necessarily divine

The Bread from HeavenJohn 6:30–40

So, they said to him, "What sign will you perform so that we may see it and trust you? What work will you do? Our ancestors ate manna in the desert as it is written: 'He gave them bread from heaven to eat.'"

Then Yeshua said to them, "Amen, amen I say to you: It was not Mosheh who gave you the bread from heaven, but it is my Father who gives you the true bread from heaven. For the bread of Elohim is that which comes down from the heavens and gives life to the world."

Then they said to him, "Master, give us this bread always."

Yeshua said to them: "I am the bread of life. Whoever comes to me will never go hungry, and whoever places their faith in me will never thirst. But I said to you: You have seen me, and yet you do not trust. All that the Father gives me will come to me, and the one who comes to me I will never turn away. For I have come down from heaven not to do my own will, but the will of Him who sent me. And this is the will of the One who sent me: That I should lose none of those He has given me but raise them up at the last day. For this is the will of my Father: That everyone who sees the Son and trusts in him should have life in the world to come, and I will raise him up on the last day."

The Living Bread from HeavenJohn 6:41–51

Then the Yehudim began to grumble about him because he said, "I am the bread that came down from the heavens." And they said, "Is this not Yeshua, the son of Yosef, whose father and mother we know? How then does he say, 'I have come down from heaven'?"

Yeshua answered and said to them, "Stop murmuring among yourselves. No one is able to come to me unless the Father who sent me draws him—and I will raise him up on the last day. It is written in the prophets: 'And they shall all be taught by Elohim.' Everyone who hears and learns from the Father comes to me. Not that anyone has seen the Father—except the one who is from Elohim; he has seen the Father.

"Amen, amen I say to you: Whoever trusts has life in the world to come. I am the bread of life. Your ancestors ate the manna in the wilderness, and they died. This is the bread that comes down from the heavens, so that one may eat it and not die. I am the living bread that came down from the heavens. If anyone eats this bread, he will live forever. And the bread that I will give is my flesh, offered for the sake of the life of the world."

Hebraic Nuance:
"Murmuring" – evokes Exodus 16, when Israel grumbled about the manna
"Draws him" – divine initiative (cf. Jer 31:3, "With cords of love I drew you")
"They shall all be taught by Elohim" – Isaiah 54:13; messianic age expectation that Elohim would teach His people directly
"Flesh offered for the world" – not literal cannibalism, but a prophetic idiom of self-sacrifice (cf. Isaiah 53:10, Psalm 22)

The Bread and the Blood of Life   John 6:52–59

Then the Yehudim began disputing among themselves, saying, "How can this man give us his flesh to eat?"

So, Yeshua said to them, "Amen, amen I say to you: Unless you eat the flesh of the Son of Man and drink his blood, you have no life in you. Whoever eats my flesh and drinks my blood has life in the world to come and I will raise him up on the last day. For my flesh is true food, and my blood is true drink. Whoever eats my flesh and drinks my blood dwells in me, and I in him. Just as the living Father sent me, and I live because of the Father, so the one who partakes of me will live because of me. This is the bread that came down from the heavens—not like the bread your fathers ate and died. Whoever eats this bread will live forever." He said these things while teaching in the synagogue at Kfar Nachum.

Hebraic Context Notes	Talmudic Parallel
"Eat flesh, drink blood" — This is not meant literally but follows a common prophetic idiom where consuming something symbolizes internalization. Compare: 1. Jeremiah 15:16 – "Your words were found, and I ate them…" 2. Ezekiel 3:1–3 – "Eat this scroll and go speak…" 3. Psalm 34:9 – "Taste and see that Adonai is good."	Sanhedrin 98b: Rabbi Hillel said: "There shall be no Moshiach for Israel, because they already consumed him in the days of King Hezekiah." This is interpreted not to deny the concept of Messiah entirely, but to say that the generation already received the spiritual benefit of the Messiah through a righteous man (Hezekiah), and "ate" of him — i.e., they consumed his merit or essence.
"Dwells in me, and I in him" – This reflects the Hebraic concept of devekut (דבקות), spiritual cleaving or intimacy with the righteous and with the Divine through Torah observance and spiritual discipline.	This mirrors Yeshua's language: " If you do not eat of me, you have no life…" i.e., if you do not fully partake of the path and inner teachings, you miss what Elohim has offered your generation.
"Lives because of me" – As Yeshua walks in perfect alignment with Elohim's will, to partake of him is to partake in that alignment — i.e., the living Torah path.	In Jewish mysticism and rabbinic thought, "eating" the righteous one can refer to the generation having already drawn spiritual benefit (merit) from a divinely appointed leader.

A Dividing Word Among the Disciples   John 6:60–71

Many of Yeshua's talmidim, when they heard this, said, "This teaching is difficult—who is able to accept it?"

But Yeshua, knowing within himself that his talmidim were murmuring about this, said to them, "Does this cause you to stumble? What then if you were to see the Son of Man ascending to where he was before? It is the spirit that gives life—the flesh is of no benefit. The words I have spoken to you are spirit and are life. Yet there are some among you who do not trust." For Yeshua knew from the beginning who did not trust and who would betray him.

Then he said, "For this reason I told you: No one is able to come to me unless it is granted to him by the Father." From that time, many of his talmidim turned back and no longer walked with him.

Then Yeshua said to the Twelve, "Do you also want to leave?"

Shim'on Kefa answered him, "Master, to whom shall we go? You have ha'davar chayim (the words of life) in the world to come. We have trusted and have come to know that you are the Holy One of Elohim."

Yeshua answered them, "Did I not choose you—the Twelve? Yet one of you is an adversary." He spoke of Yehudah from Qeriyot, son of Shim'on. For he, one of the Twelve, was going to betray him.

Chapter 12: Yeshua's Second Year of Ministry

Confrontation Over Tradition Matthew 15:1–9 | Mark 7:1–13

Then the Prushim (Pharisees) and scribes came to Yeshua from Yerushalayim, and when they saw some of his disciples eating bread with defiled hands (unwashed), they found fault. For the Prushim and all the Yehudim, unless they wash with a fist (netilat yadayim), do not eat—holding fast the traditions of the elders. And coming from the marketplace, they do not eat unless they are immersed. And there are many other traditions which they received to hold: washings of cups, pots, copper vessels, and couches.

So, the Prushim and scribes asked him, "Why do your disciples transgress the tradition of the elders? For they do not wash their hands before they eat bread."

But Yeshua answered and said to them: "Why do you transgress the command of Elohim for the sake of your tradition? For Elohim said, 'Honor your father and your mother,' and 'He who speaks evil of father or mother must surely die.' But you say, 'If a man says to his father or his mother, "What you would have received from me is Korban (a gift to Elohim)," then he is no longer bound to honor his father or mother.' In this way you nullify the word of Elohim through your tradition, which you passed down. And many such things you do. Hypocrites! Yesha'yahu (Isaiah) prophesied rightly about you, saying: 'These people honor Me with their lips, but their heart is far from Me. In vain do they worship Me, teaching as doctrines the commandments of men.'"

Talmudic Parallels and Discussions

1. Korban vs. Honoring Parents – Mishnah Nedarim 9:1–7
Mishnah Nedarim 9:1–7 (and Gemara Nedarim 30a–36b) discusses vows that conflict with Torah obligations, including honoring one's parents.

Key Point:
The Mishnah allows a person to make a vow that restricts another's benefit—even a parent's. However, the Talmudic discussion wrestles with limiting such vows if they violate greater Torah obligations, like kibbud av va'em (honoring father and mother).

Nedarim 30b:
"A vow that violates the words of the Torah is not upheld."

Nedarim 30b:
 "A vow that contradicts Torah is not binding."

Nedarim 35a
Explains how vows must be treated carefully so as not to nullify Torah law.

2. Halachic Rebuke – Yevamot 90b
Yevamot 90b: Warns that "a decree that leads to Torah being uprooted is invalid."

Yeshua's rebuke would align with this: if a tradition (like Korban) undermines Torah, it is invalid, even if rabbinically sanctioned.

3. Rebuking Sages – Shabbat 96b
Moshe rebukes the sages (elders) for not acting properly, and Rav Nachman says: "One may rebuke even one's teacher if Torah is at stake."

Also:
Pesachim 66a shows Hillel rebuking the sons of Betheira, when they failed to rule properly on the Korban Pesach question.

What Truly Defiles a Person Matthew 15:10–14 | Mark 7:14–23

Then Yeshua called the crowd near and said to them, "Listen to me, everyone, and understand: There is nothing outside a man that, entering into him, can defile him; but the things that come out of the man—those are what defile him. Let anyone who has ears to hear, let him hear."

Later, when Yeshua entered the house away from the crowd, his disciples asked him about the parable. Kefa said to him, "Explain this parable to us."

He said to them, "Are you also still without understanding? Do you not see that whatever enters into a man from the outside cannot defile him? Because it does not go into his heart, but into his belly, and then is expelled into the latrine." In saying this, he was declaring that food, as defined by Torah, is not defiled by hands alone.

Then he said, "What comes out of a man's mouth—that is what defiles him. For from within, out of the heart of men, proceed: evil thoughts, sexual immorality, thefts, murders, adulteries, greed, wickedness, deceit, sensuality, envy, slander, pride, and foolishness. All these evil things come from within and defile a man. But to eat with unwashed hands does not defile him."

Then his disciples came to him and said, "Do you know that the Prushim were offended when they heard this teaching?"

Yeshua replied, "Every plant that my heavenly Father has not planted will be uprooted. Let them be—they are blind guides of the blind. And if the blind lead the blind, both will fall into a pit."

The Faith of a Gentile Woman Matthew 15:21–31 | Mark 7:24–30 | Mark 7:31–37

Then Yeshua rose and withdrew from there, journeying northward to the coastal region of Tzor (Tyre) and Tzidon (Sidon), far from the crowds of the Galil. He entered a house, desiring privacy, hoping for rest and silence—but even here, his presence could not remain hidden. Word of his arrival whispered through the streets like wind through dry reeds.

Soon, a woman—Kena'anit by lineage, a native of those gentile coasts—came seeking him. Her heart burned with anguish, her voice trembling as she cried out, "Master, son of David! Have mercy! My little daughter is gripped and tormented by a cruel spirit!"

But Yeshua answered her not a word. The silence lingered heavy between them. Yet she would not be moved. She cried all the more, her pleas piercing the hush like a shofar's blast in the wilderness. The talmidim, uncomfortable and impatient, came to him and urged, "Send her away—she keeps shouting after us."

But he turned and replied, his voice solemn with purpose: "I was not sent except to the lost sheep of house of Israel."

Still she did not turn back. With tears upon her face and desperation in her bones, she knelt before him and said, "Lord, help me."

He looked upon her, and in words wrapped with testing, he said, "Let the children be filled first. It is not right to take the children's bread and cast it to the dogs."

But she met his eyes without fear and said, "Yes, Master—but even the dogs eat the crumbs that fall from their masters' table." A holy silence fell upon the moment.

Then Yeshua's expression softened, and his voice rose with wonder: "Woman, great is your faith! Because of this word—go. The demon has left your daughter." And from that very hour, her child was made whole. When she returned to her home, she found the little one lying peacefully upon her bed—the spirit gone, the torment ended.

Healings in the Decapolis Mark 7:31–37; Matthew 15:29–31

Yeshua departed from the borders of Tzor, traveling through the territory of Tzidon, and made his way down toward the Sea of Galil. He entered the region of the Decapolis—a land of mixed peoples, where pagan shrines dotted the hills and Roman influence lingered. There, upon a hillside, Yeshua sat—alone, quiet, waiting.

But the people found him. Great crowds surged to him, bringing their wounded, their afflicted, their forgotten: the lame and the blind, the crippled and the mute, the twisted and the broken. They laid them at his feet like offerings upon an unseen altar—and Yeshua healed them all. And the people marveled. They beheld the mute speaking, the crippled restored, the lame walking, and the blind seeing. Awe rippled through the multitude like waves upon the sea. And they gave kavod (glory) not to idols or emperors—but to the Elohim of Yisrael.

Healing the Deaf Mute and Feeding the Four Thousand Mark 7:32–37 | Mark 8:1–10 | Matthew 15:32–39

Then they brought to him a man who was deaf and could barely speak, and they begged him to lay his hand on him. Yeshua took him aside privately, away from the crowd. He put his fingers into the man's ears, then spit and touched his tongue. Looking up toward the heavens, he sighed deeply and said to him, "Ephatach!"—that is, "Be opened!" Immediately his ears were opened, his tongue was loosened, and he began to speak plainly.

Yeshua instructed them not to tell anyone. But the more he told them not to, the more they spread the news. People were overwhelmed with amazement, saying, "He has done all things well! He makes the deaf hear and the mute speak!"

Now Yeshua, seeing the great crowd that had remained with him for three days and had nothing to eat, called his talmidim and said, "I have compassion for this people. They have remained with me now for three days and have nothing left to eat. If I send them away hungry, they will faint on the way—some of them have come from far distances."

His talmidim answered him, "Where in this remote place can anyone find enough bread to satisfy such a large crowd?"

Yeshua asked them, "How many loaves do you have?"

They said, "Seven." Then he instructed the crowd to recline on the ground. Taking the seven loaves and giving thanks to El Elyon, he broke them and began giving them to his talmidim to set before the people, and they served the crowd. They also had a few small fish. He gave thanks to them as well and had them served. So, the people ate and were satisfied. And the talmidim picked up seven large baskets full of what was left over. The number of men who ate was about four thousand, not including women and children. Then Yeshua dismissed the crowd, and immediately he got into the boat with his talmidim and came to the region of Magadan (called Dalmanutha in another account).

Symbolism in the Feeding of the 4,000		

1. Seven Loaves
   A. Seven Noahide Laws (Universal Ethics)
These are the universal commandments given to all of humanity through Noach (Sanhedrin 56a):
-No idolatry, No blasphemy, No murder, No sexual immorality, No theft, No eating flesh from a living animal and Establish courts of justice
Feeding the Gentiles with seven loaves symbolizes Torah-based nourishment for the nations through moral law and emunah (faith).
 	
   B. Seven Canaanite Nations (Deut. 7:1)
The seven nations that once inhabited the Land represent the nations of the world, which will be transformed in the Messianic future.
The feeding of the Gentiles with seven loaves points toward redemption and rectification of the nations who were once hostile to Israel.
 	
   C. Seven Days of Creation / Completion
In Torah thought, seven represents spiritual completeness and divine order (Shabbat, Menorah, Omer count, festivals, etc.).
 	
The seven loaves imply that even among the nations, Elohim's creative purpose is unfolding — their spiritual hunger is part of His plan.
	2. Few Small Fish
	   A. Spiritual Humility
	The fish are described as "few and small," implying the humble beginnings of Gentile faith. Just as the Syrophoenician woman asked for crumbs, the small fish reflect a posture of spiritual lowliness and a desire to be included.
	
	   B. Hidden Wisdom / Inner Potential
	Fish live beneath the surface and are hidden from view, just like sparks of holiness among the nations (Zohar II:172b). The small fish may symbolize the inner wisdom that exists among the Goyim, waiting to be elevated through faith in the true Elohim.
	
	   C. Righteous Gentiles
	In Talmudic and Midrashic thought, fish are also used to describe tzaddikim, especially those who swim upstream. These fish may point to the righteous among the nations who will cleave to Yisrael's Elohim (cf. Zech 8:23).
		3. Seven Large Baskets Left Over
		   A. Provision for the Nations
		The baskets used here are spyrides (large Gentile-style baskets), unlike the Jewish kophinoi in the Feeding of the 5,000.
		
		This suggests abundant provision for the Gentiles, symbolizing their eventual full inclusion in the blessing of the covenant.
		
		   B. Spiritual Overflow
		The leftovers are not waste — they are surplus spiritual nourishment that points to the abundance of Torah, even beyond Israel's initial portion.
		
		This connects to the idea that Torah will go forth from Zion, and many nations will come to learn (Isa 2:2–3).

The Sign of Yonah and the Healing at Beit-Tzaidah   Matthew 16:1–12 | Mark 8:11–26

Then the Prushim (Pharisees) and Tzedukim (Sadducees) came and began to argue with Yeshua, testing him. They asked him to show them a sign from the heavens — something undeniable, a proof that would vindicate his authority. Yeshua sighed deeply in his spirit and said, "Why does this generation seek a sign? When evening comes, you say, 'It will be fair weather, for the sky is red.' And in the morning, 'Today will be stormy, for the sky is red and overcast.' You know how to read the face of the heavens, but you cannot discern the signs of the times." He looked at them and said: "A wicked and unfaithful generation seeks after a sign, but no sign will be given to it except the sign of Yonah the prophet." And he left them, got back into the boat with his talmidim, and departed to the other side.

As they crossed to the other side, the talmidim had forgotten to bring bread — they had only one loaf with them in the boat. Yeshua warned them, saying: "Be on guard. Watch out for the leaven of the Prushim and the Tzedukim — and the leaven of Herod."

But they began discussing among themselves, saying, "It's because we didn't bring bread…"

Aware of this, Yeshua said to them: "Why are you talking about not having bread? Do you still not understand or perceive? Are your hearts so dull? You have eyes — don't you see? Ears — don't you hear? Don't you remember? When I broke the five loaves for the five thousand, how many baskets did you gather?"

They answered, "Twelve."

"And the seven loaves for the four thousand — how many baskets full did you take up?"

They said, "Seven."

"Do you still not understand?"

Then they understood that he was not speaking about physical bread, but about the teaching (lechem ruchani, spiritual bread) — the corrupt doctrines of the Prushim, the Tzedukim, and the influence of Herod. And they came to Beit-Tzaidah. Some people brought to Yeshua a man who was blind and begged him to touch him. Yeshua took the blind man by the hand and led him outside the village. He spat in his eyes, laid his hands on him, and asked, "Do you see anything?"

The man looked up and said, "I see people, but they look like trees walking around."

Then Yeshua placed his hands on the man's eyes again. He looked intently, and his sight was restored — he could see everything clearly. Yeshua sent him home and said, "Do not even enter the village."

The Great Confession of Shimon Kefa   Matthew 16:13–20 | Mark 8:27–30 | Luke 9:18–21

Now Yeshua went out with his talmidim, journeying north to the scattered villages surrounding Kesarya Shel Pilipos (Caesarea Philippi), a city nestled at the foot of Mount Hermon, where the waters of the Hermon sprang forth into the Jordan—a land filled with idols, altars to Pan, and shadows of pagan rule.

As they walked, Yeshua turned aside to pray. And while he prayed alone, his talmidim drew near and walked with him. Along the way, as the road wound through trees and rock, he turned to them and asked, "Who do the people say that I, the Son of Man, am?"

They answered, repeating the murmurs of the crowds: "Some say Yochanan the Immerser; others, Eliyahu; and still others, Yirmeyahu or one of the nevi'im (prophets) raised from the dead."

Then Yeshua stopped in his tracks. His gaze pierced deeper now—not into the world, but into their hearts. "But you," he said, "Who do you say that I am?"

There was a pause. Then Shimon Kefa stepped forward, his eyes filled with conviction, and he declared, "You are the Mashiach—the Anointed One—the Son of the living Elohim."

And Yeshua looked upon him with joy and said: "Ashrekha (blessed are you), Shimon son of Yonah! For flesh and blood did not reveal this to you, but my Father in the heavens. And I tell you this: You are Kefa (Rock), and upon this rock I will build my kehillah (assembly), and the gates of She'ol will not overcome it. I will give you the keys of the Kingdom of the Heavens—whatever you bind on earth will be bound in the heavens, and whatever you loose on earth will be loosed in the heavens."

"Binding and loosing": A rabbinic idiom for halakhic authority — the power to permit or forbid behavior (cf. Talmud, Berakhot 19b).
"Son of the living Elohim": Not a declaration of divinity, but a royal Messianic title (cf. 2 Sam 7:14, Ps 2:7).

Yeshua Foretells His Suffering and Confronts Kefa Matthew 16:21–23 | Mark 8:31–33 | Luke 9:22

From that moment forward, as they continued walking along the dusty roads near Kesarya Shel Pilipos, Yeshua began to open the veil for his talmidim. He spoke plainly—without parable, without metaphor. "It is necessary," he said, "for the Son of Man to go up to Yerushalayim—to suffer many things at the hands of the elders, the chief priests, and the scribes. He will be rejected. He will be killed. And on the third day, he will rise again." The words fell heavy. They did not understand, and their hearts resisted the sorrow that hovered like a storm cloud over their joy.

Then Kefa, shaken and grieved, took Yeshua aside. He pulled him gently away from the others and began to rebuke him. "Far be it from you, Adoni! This must never happen to you!"

But Yeshua turned, his eyes burning with holy resolve. He looked not only at Kefa, but beyond him—at the unseen hand that whispered doubt and fear. And he said with authority, "Get behind me, accuser (satan)! You are a stumbling block to me. For your thoughts are not on the things of Elohim, but on the ways of men." The words pierced the moment like a blade. And Kefa stood silent, his zeal confronted by the higher wisdom of heaven.

The Cost of Discipleship and the Coming Glory   Matthew 16:24–28 | Mark 8:34–9:1 | Luke 9:23–27

Then Yeshua called to both the crowd and his talmidim and said to them all: "If anyone desires to become my talmid, let him deny his flesh, take up his cross daily, and follow me. For whoever desires to save his life will lose it, but whoever loses his life for my sake and for the sake of the good news will save it. What does it profit a man if he gains the whole world but loses or forfeits his soul? Or what will a man give in exchange for his soul?

For whoever is ashamed of me and of my words in this adulterous and sinful generation, the Son of Man will also be ashamed of him when the Son of Man is going to come in the kavod (glory) of his Father with the set-apart messengers and will repay each person according to his deeds. Truly I say to you: There are some standing here who will not taste death until they see the Kingdom of Elohim come with power."

The Transfiguration and the Mystery of Eliyahu   Matthew 17:1–13 | Mark 9:2–13 | Luke 9:28–36

It came to pass, about six days after these words, Yeshua took with him Kefa, Yaakov, and Yochanan his brother, and led them up a high mountain by themselves to pray. And while he was praying, the appearance of his face was changed, and his garments became radiant — dazzling white, shining like the sun, exceedingly white, so much so that no one on earth could bleach them.

And behold — two men were speaking with him: Moshe and Eliyahu. They appeared in kavod (glory), and they were speaking with Yeshua about his departure, which he was about to complete in Yerushalayim. But Kefa and those with him were weighed down with sleep, and when they became fully awake, they saw his kavod, and the two men standing with him. As Moshe and Eliyahu were departing from him, Kefa said to Yeshua, "Master, it is good for us to be here. If you wish, let us make three sukkot—one for you, one for Moshe, and one for Eliyahu." He did not know what he was saying, for he was overwhelmed with fear.

While he was still speaking, a bright cloud enveloped them, and they were afraid as they entered the cloud. Then a voice came out of the cloud, saying: "This is my Son, my chosen one, in whom I delight. Listen to him."

When the talmidim heard this, they fell on their faces and were very afraid. And Yeshua came to them, touched them, and said, "Rise, and do not be afraid." And suddenly, when they looked up, they saw no one but Yeshua alone with them. As they were coming down the mountain, he commanded them not to tell anyone what they had seen until the Son of Man had risen from the dead. They kept this word among themselves, questioning what "rising from the dead" might mean. And they were silent and told no one in those days what they had seen.

And his talmidim asked him, saying, "Why then do the scribes say that Eliyahu must come first?"

Yeshua answered them, "Indeed, Eliyahu comes first to restore all things. But I say to you: Eliyahu has already come, and they did not recognize him, but did to him whatever they wished, just as it is written about him." Then the talmidim understood that he was speaking to them about Yochanan the Immerser. And Yeshua said, "Likewise, the Son of Man is going to suffer many things and be treated with contempt."

The Healing of the Possessed Boy Matthew 17:14–21 | Mark 9:14–29 | Luke 9:37–43

It came to pass on the next day, when they had come down from the mountain, Yeshua came near to the rest of his talmidim. He saw a large crowd gathered around them, and some of the scribes were arguing with them. And immediately, when the crowd saw him, they were amazed and ran to greet him. Yeshua asked them, "What are you discussing with them?"

And a man from the crowd approached and fell to his knees before him, crying out, "Rabbi, I beg you, look upon my son—my only child! For he is seized by a spirit, and wherever it takes hold of him, it throws him down. He foams at the mouth, grinds his teeth, and becomes rigid. Often it throws him into the fire or into water to kill him. It suddenly cries out, convulses him so that he foams at the mouth, and it scarcely leaves him, oppressing him. I brought him to your talmidim, but they could not drive it out."

Yeshua answered and said, "O faithless and twisted generation—how long shall I remain with you? How long shall I bear with you? Bring the boy here to me." So, they brought the boy to him. And when the spirit saw Yeshua, immediately it threw the boy into convulsions. He fell to the ground and rolled about, foaming at the mouth.

Yeshua asked the father, "How long has this been happening to him?"

The father's voice trembled as he answered, his eyes fixed on his tormented son. "From infancy," he said. "If you are able to do anything, have compassion on us... help us!"

Yeshua looked at him—not with rebuke, but with a piercing love that awakened what was buried deep. "If you are able?" he repeated. "All things are possible for the one who believes."

At once, the man broke. The façade crumbled. With tears streaming from his face and the cry of a soul laid bare, he exclaimed, "I do believe! Help my lack of emunah (faith)!"

Yeshua turned toward the boy, who even now was being shaken by the unclean spirit. The crowd was gathering quickly. He stood firm, and with the authority of heaven, he rebuked the spirit: "You deaf and mute spirit—I command you: Come out of him and never enter him again!"

There was a shriek, a violent convulsion, and the boy collapsed. He lay still, his body limp. The people gasped. "He's dead," they whispered.

But Yeshua walked to him, knelt down, and took his hand. He lifted him gently—and life surged back into the boy. His eyes opened. He stood up. Yeshua placed him in his father's arms. A wave of awe washed over the crowd. They marveled—not merely at the miracle, but at the greatness of Elohim who brings the dead back to life.

Later, when they had entered the house, the talmidim approached Yeshua privately, humbled. "Rabbi," they asked, "why couldn't we cast it out?"

He looked at them with both compassion and truth. "Because of your lack of emunah," he said. "Amen, I tell you: If you have emunah like a mustard seed, you will say to this mountain, 'Move from here to there,' and it will move. Nothing will be impossible for you."

Then he added quietly, "This kind does not come out except by prayer and fasting."

Yeshua Foretells His Death Again   Matthew 17:22–23 | Mark 9:30–32 | Luke 9:43b–45

As they were quietly passing through the hills and valleys of the Galil, Yeshua did not want anyone to know where they were, for he was devoting this journey to the private instruction of his talmidim. His voice was somber, and his steps slow with the weight of what lay ahead.

He turned to them and said, "Let these words sink deep into your ears and settle in your hearts: The Son of Man is about to be delivered into the hands of men. They will kill him—and on the third day, he will be raised up."

A heavy silence fell upon the group. The talmidim were distressed—deeply shaken and grieved—but the meaning of his words was veiled from their understanding. It was as if a divine concealment had settled over their minds, for the time of full revelation had not yet come. And though their hearts were troubled, they were afraid to ask him what he meant.

Who Is the Greatest in the Kingdom?   Matthew 18:1–5 | Mark 9:33–37, 38–41 | Luke 9:46–48

They came to K'far Nachum (Capernaum), the familiar village along the northern shore of the Sea of Galil. When they entered the house—the home where they had often gathered—Yeshua, perceiving the thoughts stirring within their hearts, turned to his talmidim and asked, "What were you discussing along the way?" But a hush fell over them. Embarrassed, they remained silent. For on the road they had been arguing among themselves—each one contending for honor, asking in prideful whispers who among them was the greatest.

Yeshua sat down, the traditional posture of a rabbi ready to teach, and called the Twelve near. With calm authority, he said to them, "If anyone desires to be first, he must become the last of all, and the servant of all."

At that time, some of the disciples approached him and asked aloud, "Who then is the greatest in the Kingdom of the Heavens?"

Yeshua, looking around, called over a young child from nearby and placed him in their midst. Then he lifted the child into his arms and said to them, "Amein, I tell you: Unless you turn and become like little children—free of pride, full of trust—you will never enter the Kingdom of the Heavens. Whoever humbles himself like this child is the greatest in the Kingdom. And whoever receives one such child in my name receives me. And whoever receives me does not receive me alone, but the One who sent me. For the one who is least among you all—he is the greatest."

Then Yochanan spoke up and said, "Rabbi, we saw someone casting out demons in your name, and we tried to stop him, because he does not follow us."

But Yeshua replied, "Do not stop him. For there is no one who will perform a mighty work in my name and then be able quickly to speak evil of me. Whoever is not against us is for us. Truly I say to you: Whoever gives you even a cup of water to drink because you bear the name of a talmid of the Anointed One—amen, I say to you—he will certainly not lose his reward."

Woe to Those Who Cause Others to Stumble   Matthew 18:6–7 | Mark 9:42

Yeshua turned again to the gathered talmidim, now holding the child as a living parable, and said with stern compassion: "Whoever causes one of these little ones—those who trust in me—to stumble, it would be better for him if a great millstone were hung around his neck and he were drowned in the depths of the sea. Such a one would be cast down swiftly, never to rise again. Woe to the world because of stumbling blocks! For stumbling blocks must come—it is the nature of a broken world—but woe to the person through whom the stumbling comes!"

Cut Off What Causes You to Stumble   Matthew 18:8–9 | Mark 9:43–48

His voice grew heavier, weighed with sorrow, as he continued: "If your hand causes you to stumble, cut it off. It is better for you to enter into the life maimed than to have two hands and go into Gei-Hinnom (the Valley of Judgment), into the unquenchable fire—where their worm does not die and the fire is not quenched. And if your foot causes you to stumble, cut it off. It is better for you to enter life lame than to have two feet and be thrown into Gei-Hinnom. And if your eye causes you to stumble, tear it out and cast it from you. It is better for you to enter into the kingdom of Elohim with one eye than to have two eyes and be thrown into the fire of Gei-Hinnom—where their worm does not die and the fire is not quenched."

Everyone Will Be Seasoned with Fire   Mark 9:49–50

Yeshua then looked each of them in the eye and said: "Everyone will be seasoned with fire. Every soul will be tested. Salt is good—but if the salt becomes tasteless, with what will you restore its flavor? Have salt within yourselves—preserve righteousness within—and be at shalom with one another."

The Worth of EveryMatthew 18:10–14

He returned his gaze to the child and said: "See that you do not look down on one of these little ones, for I tell you that their malakhim (messengers, angels) in the heavens continually behold the face of Avi (my Father) who is in the heavens. For the Son of Man came to save what was lost."

He continued with a parable: "What do you think? If a man has a hundred sheep, and one of them goes astray, does he not leave the ninety-nine on the hills and go in search of the one that wandered away? And if he finds it—amen, I tell you—he rejoices over it more than over the ninety-nine that did not go astray. In the same way, it is not the desire of your Father in the heavens that even one of these little ones should perish."

How to Deal with a Sinning BrotherMatthew 18:15–17

Yeshua then taught them how to maintain righteousness within the brotherhood of the faithful: "If your brother sins against you, go and reprove him privately. Speak to him in humility and truth. If he listens to you, you have gained your brother back. But if he will not listen, take with you one or two others, so that every matter may be established by the mouth of two or three witnesses, as Torah commands. And if he refuses to listen to them, bring it before the kehillah (assembly). If he still refuses to listen even to the community, let him be to you as a pagan and a tax collector—outside the covenant until repentance is found."

Where Two or Three Are GatheredMatthew 18:18–20

Yeshua lifted his voice with solemnity and said, "Amen, I tell you: whatever you bind on earth will be bound in the heavens, and whatever you loose on earth will be loosed in the heavens. Again, amen, I say to you: if two of you agree on earth concerning anything they ask, it will be done for them by my Father in the heavens. For where two or three are gathered together in my name, there I am in their midst."

A Question About ForgivenessMatthew 18:21–22

Then Kefa stepped forward, the weight of the Master's teachings stirring deeply in his soul. With the sincere concern of one seeking righteousness, he asked, "Master, how many times shall I forgive my brother who sins against me? Up to seven times?"

Yeshua turned to him with eyes that searched the heart, and replied, "I do not say to you seven times, but seventy times seven."

The Parable of the Unforgiving Servant Matthew 18:23–35

And Yeshua continued, lifting a parable to heaven like incense: "Therefore, the kingdom of the heavens is like a great king who desired to settle accounts with his servants. When he began the reckoning, one man was brought before him who owed him ten thousand talents—a debt beyond imagination, the weight of many lifetimes. And since he had no means to pay, the king gave command that he be sold—along with his wife, his children, and all that he possessed—so that payment might be made. The servant fell to the ground, trembling and broken. With his face in the dust, he prostrated himself and pleaded, 'Be patient with me, and I will repay you everything!'

And the heart of the king was stirred with mercy. He looked upon the man with compassion, released him, and forgave the entire debt. But that servant—having just tasted the sweetness of mercy—went out and found one of his fellow servants who owed him a mere hundred denarii. Seizing him by the throat, he began to choke him, shouting, 'Pay back what you owe!' The fellow servant fell to his knees and pleaded with him, 'Be patient with me, and I will repay you!' But he was not willing. Instead, he cast him into prison until the debt should be paid in full.

When their fellow servants saw what had happened, they were deeply grieved. They went and reported all these things to their master. Then the king summoned the man and said, 'Wicked servant! I forgave you all that debt because you pleaded with me. Should you also not have had compassion on your fellow servant, just as I had mercy on you?' And in his righteous anger, the master delivered him over to the tormentors until he should pay all that was owed. So too," Yeshua concluded, "will my Father in the heavens do to you—unless each one of you forgives his brother from the depths of your heart."

Chapter 13 Yeshua Begins His Judean Ministry

Yeshua and the Festival of Sukkot — John 7:1–10

After this, Yeshua continued walking in the region of the Galil, choosing not to journey into Yehudah, for the Yehudim there were already plotting his death. Their hearts had hardened, and the storm clouds of opposition gathered with growing fury. Now the Festival of Sukkot—the pilgrimage feast of the Yehudim—was drawing near, the season when the people of Yisrael would dwell in booths and remember the wilderness journey, rejoicing before Adonai with palm branches and living water.

His brothers, who still did not fully believe in him, approached with words cloaked in challenge:
"Leave here and go to Yehudah, so your talmidim there can see the works you are doing. No one does things in secret if he wants to be known openly. If you truly do these things, reveal yourself to the world." But their eyes were veiled from seeing the deeper mission that burned within him.

Yeshua said to them, "My appointed time has not yet come, but your time is always ready. The world cannot hate you, but it hates me—because I bear witness against it, that its works are evil. You go up to the festival. I am not going up to this festival yet, because my time has not yet been fulfilled." And with those words, he remained behind in the Galil. Yet after his brothers had gone up to Yerushalayim for the festival, Yeshua also went—but not with a public procession or acclaim. He traveled in quietness, concealed from the eyes of the crowd, for his hour had not yet come.

Teaching in the Temple at Sukkot — John 7:11–24

At the festival, the Yehudim were searching for him, whispering urgently among themselves, "Where is that man?" Their eyes darted about the crowd, hoping to catch a glimpse of the controversial teacher who stirred the multitudes and confounded the elders.

There was much quiet murmuring throughout the masses. Some whispered, "He is good." Others countered, "No—he is leading the people astray." Yet despite the lively debate burning just beneath the surface, no one dared to speak of him openly, for fear of the Yehudim leaders.

But about halfway through the Feast—when the city of Yerushalayim was alive with pilgrims and the courts of the Temple rang with voices and footsteps—Yeshua ascended into the Temple courts and began to teach. His voice carried through the air like a sharp wind, cutting through the noise and drawing all eyes to him.

The Yehudim were astonished. They murmured among themselves, "How does this man know the writings so well, never having studied under one of our schools?" They could not comprehend how a Galilean craftsman, not trained in their yeshivot, could speak with such clarity, authority, and command of the sacred texts.

Yeshua answered them, "My teaching is not my own, but from the One who sent me. If anyone desires to do His will, he will recognize whether my teaching is from Elohim or if I speak from myself. The one who speaks on his own seeks his own kavod (honor), but the one who seeks the kavod of the One who sent him is true, and there is no avlah (crookedness, injustice) in him."

He looked directly at them and declared, "Did not Moshe give you the Torah? Yet none of you is truly shomer (faithful) to the Torah. Why then are you seeking to put me to death?"

The crowd was stunned. Some shouted back defensively, "You have a shed (unclean spirit)! Who is trying to kill you?"

But Yeshua, undeterred, answered, "I performed one deed, and all of you marvel. Moshe gave you the mitzvah of circumcision—not that it originated with Moshe, but with the avot (patriarchs)—and you circumcise a male child even on the Shabbat. If a child receives brit milah (circumcision) on Shabbat, so that the Torah of Moshe will not be broken, why are you angry with me for making a man entirely whole on Shabbat? Do not judge by outward appearances but render mishpat tzedek—righteous judgment."

The Crowd Divided John 7:25–39

Then some of the people of Yerushalayim began whispering among themselves, casting wary glances toward the Temple courts: "Isn't this the one they are trying to kill? Look! He is speaking openly—without fear—and they are saying nothing to him. Could it be… have the leaders truly come to recognize that this one is the Mashiach?"

But others among them scoffed, saying, "We know where this man is from—and when the Anointed One comes, no one will know from where he comes." Confusion stirred among the people, as expectation clashed with skepticism.

Then Yeshua lifted his voice and cried out in the Temple as he was teaching, his words ringing like the blast of a shofar: "You know me, and you know where I am from? Yet I have not come on my own. The One who sent me is true—but you do not know Him. I know Him, for I am from Him, and He has sent me."

At these words, tension rippled through the crowd. Some clenched their fists, others looked around nervously. They sought to seize him, yet no one laid a hand on him—for his appointed time had not yet come. The unseen hand of Heaven restrained them. Still, many among the crowd believed in him and said, "When the Anointed One comes, will he perform more signs than this man has done?"

The Prushim (Pharisees) heard the crowd murmuring these things—an undercurrent of belief spreading through the people. Alarmed, the chief priests and the Prushim dispatched attendants to seize him.

But Yeshua, knowing their intent, said calmly, "Yet a little while I am with you, and then I go to the One who sent me. You will seek me, but you will not find me; and where I am, you are not able to come."

The Yehudim turned to one another, confused and incredulous: "Where is he intending to go, that we will not find him? Will he go to those scattered among the nations and teach the goyim (Gentiles)? What is this saying he said: 'You will seek me, and not find me,' and 'Where I am, you are not able to come'?" Then came the last day—the great day of the Festival of Sukkot, when the water libation was poured out with joy and the people danced before the altar with willows and palm branches.

On that climactic day, Yeshua stood and cried out in the midst of the crowds, "If anyone thirsts, let him come to me and drink! The one who trusts in me, as the Scripture has said—from within him will flow rivers of mayim chayim (living water)!"

He spoke this concerning the Ruach (Spirit), which those who trusted in him were going to receive. For the Ruach had not yet been poured out, because Yeshua had not yet been esteemed.

Historical Commentary

Simchat Beit HaSho'eivah — The Joy of the Water-Drawing

During the days of Sukkot, the Temple in Yerushalayim hosted one of the most joyous and spiritually rich ceremonies in the Jewish calendar: the Simchat Beit HaSho'eivah ("Rejoicing at the Place of the Water-Drawing"). Each morning (except Shabbat), a solemn procession of priests descended from the Temple to the Pool of Shiloach to draw mayim chayim (living water) in a golden pitcher. This water was brought up to the altar, where it was poured into a silver basin during the Tamid (daily burnt offering), alongside a libation of wine.

The people, waving lulavim and singing Hallel, celebrated not only the gift of physical rain, but the spiritual outpouring of the Ruach HaKodesh (Holy Spirit), as hinted in the verse: "With joy you shall draw water from the wells of salvation." (Isaiah 12:3)

This ceremony, while not commanded in the written Torah, was a cherished Temple tradition rooted in prophetic symbolism and deeply mystical expectation. The Talmud states: "Whoever has not seen the joy of the Simchat Beit HaSho'eivah has never seen joy in their life." (Sukkah 51a)

The water-pouring was a prayerful appeal to Elohim for rain, sustenance, and ultimately redemption. It was believed to open the gates of divine flow (shefa), invoking the future era when living waters would flow from Yerushalayim to heal the nations (cf. Zechariah 14:8, Ezekiel 47).

It is precisely on the last day of Sukkot — known as Hoshana Rabbah — that Yeshua stood and cried out: "If anyone thirsts, let him come to me and drink... whoever believes in me, as the Scripture has said, rivers of living water will flow from within him." (John 7:37–38)

This statement is not metaphorical poetry — it is a prophetic commentary on this exact ritual, marking him as one who channels the Torah, the Ruach, and the healing waters of the World to Come.

Division Among the People   John 7:40–52

When the crowd heard these words, a murmur spread like wind through the festival booths. Many began to respond with rising excitement. Some said, "This man is truly the Navi

(Prophet), the one like Moshe who was to come into the world." Others declared with conviction, "He is the Anointed One!"

But still others scoffed and said, "Can the Anointed One come from the Galil (Galilee)? Does not the Scripture say that the Anointed One is to come from the seed of David, and from Beit-Lechem (Bethlehem), the village where David was born?"

And so, the crowd was torn. There was division among the people because of him—some drawn by his words, others hardened by doubt. A few, in their zeal, even sought to seize him. Yet again, no one laid a hand on him—his hour had not yet arrived.

Meanwhile, the officers of the Temple guard, who had been sent to arrest him, returned to the chief priests and the Prushim (Pharisees) empty-handed. The leaders demanded, "Why didn't you bring him?"

The officers, visibly shaken and moved, replied, "No man has ever spoken the way this man speaks."

The Prushim, scowling with disdain, rebuked them: "Have you also been deceived? Have any of the rulers or any of the Prushim believed in him? This crowd—this am ha'aretz (people of the land) that does not know the Torah—they are cursed!"

But then a voice of courage rose from among them—Nakdimon (Nicodemus), the one who had come to Yeshua by night and who was himself a member of the Sanhedrin. He said, "Does our Torah judge a man before it hears him and knows what he is doing?"

They turned on him, sneering, "Are you also from the Galil? Search the Scriptures and see—no prophet arises out of the Galil!" And so, their hearts remained closed, though the Word of Life had spoken plainly in their midst.

The Woman Caught in Adultery — John 8:1–11

Yeshua went out to the Mount of Olives, a place of quiet and prayer, where prophets and kings had once sought the presence of Elohim. And at dawn, as the city stirred to life and the smoke of morning offerings rose from the Temple, he returned again to the courts of the House of Elohim. All the people came to him, gathering around like sheep around their shepherd, and he sat down to teach them — as was the custom of the sages of Yisrael.

In the midst of his teaching, the hush of learning was broken. A stir arose as the scribes and Prushim (Pharisees) approached, dragging with them a woman — disheveled and trembling — caught in the very act of adultery. They placed her in the center of the crowd, the place of shame, turning the sacred court into a courtroom. The woman stood there trying to cover herself hiding her face in shame and some anger at being trapped into a sin by the very ones who stood trying to accuse. She was scared she was about to pronounced guilty and be stoned to death.

They said, "Rabbi, this woman was seized while committing adultery. In the Torah, Moshe commands us to stone such a woman. What then do you say?"

But this was not a question born of love for the Torah or concern for righteousness — it was a snare, a trap set with cruel cunning, so that they might have grounds to accuse him whether he upheld the sentence or refused it. Yeshua, silent and calm, bent down and began to write on the ground with his finger — as though ignoring them, as though writing judgment not on stone but in dust, in the same dust from which man was formed. Yet they continued pressing him, voices rising, hearts hardened.

Then he stood up and said to them, his words like a sword cutting through their hypocrisy: "Let the one among you who is without sin be the first to cast a stone at her." And again he stooped down and continued writing in the dust — unmoved, unshaken, as eternity held its breath.

One by one, the stones fell from their hands. Consciences awakened, hearts pierced, they departed — beginning with the elders, the most learned and aged, and then the younger ones followed — until none remained but Yeshua, and the woman still standing in the center relief and uncertainty in her mind and posture.

He rose and looked upon her with eyes of compassion. "Woman, where are they? Has no one condemned you?"

She shifted her stance a little nervously and lifted her eyes and whispered in a cracked voice, "No one, master."

And Yeshua said, "Then neither do I condemn you. Go, and do not return to sin.

Yeshua as Halachic Judge — Disqualification of Witnesses

Yeshua's handling of the woman accused of adultery reflects a profound knowledge of Torah and halacha. According to Deuteronomy 22:22, both the man and woman caught in adultery must be judged together. Yet only the woman is brought — violating Torah.

Furthermore, capital cases under Deuteronomy 17:8–13 require a proper beit din (court) and two or more valid, righteous witnesses (Deut. 19:15; Sanhedrin 42b–45a). By testing the accusers' moral standing with the phrase, "Let the one among you who is without sin cast the first stone," Yeshua effectively performs the role of a halachic judge — interrogating and then disqualifying the witnesses as unfit.

His ruling exposes their hypocrisy while upholding Torah law. Rather than abrogate the law, Yeshua preserves its integrity by ensuring it is not misused for entrapment or partiality (cf. Exodus 23:1–9). This scene demonstrates his judicial wisdom, not leniency — and reflects righteous judgment in accordance with Torah and Talmud.

The Light of the World   John 8:12

Then Yeshua spoke to them again — to the crowds still gathered in the Temple courts, to the hearts stirred by mercy and awakened by truth — and he lifted his voice, saying: "I am the light of the world. The one who follows me will not walk in darkness but will have the light of life."

His words echoed through the colonnades of the Temple like the flame of the menorah in the Holy Place — a light not kindled by man but burning from the heart of Elohim Himself. For just as the pillar of fire led the children of Yisrael through the wilderness by night, so would Yeshua lead those who follow him through the shadows of this world into the life of the world to come.

Historical Commentary

The Illumination of the Temple during Sukkot (Beit HaSho'eivah Nights) Each night of Sukkot in the Second Temple period, the Court of the Women in the Beit HaMikdash (Temple) was transformed into a site of extraordinary light and joy during the festive nights of the water-drawing celebration — called Beit HaSho'eivah. According to Mishnah Sukkah 5:2–4, four immense golden lampstands were erected, each with four large oil basins atop them. The old priestly garments were used as wicks, and young kohanim (priests) climbed tall ladders to refill the lamps nightly. The result was breathtaking: "There was not a courtyard in Jerusalem that was not lit by the light of the Beit HaSho'eivah." (Mishnah Sukkah 5:3)

> The Levites stood on the 15 steps leading from the Court of the Women to the Court of Israel, playing lyres, harps, cymbals, trumpets, and singing psalms of joy. The righteous and sages danced with torches in hand, performing acrobatic displays of devotion. This illumination was not merely decorative — it symbolized the light of the Shechinah, the Divine Presence that once filled the Temple. It also recalled the pillar of fire that led Israel through the wilderness, a reminder that Elohim's guidance and glory remain with His people.
>
> Many in the Second Temple period believed this light prefigured the coming of the Messianic age, when: "At evening time, there shall be light." (Zechariah 14:7) It was in this setting — just after the lights had been extinguished at the end of the festival — that Yeshua stood in the Temple and declared: "I am the light of the world. Whoever follows me will not walk in darkness but will have the light of life." (John 8:12) This declaration would not have been missed. Yeshua was not claiming divinity, but Torah-authentic authority — speaking as a tzaddik and light-bearing teacher, pointing to the illumination of Torah, the guidance of the Shechinah, and the life-giving clarity of halachic righteousness.

Peshat (Plain Meaning)	Remez (Hint)	Derash (Midrash / Talmudic)	Sod (Mystical / Kabalistic)
Yeshua declares himself to be "the light of the world", a claim deeply rooted in biblical imagery. He is speaking publicly in the Temple courts, likely still during Sukkot, just after the water-drawing and illumination ceremonies. In this context, "light" signifies Divine revelation, Torah, and the path of righteousness.	Yeshua's language echoes several Tanakh verses: Psalm 119:105 "Your word is a lamp to my feet and a light to my path." The Torah is the true light. Yeshua, as its embodiment and teacher, is pointing to obedience and faithful halachic walking in its light. Isaiah 2:5 "Come, O house of Jacob, let us walk in the light of YHWH." Proverbs 6:23 "For the commandment is a lamp and the Torah is light; reproofs of discipline are the way of life." ↳ "Light of life" = Torah lived out.	Talmud Bavli, Bava Batra 10a says: "The righteous are called light, as it is said: 'Then shall your light break forth like the dawn' (Isaiah 58:8)." Yeshua calls those who follow him to walk in that same light — which means walking in righteous deeds, justice, and obedience to mitzvot. Further, the Festival of Sukkot included the illumination of the Temple court during the nights of the festival — four great lampstands with blazing torches. The "light of the world" may allude directly to this Temple ceremony.	Zohar (I:50b): "Orayta (Torah) and the Holy One, blessed be He, are one...The light that proceeds from Torah is the light that illuminates all worlds." Yeshua's declaration is a Sod-level teaching, identifying himself with the emanated light of Torah, the Shechinah's reflection through a tzaddik who is a vessel. The "light" is Torah consciousness — accessible through attachment to the righteous (devekut). To "follow him" is to follow the derekh (path) he walks — a life of Torah-faithfulness, humility, and purity. Tanya, Likkutei Amarim, Chapter 4: "The Torah and mitzvot are garments for the Divine light, enabling the soul to be united with the Or Ein Sof." So, Yeshua's call is not just to believe in him — but to walk as he walks, which is Torah-obedient light.

The Father Bears Witness — John 8:13–20

Then the Prushim (Pharisees), standing among the crowds with arms folded and brows furrowed, said to him, "You are testifying about yourself; your testimony is not valid [ne'eman]!"

Yeshua answered them with calm authority: "Even if I testify about myself, my testimony remains true, because I know where I came from and where I am going. But you— you do not know where I come from or where I am going. You judge according to the flesh, through outward appearances and surface reasoning. I judge no one in this way. And even if I do pass judgment, my judgment is true, because I am not alone—but I and the One who sent me bear witness together.

"Even in your Torah it is written that the testimony of two witnesses is valid. I am one who testifies concerning myself—and the Father who sent me also testifies concerning me."

At this, they said to him mockingly, "Where is your father?"

Yeshua replied, "You know neither me nor my Father. If you had truly known me, you would have known my Father also." He spoke these words in the treasury, within the Court of the Women in the Temple, where the offering boxes were placed. Yet though his words stirred offense, no one laid hands on him—for his hour had not yet come.

The Truth Will Set You Free — John 8:21–32

Then Yeshua said to them again, his voice filled with solemn urgency, "I am going away, and you will seek me, yet you will die in your sin. Where I go, you are not able to come."

Confused and cynical, the Yehudim whispered among themselves, "Will he kill himself? Is that why he says, 'Where I go, you are not able to come'?"

But Yeshua, perceiving their hearts, said to them, "You are from below; I am from above. You are of this world—I am not of this world. That is why I said to you: you will die in your sins. For unless you believe that I am he, you will surely die in your sins."

They challenged him again, "Who are you?"

Yeshua answered, "What have I been saying to you from the beginning? I have many things I could say—many judgments I could render concerning you—but the One who sent me is true. And whatever I have heard from Him; these are the things I speak to the world." But still, they did not grasp that he was speaking about the Father.

So Yeshua said, "When you have lifted up the Son of Man, then you will know that I am he, and that I do nothing from myself, but speak just as the Father has taught me. And the One who sent me is with me. He has not left me alone, for I always do what is pleasing to Him." As he was speaking these words, many among them began to believe, their hearts pierced by the authority of his words. Then Yeshua turned to those Yehudim who had trusted in him and said, "If you remain in my word, then you are truly my talmidim. And you will know the truth—and the truth will set you free."

PaRDeS Interpretation			
Peshat	Remez	Derash	Sod
Yeshua is speaking to the Prushim and those listening in the Temple court. He states that when they "lift up the Son of Man" (i.e., crucify the messiah), they will realize who he is—not acting independently, but sent and taught by Elohim.	Psalm 119:142: "Your Torah is truth." Proverbs 6:23: "The mitzvah is a lamp, and Torah is light…" This implies that the "truth" Yeshua is referring to is Torah, particularly its true interpretation, as he teaches it.	"The words of Torah were given in black fire on white fire…" (Yerushalmi Shekalim 6:1) "In the future, the Holy One will sit and expound on the new Torah—that is, the hidden dimensions not yet revealed." (Vayikra Rabbah 13:3) Yeshua's statement "If you remain in my word… you will know the truth" echoes this. He is positioning himself as the Messianic teacher who reveals the inner meaning of Torah—not replacing it, but unlocking its fullness. Freedom Through Torah Yaakov (James) 1:25: "But the one who looks into the perfect Torah, the Torah of freedom, and continues in it…" Son of Man and Rejected Messiah: In Sukkah 52a, the sages wrestle with Zechariah 12:10 and the "one who was pierced" and conclude: "This refers to Messiah ben Yosef, who will be slain." Yeshua's reference to being "lifted up" as the Son of Man echoes the role of Messiah ben Yosef, whose mission involves suffering, rejection, and atonement—before the coming of Messiah ben David.	The Zohar says: "The Torah is the name of the Holy One, blessed be He, in another form." (Zohar II, 90b) To know the "truth" through discipleship is to be united with the Divine will, which is freedom from the klipot (husks) of sin, ego, and illusion.

The Sons of Avraham and the Son of Elohim John 8:33–59

They answered him with indignation, "We are offspring of Avraham and have never been enslaved to anyone! How can you say, 'You will become free'?"

Yeshua said to them, his voice steady and piercing, "Amein, amein, I tell you: everyone who practices sin is a slave to sin. And a slave does not remain in the house forever, but the son remains forever. So if the Son sets you free, you will truly be free indeed.

I know that you are the physical seed of Avraham—yet you seek to kill me because my word finds no room within you. I speak what I have seen while in the presence of the Father, but you—you do what you have heard from your father."

They answered, holding to their lineage, "Avraham is our father!"

But Yeshua replied, "If you were truly the children of Avraham, you would be doing the deeds of Avraham. But now you are seeking to kill me—a man who has told you the truth that I heard from Elohim. Avraham did not do such things. No—you are doing the works of your father."

They retorted, offended, "We were not born of fornication! We have one Father—Elohim Himself!"

Yeshua said to them, "If Elohim were truly your Father, you would love me, for I came forth from Elohim and have now come into the world. I did not come of my own initiative—but He sent me. Why do you not understand what I say? Because you are not able to listen to my words.

You are from your father—the accuser (ha-satan)—and it is his desires that you want to carry out. He was a murderer from the beginning and does not stand in the truth, because there is no truth in him. When he lies, he speaks from his own nature, for he is a liar and the father of lies. But because I speak the truth—you do not believe me. Which one of you convicts me of sin? If I speak the truth, why do you not believe me? Whoever is from Elohim hears the words of Elohim. This is why you do not hear—because you are not from Elohim."

The Yehudim, enraged, lashed out, "Are we not right in saying that you are a Shomroni (Samaritan) and have a demon?"

Yeshua answered calmly, "I do not have a demon. I honor my Father—and you dishonor me. Yet I do not seek my own kavod (glory); there is One who seeks it, and He is the judge. Amein, amein, I tell you: if anyone keeps my word, he will never see death."

The Yehudim scoffed, "Now we know you have a demon! Avraham died, and so did the prophets—yet you say, 'If anyone keeps my word, he will never taste death.' Are you greater than our father Avraham, who died? The prophets died too! Who do you make yourself out to be?"

Yeshua answered them, "If I glorify myself, my kavod is nothing. It is my Father who glorifies me—the One of whom you say, 'He is our Elohim.' Yet you do not know Him, but I know Him. And if I were to say, 'I do not know Him,' I would be a liar like you. But I do know Him—and I keep His word.

Your father Avraham rejoiced to see my day. He saw it—and was glad."

They laughed in disbelief, "You are not even fifty years old—and you have seen Avraham?"

Yeshua said to them, with authority burning in his voice, "Amein, amein, I tell you: before Avraham was—I am." At this, they were seized with fury and picked up stones to hurl at him. But Yeshua concealed himself and slipped away from the Temple, passing through their midst, unharmed.

Yeshua is claiming preeminence, not pre-existence. The phrase "before Avraham was" contrasts with "I am", which is present tense. This does not require ontological preexistence, but rather: That his mission, identity, or role was foreordained before Avraham's time, Or that Avraham prophetically saw his day (v.56), as in Midrashic or prophetic vision. In Hebrew idiom, "to be" (hayah) is often about destiny, role, or appointment, not metaphysical existence.

Avraham "Saw His Day" (John 8:56)
When Yeshua says, "Avraham rejoiced to see my day; he saw it and was glad," he refers to more than one prophetic experience in Avraham's life. The most significant are:

1. Genesis 22 – The Akeidah (Binding of Yitzchak)
Avraham sees the ram caught in the thicket—a substitute offering—which becomes a foreshadowing of redemptive sacrifice.

The sages connect this with Messianic expectation. See Pesikta Rabbati 36 and Targum Pseudo-Jonathan, which interpret this event as Avraham prophetically seeing the coming of the Messiah.

2. Genesis 15 – The Covenant Between the Pieces
"A deep sleep fell upon Avram... and behold, a dread and great darkness fell upon him." (Gen. 15:12)

In this dream-vision, Hashem foretells the future exile and redemption of Avraham's descendants.

The vision includes:
   -A smoking furnace and a burning torch passing between the divided pieces (15:17), symbolizing the Divine presence and covenant ratification.
   -Prophetic insight into future redemptions, including Messianic expectation. This is seen by commentators as a multi-layered vision reaching far beyond Egypt and into the end of days.

3. Midrashic and Rabbinic Support
Genesis Rabbah 44:23: "Avraham saw the kingdom of the Messiah and rejoiced."

Pirkei deRabbi Eliezer 31: Suggests that Avraham foresaw both the First and Second Temples, and the final redemption.

In this light, Yeshua's claim is that Avraham foresaw "my day"—the day of the Redeemer's appearance—not by seeing Yeshua physically, but through a Divine prophetic revelation.

The Healing of the Man Born Blind   John 9:1–41

As Yeshua was passing by, his eyes fell upon a man who had been blind from birth. His talmidim, curious and burdened with the questions of human suffering, asked him, "Rabbi, who sinned—this man or his parents—that he was born blind?"

Yeshua answered them with compassion and insight: "Neither this man nor his parents sinned. Rather, this happened so that the works of Elohim might be made manifest in him. We must do the works of the One who sent me while it is still day. Night is coming when no one will be able to work. As long as I am in the world, I am the light of the world."

After saying this, Yeshua stooped to the ground. He spat upon the earth and made a mixture of mud with his saliva. With his hands, he gently anointed the blind man's eyes with the clay and said to him, "Go, wash in the Pool of Shiloach" (which means Sent).

The man obeyed. He went down to the pool, washed his eyes—and returned, seeing. When the people saw him walking with open eyes, no longer groping in darkness, his neighbors and those who had known him as a beggar began to whisper in astonishment. "Isn't this the one who used to sit and beg?" they asked.

Some said, "Yes, it's him." Others insisted, "No, it only looks like him."

But he kept declaring, "I am that man."

They asked him, "Then how were your eyes opened?"

He answered simply, "The man called Yeshua made mud, put it on my eyes, and told me, 'Go to Shiloach and wash.' So I went and washed—and now I see."

They asked him, "Where is he?"

He replied, "I don't know."

They brought the man who had once been blind to the Prushim (Pharisees), for it was on a Shabbat that Yeshua had made the mud and healed his eyes. The Prushim also questioned him about how he had received his sight.

He answered them again, "He put mud on my eyes. I washed—and now I see."

Some of the Prushim scowled and said, "This man is not from Elohim, for he does not guard the Shabbat."

But others countered, "How can a man who is a sinner perform such miraculous signs?" So there arose a division among them.

They turned again to the man and asked, "What do you say about him, since it was your eyes he opened?"

He replied boldly, "He is a prophet."

But the Sadducees and some among the leaders refused to believe that the man had really been born blind and received his sight—so they summoned his parents.

They asked them, "Is this your son, the one you say was born blind? Then how does he now see?"

His parents answered cautiously, "We know this is our son, and we know that he was born blind. But how he sees now—we do not know. Nor do we know who opened his eyes. Ask him—he is of age. He can speak for himself."

They answered in this way out of fear, for the leaders of the Yehudim had already decided that anyone who acknowledged Yeshua as the Anointed One would be expelled from the synagogue. That is why they said, "He is of age—ask him."

So they called the man back a second time and said to him, "Give glory to Elohim! We know this man is a sinner."

But the man replied, "Whether he is a sinner, I do not know. One thing I do know: I was blind—and now I see."

They pressed him again, "What did he do to you? How did he open your eyes?"

He answered with sharpness, "I already told you—and you did not listen! Why do you want to hear it again? Do you also want to become his talmidim?"

At this, they reviled him. "You are his talmid—but we are talmidim of Moshe! We know that Elohim spoke to Moshe, but as for this man, we do not even know where he comes from!"

The man, unfazed, answered, "This is utterly amazing! You do not know where he is from—and yet he opened my eyes! We know that Elohim does not listen to sinners, but if someone fears Elohim and does His will, He hears him. Since the beginning of the world, no one has ever heard of anyone opening the eyes of a man born blind. If this man were not from Elohim—he could do nothing."

Furious, they shouted, "You were born entirely in sin—and you're teaching us?" And they cast him out of the synagogue.

When Yeshua heard that they had driven him out, he sought the man and found him. He looked into his eyes and asked, "Do you trust in the Son of Man?"

The man answered sincerely, "Who is he, Adoni, that I may trust in him?"

Yeshua said to him, "You have seen him—and he is the one speaking with you now."

Then the man fell to his knees and said, "I do trust, Adoni." And he worshiped him.

Yeshua said, "For judgment I have come into this world: so that those who do not see may see—and those who claim to see may be made blind."

Some of the Prushim who were nearby heard this and asked him, "Are we blind also?"

Yeshua replied, "If you were truly blind, you would be without guilt. But now that you say, 'We see,' your guilt remains."

Historical Profile: The Man Born Blind

- 1. Blindness and Social Status in First Century Judea In ancient Israel, blindness was:
  - Considered a permanent physical blemish (Lev. 21:18)
  - Excluded a man from serving as a priest or offering sacrifices
  - Often associated with divine judgment (John 9:2 shows this mindset)
  - Carried serious economic consequences, since the blind could not perform most labor

There were no state welfare systems. A blind person relied on family or public alms for survival.

- 2. He Was Likely Very Young, John 9:21–23 suggests the man was:
  - Just "of age" by Jewish standards—meaning 13 years or slightly older
  - Old enough to be bar mitzvah, legally responsible for Torah commands and testimony
  - Young enough that his parents were still socially involved, and known to the community

The combination of his age and disability made him especially vulnerable and dependent.

- 3. Why Was He Begging? John 9:8 "Isn't this the one who used to sit and beg?" The Temple area was the best place to beg:
  - Pilgrims came to give tzedakah (charity) as a spiritual act
  - Torah commands almsgiving to the poor (Deut. 15:7–11)
  - The Temple system included charity boxes and expected public generosity

This boy likely sat in a public gate or courtyard of the Temple, as Acts 3:2 shows another man doing.
  - His begging implies:
    a) Extreme poverty
    b) Possibly no ability of his parents to support him fully
    c) Social approval of almsgiving to the disabled

- 4. Parental Fear and Social Pressure John 9:22 explains that: "His parents said this because they were afraid of the Judeans..."

The threat was excommunication from the synagogue, which meant:
  - Loss of communal identity
  - Loss of economic protection (charity, work, etc.)
  - Social shame and ostracism

> In a poor family, this could be devastating. So, his parents, while recognizing the miracle, distanced themselves to avoid punishment.
>
> - 5. Legal and Religious Implications, At around 13 years old, the boy:
>   - Could testify on his own behalf
>   - Was liable for mitzvot under Torah law
>   - Could enter the synagogue courts and participate in legal discussions
>
> Despite his youth, the leaders interrogated him directly, expecting full accountability. Prushim insisted that Yeshua violated Shabbat by making mud and healing. The boy defended Yeshua's integrity and power, calling him: "A prophet" (John 9:17)and "[One] from Elohim" (John 9:33) His simple, bold testimony enraged the religious elites.
>
> - 6. What this tells us about the Times. This one short story tells us much about Jewish life in the late Second Temple period:
>   - Disabilities led to poverty and public shame
>   - Children could be legally independent by 13, but were still socially dependent
>   - Synagogue excommunication was a powerful fear, used by authorities to control dissent
>   - Temple culture revolved around public piety, offerings, and almsgiving
>   - Ordinary people, even poor teenagers, could challenge religious authority when empowered

The Good Shepherd and the Gate   John 10:1–21

Then Yeshua lifted his voice once more and said to them, "Amen, amen, I tell you: The one who does not enter the sheepfold by the gate but climbs in by another way—he is nothing but a thief and a robber. But the one who enters by the gate is the true shepherd of the sheep. The gatekeeper opens the gate for him, and the sheep hear his voice. He calls his own sheep by name—each one—and leads them out. When he has gathered all that are his, he walks ahead of them, and the sheep follow him, because they know his voice.

"They will not follow a stranger. Instead, they will flee from him because they do not recognize the voice of strangers." Yeshua spoke this mashal—parable—but they did not understand what he was saying to them.

So again, he said to them, "Amen, amen, I tell you: I am the gate for the sheep. All who came before me were thieves and robbers—but the sheep did not listen to them. I am the gate—if anyone enters through me, he will be saved. He will come in and go out and find pasture. The thief comes only to steal, to slaughter, and to destroy. But I have come that they may have life—true life—and have it abundantly.

"I am the Good Shepherd. The Good Shepherd lays down his life for the sheep. The hired hand, who is not a shepherd and does not own the sheep, sees the wolf coming—and he abandons the flock and flees. Then the wolf pounces—he snatches them and scatters them. The hired hand flees because he is only a hired servant and does not care for the sheep.

"I am the Good Shepherd. I know those who are mine, and they know me—just as the Father knows me and I know the Father. And I lay down my life for the sheep. I have other sheep—not of this fold. I must bring them also. They will hear my voice, and there will be one flock and one Shepherd. For this reason, the Father loves me—because I lay down my life, so that I may take it up again. No one takes it from me. I lay it down of my own free will. I have authority to lay it down—and I have authority to take it up again. This command I received from my Father." At these words, once again, a division arose among the Judeans.

Many of them scoffed and said, "He has a demon and is insane. Why even listen to him?" But others said, "These are not the words of someone who is possessed by a demon. Can a demon open the eyes of the blind?"

The Shepherd Reveals His Identity at Chanukah John 10:22–42

At that time, it was the Festival of Chanukah in Yerushalayim. The winter wind swept through the Temple courts, and Yeshua walked under the shelter of Solomon's Colonnade, his footsteps echoing beneath the great stone pillars. The Judeans gathered around him, encircling him with pressure and expectation. "How long will you keep us in suspense?" they demanded. "If you are the Moshiach, tell us plainly!"

Yeshua answered them, "I told you—and you do not believe. The works that I do in the name of my Father—they bear witness about me. But you do not believe, because you are not among my sheep. My sheep hear my voice. I know them, and they follow me. I give them eternal life, and they will never perish—ever. No one can snatch them out of my hand. My Father, who has given them to me, is greater than all. No one is able to snatch them out of the Father's hand. I and the Father are echad (one, united)."

At this, rage ignited in the hearts of his listeners. The Judeans again reached down to pick up stones—to strike him down then and there. But Yeshua stood firm and said to them, "I have shown you many good works from my Father. For which one of these do you stone me?"

They answered, "We are not stoning you for a good work, but for blasphemy—because you, being a man, make yourself Elohim."

Yeshua replied, "Is it not written in your Torah: 'I said, you are gods'?" (He was quoting from Tehillim [Psalm] 82:6.) "If those to whom the word of Elohim came were called 'gods'—and the Torah cannot be broken—why then do you say that I blaspheme because I said, 'I am the Son of Elohim'? If I am not doing the works of my Father, then do not believe me. But if I do them—even if you do not believe me—believe the works, so that you may come to know and understand that the Father is in me, and I am in the Father." But they hardened their hearts. Again, they tried to seize him—but he slipped away from their hands.

Yeshua then departed from Yerushalayim and went across the Yarden River, to the place where Yochanan had first been immersing the people. There, in that quiet and sacred place, he remained. And many came to him. They said, "Yochanan performed no miraculous sign—but everything he said about this man has proven true." And there, in the wilderness beyond the Yarden, many put their trust in him.

CHAPTER 14 Yeshua Begins his Perean Ministry

Sending of the Seventy-Two Luke 9:51–56 | 10:1–24

When the days were drawing near for him to be taken up, Yeshua set his face like flint—firm and resolute—to go up to Yerushalayim. Though he knew suffering awaited him, he would not turn aside. He sent messengers ahead of him to prepare the way, and they entered a village of the Shomronim (Samaritans), hoping to find hospitality for their rabbi. But the people of that village would not receive him, for his face was turned toward Yerushalayim, the city they despised.

Luke 9:51–53 can be read as a midrashic reworking or spiritual elevation of Jacob's journey to Esav:
• Both stories involve journeying toward confrontation
• Both send messengers ahead
• Both are met with uncertainty or rejection
• And in both, the outcome will shape the future of a people—Jacob becoming Israel, and Yeshua ascending to offer himself for Israel.

When Yaakov and Yochanan saw the rejection, indignation burned within them. "Adoni," they said, "do you want us to call down fire from the heavens and destroy them, like Eliyahu did?"

But Yeshua turned and sharply rebuked them. His voice was steady, but grieved: "You do not know what kind of spirit you are of. The Son of Man did not come to destroy the lives of people, but to save them." And with that, he led them away toward another village.

Afterward, Yeshua appointed seventy-two others and commissioned them, sending them out two by two ahead of him, to every city and village he intended to visit. As he looked upon them, compassion filled his voice: "The harvest is great, but the laborers are few. Therefore, pray to Adonai of the harvest to send out laborers into His harvest field. Go! Behold, I am sending you out like lambs among wolves. Carry no money bag, no travel sack, no sandals—and do not greet anyone on the road. When you enter a house, say first, 'Shalom to this house.' If a son of shalom is there, your shalom will rest upon him. If not, it will return to you. Remain in that same house, eating and drinking what is set before you—for the laborer is worthy of his wages. Do not keep moving from house to house.

"When you enter a city and they receive you, eat what is set before you. Heal the sick who are there and declare to them: 'The Malchut Elohim (Kingdom of God) has come near to you.' "But when you enter a city and they do not receive you, go into its streets and proclaim, 'Even the dust of your city that clings to our feet, we wipe off against you. Yet know this: the Malchut Elohim has come near.' I tell you the truth: it will be more tolerable for Sodom on that day than for that city."

The seventy-two went out and returned rejoicing, their eyes alight with wonder. "Adoni," they said, "even the demons submit to us in your Name!"

Yeshua's face glowed with a fire from heaven. "I was watching Satan fall like lightning from the heavens. Behold, I have given you samchut (authority) to trample serpents and scorpions and over all the power of the enemy. Nothing shall harm you. Nevertheless, do not rejoice that the spirits submit to you—rejoice that your names are written in the heavens."

In that same hour, overcome with joy in the Ruach, Yeshua lifted his eyes to the heavens and declared with praise, "I praise you, Abba, Adonai of Shamayim and Eretz (heaven and earth), for you have hidden these things from the wise and the learned, and you have revealed them to little children. Yes, Abba—for this was pleasing in your sight. All things have been handed over to me by my Abba. No one knows who the Son is except the Abba, and no one knows who the Abba is except the Son—and those to whom the Son chooses to reveal Him."

Then, turning privately to his disciples, Yeshua said with quiet reverence: "Blessed are the eyes that see what you see. For I tell you: many prophets and kings longed to see what you see, but did not see it; and to hear what you hear, but did not hear it."

The Greatest Mitzvah　　　　　　　　　　　　　　　　　　　　　　　　　　　　　Luke 10:25–28

As Yeshua was teaching the people, a Torah scholar rose to his feet—his posture respectful, but his intent to test the teacher. "Rabbi," he asked, "what must I do to inherit eternal life?"

Yeshua, perceiving the heart behind the question, answered him not with rebuke but with a question of his own, pointing the scholar back to the very foundation of their shared faith. "What is written in the Torah?" he said. "How do you read it?"

The man replied with the words of the Shema and the Holiness Code, the twin pillars of love: "You shall love Adonai your Elohim with all your heart, and with all your soul, and with all your strength, and with all your mind; and your neighbor as yourself."

Yeshua's eyes lit up with affirmation, and he said to him with warmth and clarity: "You have answered correctly. Do this—and you will live."

The Parable of the Compassionate Shomeroni　　　　　　　　　　　　　　　　Luke 10:29–37

But the Torah scholar, seeking to justify himself—perhaps to draw the line where his obligation would end—pressed further. "And who is my neighbor?" he asked, hoping for a limit, a definition that would make righteousness achievable and comfortable.

Yeshua looked at him and answered with a story—one that cut through religious categories and exposed the heart. "A man was going down from Yerushalayim to Yericho," Yeshua began, describing the dangerous descent along the rocky, winding path. "And he fell among robbers, who stripped him, beat him, and went away, leaving him half dead." The listeners could almost see the man's broken form lying in the dust of the roadside.

"Now," Yeshua continued, "a kohen was traveling down that road. And when he saw him—he passed by on the other side." A hush fell over the crowd. Surely the priest, a servant of the Temple, would be expected to help. But he chose ritual cleanness over mercy.

"So too a Levite," Yeshua said, pausing. "When he came to the place and saw him, he also passed by on the other side. But" Yeshua said with a tone shift that caused the crowd to lean in, "a certain Shomeroni (Samaritan) traveler—as he journeyed—came to where the man was. And when he saw him, he was moved with rachamim (compassion)."

The Shomeroni, a man from a people despised and mistrusted by the Judeans, became the unexpected hero of the tale. Yeshua's words gave the stranger dignity: "He went to him and bound up his wounds, pouring oil and wine upon them. Then he set the man on his own animal, brought him to an inn, and took care of him. And the next day, he took out two denarii and gave them to the innkeeper, saying, 'Take care of him. And whatever more you spend; I will repay you when I return.'"

Then Yeshua turned to the Torah scholar, letting the story itself deliver the verdict. "Which of these three do you think proved to be a neighbor to the man who fell among the robbers?"

The scholar, convicted in conscience, replied simply: "The one who showed mercy on him."

Yeshua said to him, "Go—and do likewise."

Martha and Miriam   Luke 10:38–42

Now it happened, as they traveled along the way, that Yeshua entered a certain village. The sun was beginning to lower over the hills, and the air carried the scent of baked bread and olive trees. A woman named Martha welcomed him into her home with warmth and reverence. Her house, a place of comfort and hospitality, stirred with activity as she began preparing to honor her guest.

Martha had a sister named Miriam (Mary), who also came into the room and quietly took her place at the feet of Yeshua. There she remained, still and attentive, drinking in every word he spoke—her soul captivated by the wisdom and presence of the Teacher.

But Martha, bustling with preparations and responsibilities, found herself increasingly distracted and weighed down with much serving. She moved quickly from room to room, the pots clanging, the bread baking, the table needing setting—yet her heart grew burdened not only with tasks but with frustration.

Finally, she came to him flustered and said, "Adoni, do you not care that my sister has left me to serve alone? Tell her then to help me."

Yeshua turned to her with a tender voice, full of both love and correction. "Martha, Martha," he said gently, "you are anxious and troubled about many things. But one thing is necessary. Miriam has chosen the good portion—the better share—and it will not be taken away from her." His words calmed the storm in the room, as if a veil had been lifted, revealing what truly mattered: to sit at the feet of the Teacher and to listen deeply to the words of life.

Teach Us to Pray   Luke 11:1–4

While Yeshua was praying in a certain place—his voice quiet, his heart lifted before the Father—one of his talmidim approached him after he had finished and said, "Rabbi, teach us to pray, just as Yohanan taught his talmidim."

Yeshua looked upon them with warmth and lifting his eyes towards heaven his palms up in reverence said, "When you pray, say:

        'Our Father who is in the heavens,
        May Your Name be made holy.

> May Your Malchut (Kingdom) come.
> May Your will be done—on earth as it is in the heavens.
> Give us our daily bread each day.
> Forgive us our sins, for we also forgive everyone who sins against us.
> And do not bring us into testing,
> but deliver us from evil.'"

The Friend at Midnight   Luke 11:5–8

Then Yeshua said to them, his tone rich with parable and invitation, "Which of you who has a friend will go to him at midnight and say, 'Friend, lend me three loaves of bread, because a friend of mine has come to me from a journey, and I have nothing to set before him'? And suppose the one inside answers, 'Do not bother me; the door is already shut, and my children are with me in bed. I cannot get up and give you anything.' I tell you the truth: even if he will not rise and give him anything because of their friendship, yet because of the man's bold persistence—because he knocks without shame—he will rise and give him whatever he needs."

Ask and You Shall Receive   Luke 11:9–13

"So I say to you: Ask—and it will be given to you. Keep looking—and you will find. Don't stop knocking—and the door will be opened to you. For everyone who keeps asking will receive. The one who keeps seeking will find. And to the one who persists in knocking, the door will be opened.

Which father among you, if his son asks for a fish, will give him a serpent instead? Or if he asks for an egg, will he give him a scorpion? If you then, being inclined toward evil, know how to give good gifts to your children, how much more will your Father from the heavens give the Ruach HaKodesh (Holy Spirit) to those who ask Him?"

True Blessedness   Luke 11:27–28

As Yeshua was saying these things, a woman from the crowd, her voice rising above the others, called out in wonder and admiration: "Blessed is the womb that carried you, and the breasts that nursed you!"

But Yeshua, turning to the crowd with a piercing truth, replied, "Rather, blessed are those who hear the word of Elohim—and obey it."

The Sign of Yonah   Luke 11:29–32

As the crowds began to swell around him, Yeshua raised his voice and said, "This generation is an evil generation. It seeks a sign—but no sign will be given to it except the sign of Yonah. For just as Yonah became a sign to the people of Nineveh, so also will the Son of Man be to this generation.

The Queen of the South will rise up at the judgment with the men of this generation and will condemn them, for she came from the ends of the earth to hear the wisdom of Shlomo—and behold, something greater than Shlomo is here.

The men of Nineveh will rise up at the judgment with this generation and will condemn it, because they repented at the preaching of Yonah—and behold, something greater than Yonah is here."

The Lamp of the Body — Luke 11:33–36

"No one lights a lamp and then hides it in a cellar or places it under a basket. Rather, it is set upon a lampstand, so that all who enter may see its light. The lamp of the body is the eye. When your eye is sound—generous, clear, and single in purpose—then your whole body is full of light. But when your eye is evil—clouded with greed, jealousy, or darkness—then your whole body is full of shadow.

Therefore, be careful—watch closely—that the light in you is not darkness.
If your whole body is filled with light, having no part dark, then it will shine brightly, completely illumined—like a lamp that gives you light with every beam."

Woes to the Perushim and Torah Scholars — Luke 11:37–54

As Yeshua continued to speak, a Perush (Pharisee), intrigued yet testing, invited him to eat at his house. Yeshua entered without hesitation and reclined at the table. But the Perush, watching him closely, was astonished—he had noticed that Yeshua had not performed the ritual handwashing customary before meals.

Seeing into the thoughts of his host, the Master spoke plainly, without fear or flattery: "You Prushim are meticulous to cleanse the outside of the cup and the dish, yet inside you are filled with greed and hidden wickedness. Foolish ones! Did not the One who created the outside also fashion the inside? But rather, give from what is within as tzedakah (righteous charity), and behold—then everything will be clean for you.

"But woe to you, Prushim! You tithe mint and rue and every garden herb with exacting care, yet you neglect mishpat (justice) and the ahavah (love) of Elohim. These you should have practiced, without neglecting the others.

"Woe to you, Perushim! You love the chief seats in the synagogues, the places of honor, and the elaborate greetings in the marketplaces. But cursed are you—for you are like unmarked graves, and people walk over you unaware, defiled without knowing."

At this, one of the Torah scholars seated nearby bristled and said, "Rabbi, in saying these things, you also insult us!"

But Yeshua turned his piercing gaze upon him and said: "Woe to you, too, Torah scholars! You burden people with heavy loads of obligation, piling halachic weights upon their backs, yet you yourselves will not lift a single finger to ease them.

"Woe to you! You build grand tombs for the prophets—yet it was your fathers who killed them. In doing so, you bear witness against yourselves: you approve of the deeds of your ancestors. They murdered the prophets—and you complete the monument of their crimes.

"Therefore, the Chokhmah (Wisdom) of Elohim has spoken: 'I will send to them prophets and emissaries—some of whom they will kill and persecute'—so that the blood of all the prophets, poured out since the foundation of the world, will be required of this generation.

From the blood of Hevel (Abel), the righteous son of Adam, to the blood of Zecharyah, who was slain between the altar and the sanctuary—yes, I tell you, it will be required of this generation.

"Woe to you, Torah scholars! You have taken away the key of da'at (knowledge)—you yourselves have not entered in, and you have hindered those who were trying to enter." And when Yeshua departed from that house, the Torah scholars and the Prushim were inflamed with hostility. They began to oppose him fiercely, lying in wait, and bombarding him with questions—seeking to entrap him, hoping to catch him in his words and destroy him.

Warnings to the Disciples and the Parable of Greed — Luke 12:1–15

Meanwhile, the crowd continue to increase in number, pressing in upon one another to the point that people were being trampled. In the midst of the chaos, Yeshua turned first to his talmidim, speaking with sober urgency: "Guard yourselves against the chametz (leaven) of the Perushim (Pharisees)—for it is hypocrisy. Nothing is concealed that will not be unveiled, nor hidden that will not be made known. Whatever you have whispered in darkness will be heard in the light. What has been murmured in the inner rooms will be proclaimed from the rooftops."

Then, lifting his voice so all could hear, he addressed them as friends, calling them to holy courage: "I say to you, my beloved ones: Do not fear those who kill the body, and after that have no more they can do. I will show you whom you should fear—Fear the One who, after He has killed, has authority to cast into Gehinnom (the Valley of Judgment). Yes, I tell you, fear Him!

"Are not five sparrows sold for two copper coins? And yet not a single one of them is forgotten before Elohim. Even the very hairs on your head are all counted. So do not be afraid—you are worth more than many sparrows.

"I tell you truly: Everyone who acknowledges me before men, the Son of Man will also acknowledge before the malakhim (messengers) of Elohim. But whoever denies me before men will be denied before the malakhim of Elohim. Whoever speaks a word against the Son of Man—it will be forgiven. But whoever blasphemes against the Ruach HaKodesh (Holy Spirit)—that one will not be forgiven. And when they bring you before synagogues, before rulers and authorities, do not be anxious about how to defend yourselves or what to say. For the Ruach HaKodesh will teach you in that very moment what you must say."

Then suddenly, from amidst the crowd, a voice called out: "Rabbi, tell my brother to divide the inheritance with me!"

But Yeshua turned and said, "Man, who appointed me to be a judge or divider over you?" And addressing all who were gathered, he declared: "Take heed! Guard yourselves against all forms of greed—for a person's life does not consist in the abundance of his possessions."

The Parable of the Rich Fool — Luke 12:16–21

And he told them a mashal (parable): "The land of a certain rich man produced abundantly. And he thought to himself, 'What will I do, since I have nowhere to store my crops?' Then he said, 'This is what I'll do—I'll tear down my barns and build larger ones, and I'll store all my grain and my goods. And I'll say to myself, "You have plenty stored up for many years. Relax, eat, drink, and enjoy."'

But the wisdom of heaven pierced the illusion of earthly security. While the man congratulated himself in private and dreamed of ease and luxury, the voice of Elohim thundered into the night: 'Fool! This night your soul is required of you. Then who will own what you have prepared?' So, it is with the one who stores up treasure for himself and is not rich toward Elohim."

Do Not Worry   Luke 12:22–24

Then Yeshua said to his talmidim, "Because of this, I tell you: Do not worry about your life—what you will eat—nor about your body—what you will wear. Life is more than food, and the body more than clothing. His eyes turned toward the open skies, and he motioned toward the flocks of birds overhead. "Consider the ravens—they neither sow nor reap, they have no storerooms or barns, yet Elohim feeds them. How much more valuable are you than birds!"

Trusting the Father's Provision   Luke 12:25–31

And which of you by worrying can add a single hour to your life? If then you cannot do even this little thing, why do you worry about the rest? Consider how the lilies grow—they do not labor or spin. Yet I tell you, even Shlomo (Solomon), in all his glory, was not clothed like one of these. And if Elohim so clothes the grass of the field, which is here today and tomorrow is thrown into the oven, how much more will he clothe you, little of emunah (faith)!" The Master's voice was gentle, but firm, like a shepherd calling his sheep back from a cliff's edge.

"Do not seek what you will eat or what you will drink, and do not be anxious. For all the nations of the world seek these things, but your Father knows that you need them. Instead, seek His Malchut (kingdom), and these things will be added to you. Do not fear, little flock, for your Father has chosen gladly to give you the Malchut (kingdom)."

Heavenly Treasure and Watchfulness   Luke 12:33–40

"Sell your possessions and give them to tzedakah (charity). Make for yourselves purses that do not wear out—an unfailing treasure in the heavens, where no thief comes near and no moth destroys. For where your treasure is, there also your heart will be." The talmidim stood still, wide-eyed. Yeshua's words had begun to draw back the veil between heaven and earth.

"Be dressed and ready, with your lamps burning. Be like people waiting for their master to return from a wedding feast, so that when he comes and knocks, they may open to him immediately. Blessed are those servants whom the master finds alert when he comes. Amen, I say to you, he will dress himself to serve, have them recline at table, and will come and serve them.

"And if he comes in the second watch, or even the third, and finds them prepared in this way, blessed are those servants! But know this: If the owner of the house had known at what time the thief was coming, he would not have let his house be broken into. You also must be ready, for the Son of Man is coming at an hour you do not expect."

The Wise and Faithful Steward   Luke 12:41–48

Then Kefa (Peter) said to him, "Master, are you telling this mashal (parable) for us, or for everyone?"

And the Master said, "Who then is the faithful and wise steward, whom his master will put in charge of his household to give them their portion at the proper time? Blessed is that servant whom his master finds doing so when he comes. Truly I say to you, he will put him in charge of all his possessions."

"But if that servant says in his heart, 'My master is delayed in coming,' and begins to beat the male and female servants, and to eat and drink and get drunk, then the master of that servant will come on a day when he does not expect him and at an hour he does not know. He will cut him into pieces and assign him a place with the unfaithful."

"That servant who knew his master's will but did not prepare or act accordingly will receive many blows. But the one who did not know and did things worthy of punishment will receive few." The weight of his words settled on the crowd like a sudden hush over stormy waters. "From everyone who has been given much, much will be required. And to whom much has been entrusted, even more will be demanded.

Fire and Division   Luke 12:49–53

"I came to cast fire upon the earth—and how I wish it were already kindled! But I have a mikveh (immersion) to undergo, and how distressed I am until it is completed! Do you think I came to bring peace on the earth? No, I tell you—but division. From now on, there will be five in one house divided, three against two and two against three. They will be divided, father against son and son against father, mother against daughter and daughter against mother, mother-in-law against her daughter-in-law and daughter-in-law against mother-in-law."

Discerning the Times   Luke 12:54–56

Then he also said to the crowds, "When you see a cloud rising in the west, you say at once, 'A shower is coming,' and so it happens. And when you see the south wind blowing, you say, 'It will be hot,' and it happens. Hypocrites! You know how to read the appearance of the earth and the sky, but how is it you do not know how to interpret this present time?"

Settle Quickly with Your Accuser   Luke 12:57–59

"Why do you not judge for yourselves what is right? As you go with your accuser before the judge, try to settle with him on the way, lest he drag you before the judge, and the judge hands you over to the officer, and the officer throws you into prison. I tell you; you will not get out until you have paid the last perutah (small coin)."

A Call to Teshuvah (Repentance)   Luke 13:1–5

Now some were present at that time who told Yeshua about the Galilim (Galileans) whose blood Pilate had mingled with their korbanot (offerings). He answered them, "Do you think that these Galilim were worse sinners than all the other people from the Galil because they suffered such things? I tell you, no! But unless you make teshuvah (repentance), you will all likewise perish.

"Or those eighteen on whom the tower in Shiloach fell and killed them—do you think they were more guilty than all the people living in Yerushalayim? I tell you, no! But unless you make teshuvah (repentance), you will all likewise perish."

As murmurs spread among the crowd regarding these tragic events, Yeshua did not speak of fate or misfortune, but of the urgency of repentance. He saw in these disasters not mere accidents, but warnings—signs calling Israel to turn from her sins before judgment would fall on all.

The Parable of the Barren Fig Tree   Luke 13:6–9

Then he told this mashal (parable): "A man had a fig tree planted in his vineyard. He came looking for fruit on it but found none. So, he said to the gardener, 'Look, for three years I have come searching for fruit on this fig tree and haven't found any. Cut it down! Why should it even use up the soil?' But the gardener answered him, 'Master, leave it alone for one more year—until I dig around it and put in manure. If it bears fruit next year, good; but if not, then you may cut it down.'"

Thematic Breakdown	Teaching	Application
*The Vineyard Owner: Represents Elohim, who plants and tends His people like a gardener with care and expectation. The fig tree often symbolizes Israel (cf. Hosea 9:10, Jeremiah 24, Micah 7:1). *The Fig Tree: Symbolizes the people of Israel—or any individual soul within the covenant—who is expected to bear fruit, meaning righteousness, obedience, justice, and mercy (cf. Isaiah 5, Micah 6:8). *Three Years of Fruitlessness: Reflects prolonged patience. It recalls the length of Yeshua's ministry, as well as the time Elohim often gives before executing judgment (cf. Exodus 34:6–7: "slow to anger"). *"Cut it down!": The decree of judgment. Just as Elohim threatens destruction when there is persistent rebellion and no repentance. *The Gardener: A picture of an intercessor—possibly Yeshua, possibly the prophets, possibly even a priestly role. This gardener doesn't challenge the owner's judgment but asks for more time and commits to additional care. *"Leave it alone for one more year…": This echoes the middat ha'rachamim—the attribute of mercy. The intercessor pleads for delay in judgment, buying time in the hope of repentance.	This parable is not about a single act of disobedience but rather a continued failure to fulfill one's covenantal purpose. Like the fig tree using up good soil without fruit, a person (or nation) may enjoy blessings but fail to respond with righteousness. Yet, the heart of Elohim is not quick to destroy. He seeks out intercessors (Ezekiel 22:30), and He delights in mercy (Micah 7:18). Yeshua teaches here that judgment is real—but so is the power of intercession. Just as Moshe stood in the breach, so too the gardener in the parable asks: "Let me work with it a little longer." It is a call to repentance and a window of opportunity. The manure, the digging—these are uncomfortable but necessary trials or teachings designed to stir the soul into action. The message is urgent: fruit must be borne now, before the axe is laid to the root (cf. Luke 3:9).	1. For Individuals: Are you bearing fruit with the life and blessings Elohim has given you? Is your heart soft to His cultivation, or have you grown indifferent in the soil of grace? 2. For Leaders and Teachers: Are you standing in the breach like Moshe? Are you digging around the trees under your care, willing to get your hands dirty to help them grow? 3. For the Community: This is a corporate warning as well. Just as Yisra'el was spared destruction because of Moshe's prayer, so too entire communities can be preserved through the faithful prayers and labors of the righteous among them.
Closing Thought: Like the fig tree, we are all standing in the vineyard of Elohim. He walks among us, not with a spirit of condemnation, but with a desire to see righteousness blossom. May we heed the call of the intercessor and respond with repentance and fruitfulness before the time of grace is spent.		

Healing the Daughter of Avraham on Shabbat   Luke 13:10–17

Yeshua was teaching in one of the synagogues on Yom Shabbat (the Sabbath). And there was a woman who had a ruach (spirit) of weakness for eighteen years. She was bent over completely and unable to straighten up at all.

When Yeshua saw her, he was filled with compassion for her, so he called her over and said to her, "Woman, you are set free from your weakness." Then he walked over to her and laid his hands on her, and immediately she stood up straight and began to give kavod (glory) to Elohim.

The hush of the synagogue was pierced by her praise. The people looked on in awe, but not all shared her joy. The rosh hakeneset (synagogue leader), indignant because Yeshua had healed on Shabbat, responded to the crowd: "There are six days in which work should be done. Come and be healed on those days, and not on Yom Shabbat!"

But the Master answered him, "Hypocrites! Doesn't each of you untie his ox or donkey from the manger on Shabbat and lead it to drink? And this daughter of Avraham—whom the satan has bound for eighteen years—should she not be set free from this bondage on Yom Shabbat?"

As he said these things, all his opponents were put to shame, but the whole crowd was rejoicing over all the glorious things being done by him. In that moment, the synagogue became a courtroom where mercy triumphed over halachic rigidity. The chains of suffering were broken, not only for the woman, but for those whose hearts were opened to the deeper justice of Shabbat—a day not only of rest, but of release.

Parables of the Mustard Seed and the Leaven   Luke 13:18–21

Then Yeshua said, "What is the Malchut Elohim (Kingdom of God) like? And to what shall I compare it? It is like a mustard seed that a man took and sowed in his garden. It grew and became a tree, and the birds of the heavens came and nested in its branches."

And again, he said, "To what shall I compare the Malchut Elohim? It is like se'or (leaven) that a woman took and hid in three measures of flour, until it was all leavened."

> What may seem small and insignificant—like a seed or like leaven—has the power to transform everything it touches. The Kingdom begins in hidden places: buried in the soil of humble obedience or mingled invisibly into the dough of daily life. Yet, given time and proper care, it flourishes. The seed becomes a shelter. The leaven changes the whole loaf. So it is with those who receive the Word and nurture it in faith.

Healing on Shabbat and a Lesson in Compassion   Luke 14:1–6

Now it happened, when Yeshua went into the house of one of the leaders of the Perushim (Pharisees) to eat bread on Yom Shabbat (the Sabbath), they were watching him closely. There before him was a man suffering from dropsy (swelling with fluid). Yeshua spoke to the Torah scholars and the Perushim, asking, "Is it permitted to heal on Shabbat or not?" But they remained silent. So, he took hold of the man, healed him, and sent him away. Then he said to them, "Which of you, if your son or your ox falls into a well on Yom Shabbat, will not immediately pull him out?" And they were not able to reply to these things.

Though they gathered to scrutinize him, Yeshua's eyes turned to the one suffering. Without hesitation, he extended healing on the day of rest, revealing that Shabbat was made for mercy, not bondage. His question pierced their silence, laying bare their hypocrisy—they would rescue an animal, yet begrudged mercy to a human being. In that quiet house, the true spirit of Torah stood in their midst.

Parable on Choosing Honor and Humility   Luke 14:7–11

When Yeshua noticed how the guests were choosing places of honor at the table, he gave them a mashal (parable). He said, "When you are invited by someone to a wedding feast, do not sit down in the place of honor, lest someone more distinguished than you may have been invited by him. Then the one who invited both of you will come and say to you, 'Give your place to this man,' and then, with shame, you will go to the lowest place. But when you are invited, go and recline in the lowest place, so that when the one who invited you comes, he may say to you, 'Friend, move up higher.' Then you will be honored before all who sit with you. For everyone who exalts himself will be humbled, and the one who humbles himself will be exalted."

Yeshua's words settled over the gathering like a soft but stinging wind. In a culture obsessed with status and rank, he unveiled the secret of true greatness—humility. Not the kind that hides in false modesty, but the kind that trusts Elohim to raise up the lowly in due time.

Instructions for Kingdom Generosity   Luke 14:12–14

Then Yeshua also said to the one who had invited him, "When you prepare a luncheon or a dinner, do not invite your friends, your brothers, your relatives, or your rich neighbors—lest they also invite you in return and you be repaid. But when you prepare a feast, invite the poor, the crippled, the lame, and the blind. Then you will be blessed, because they cannot repay you—for you will be repaid in the resurrection of the tzaddikim (righteous)."

In the very house of a Pharisee, Yeshua turned their feast into a classroom of the Malchut Elohim. True righteousness was not found in circles of mutual favor but in the embrace of those the world forgets. For in the eyes of heaven, giving with no hope of return stores treasure in eternity.

The Great Banquet Mashal (Parable)   Luke 14:15–24

One of those reclining at the table with him heard these things and said to him, "Blessed is the one who will eat bread in the Malchut Elohim (Kingdom of God)!"

But Yeshua replied with this mashal (parable): "A certain man prepared a great banquet and invited many. At the time of the banquet, he sent his servant to tell those who had been invited, 'Come, for everything is now ready.' But they all alike began to make excuses. The first said, 'Please excuse me, I have bought a field, and I must go and see it.' Another said, 'Please excuse me, I have bought five yokes of oxen, and I am going to try them out.' Still another said, 'I have married a wife, and therefore I cannot come.' So, the servant came back and reported these things to his master.

Then the master of the house became angry and said to his servant, 'Go out quickly into the streets and lanes of the city, and bring in the poor, the crippled, the blind, and the lame.' The servant said, 'Master, what you commanded has been done, and there is still room.' Then the master said to the servant, 'Go out into the highways and the hedges, and compel them to come in, so that my house may be filled. For I tell you, none of those men who were invited will taste of my banquet.'"

The Cost of Discipleship   Luke 14:25–35

Now large crowds were going along with Yeshua, and he turned and said to them: "If anyone comes to me and does not hate his father and mother, his wife and children, his brothers and sisters—yes, even his own life—he is not able to be my talmid (disciple). Whoever does not carry his cross and comes after me cannot be my talmid.

"For which of you, wanting to build a tower, does not first sit down and calculate the cost, to see if he has enough to complete it? Otherwise, if he has laid the foundation and is not able to finish it, everyone who sees it will begin to mock him, saying, 'This man began to build and was not able to finish.'

"Or what king, going out to make war against another king, does not first sit down and consider whether he is able with ten thousand to face the one coming against him with twenty thousand? And if not, while the other is still far off, he sends a delegation and asks for shalom.

So therefore, every one of you who does not renounce all that he possesses cannot be my talmid. Salt is good—but if the salt becomes tasteless, with what will it be seasoned? It is no longer fit for the soil or the manure heap—it is thrown away. Let the one who has ears to hear, hear!" Though the crowd swelled with curiosity and excitement, Yeshua's words cut like a plowshare—he did not court followers with promises of ease, but summoned them to radical loyalty.

The Parable of the Lost Sheep   Luke 15:1–7

Now all the tax collectors and the sinners were drawing near to listen to him. But both the Perushim (Pharisees) and the Torah scholars were grumbling, saying, "He welcomes sinners and eats with them!"

So, Yeshua spoke this mashal (parable) to them: "Which man among you, if he has a hundred sheep and loses one of them, does not leave the ninety-nine in the wilderness and go after the one that is lost until he finds it? When he has found it, he lays it on his shoulders, rejoicing. And when he comes home, he calls together his friends and neighbors and says to them, 'Rejoice with me, for I have found my sheep that was lost!'"

Yeshua's voice softened with compassion as he looked upon those who judged others harshly. They had forgotten what Elohim truly delights in—the return of a soul. He continued: "I tell you, in the same way there will be more joy in the Shamayim (heavens) over one sinner who makes teshuvah (repentance) than over ninety-nine tzaddikim (righteous ones) who do not need teshuvah."

The Parable of the Lost Coin   Luke 15:8–10

"Or what woman, if she has ten silver coins and loses one coin, does not light a lamp, sweep the house, and search carefully until she finds it? When she has found it, she calls together her friends and neighbors, saying, 'Rejoice with me, for I have found the coin I had lost!'"

"Just as the Good Shepherd seeks the sheep, the woman's diligent search revealed the passion of heaven—a Father who does not give up until what was lost is found. In the same way, I tell you, there is joy before the malakhim (messengers) of Elohim over one sinner who makes teshuvah."

The Parable of the Lost Son — Luke 15:11–32

Then he said, "A certain man had two sons. The younger of them said to his father, 'Father, give me the share of the estate that falls to me.' So, he divided his property between them. Not many days later, the younger son gathered everything he had and went on a journey to a distant country, and there he squandered his estate in wild living. After he had spent everything, a severe famine arose in that land, and he began to be in need.

So, he went and hired himself out to one of the citizens of that country, who sent him into his fields to feed pigs. He longed to fill his stomach with the pods that the pigs were eating, but no one gave him anything. It was in that moment—broken, starving, and far from his father's house—that he awoke to the truth.

"When he came to his senses, he said, 'How many of my father's hired workers have food in abundance, but I am dying here with hunger! I will get up, go to my father, and say to him, "Father, I have sinned against the heavens and before you. I am no longer worthy of being called your son. Make me like one of your hired workers."'

"So, he got up and went to his father. But while he was still far away, his father saw him and felt compassion. He ran, fell on his neck, and kissed him.

The son said to him, 'Father, I have sinned against the heavens and before you. I am no longer worthy to be called your son.'

But the father said to his servants, 'Quick! Bring out the best robe and clothe him. Put a ring on his hand and sandals on his feet. Bring the fattened calf and kill it. Let's eat and celebrate! For this son of mine was dead and has come back to life—he was lost and is found.' And they began to celebrate.

"Now his older son was out in the field. As he came near the house, he heard music and dancing. So, he called one of the servants and asked what was going on. The servant said to him, 'Your brother has come, and your father has killed the fattened calf because he got him back safe and sound.'

But the older son was angry and refused to go in. So, his father came out and pleaded with him. But he answered and said to his father, 'Look, these many years I've served you, and I never disobeyed your command—yet you never gave me a young goat so I could celebrate with my friends. But when this son of yours comes—who has devoured your property with prostitutes—you killed the fattened calf for him!'

"Then the father said to him, 'Son, you are always with me, and everything that is mine is yours. But we had to celebrate and rejoice, for this brother of yours was dead and has come back to life—he was lost and is found.'"

The Parable of the Dishonest Steward   Luke 16:1–13

Then Yeshua also said to his talmidim, "There was a certain rich man who had a steward. Accusations were brought to him that this man was squandering his possessions. So, he called him and said, 'What is this I hear about you? Turn in the report of your stewardship, for you can no longer be steward.'

Then the steward said to himself, 'What will I do? My master is taking the stewardship away from me. I am not strong enough to dig, and I am ashamed to beg. I know what I'll do, so that when I am removed from my stewardship, people will welcome me into their homes.'

"So, he called in each one of his master's debtors. He said to the first, 'How much do you owe my master?' The man replied, 'A hundred measures of olive oil.' He said to him, 'Take your bill, sit down quickly, and write fifty.' Then he said to another, 'And how much do you owe?' He replied, 'A hundred measures of wheat.' He said to him, 'Take your bill and write eighty.' Then the master praised the dishonest steward because he acted with chochmah (wisdom), for the sons of this world are shrewder in dealing with their own kind than are the sons of the light.

"I tell you," Yeshua continued, "make friends for yourselves with the mammon ha-risha (unrighteous wealth), so that when it fails, they may welcome you into eternal dwellings. The one who is faithful in very little is also faithful in much, and the one who is dishonest in very little is also dishonest in much. So, if you have not been faithful with mammon ha-risha (unrighteous wealth), who will entrust you with the true riches? And if you have not been faithful with what belongs to someone else, who will give you what is your own?

"No servant can serve two masters. Either he will hate one and love the other, or he will cling to one and despise the other. You cannot serve both Elohim and mammon (wealth)."

A Rebuke to the Lovers of Money   Luke 16:14–17

Now the Perushim, who were lovers of money, were listening to all these things and were sneering at him. But he said to them, "You are the ones who justify yourselves before men, but Elohim knows your hearts. For what is exalted among men is detestable in the sight of Elohim. The Torah and the Nevi'im (Prophets) were until Yochanan. From then on, the Malchut Elohim (kingdom of God) is proclaimed, and everyone is forcing his way into it. But it is easier for the heavens and the earth to pass away than for one tiny stroke of a letter in the Torah to fall."

Though the crowd marveled at Yeshua's wisdom, the Perushim scoffed in contempt. But Yeshua, seeing into their hearts, exposed the hidden rot behind their pious faces. They cloaked their greed in righteousness, yet Elohim was not deceived. His kingdom could not be entered by wealth, status, or clever manipulation—but only through humble surrender and truth.

The Parable of the Rich Man and El'azar   Luke 16:19–31

Then he said: "There was a certain rich man who was clothed in purple and fine linen, feasting luxuriously every day. At his gate was laid a poor man named El'azar (Lazarus), covered with sores. He longed to be fed with the crumbs that fell from the rich man's table. Even the dogs came and licked his sores.

"Now it happened that the poor man died and was carried away by the malakhim (messengers) to Avraham's side. The rich man also died and was buried. In She'ol, being in torment, he lifted up his eyes and saw Avraham far off with El'azar at his side.

"He cried out, 'Father Avraham, have mercy on me! Send El'azar to dip the tip of his finger in water and cool my tongue, because I am in anguish in this flame!'

"But Avraham said, 'Son, remember that you in your lifetime received your good things, and El'azar likewise received bad things. But now he is comforted here, and you are in anguish. Besides all this, a great chasm has been fixed between us and you, so that those who want to pass from here to you cannot, and no one can cross from there to us.'

"Then the rich man said, 'Then I beg you, father, send him to my father's house—for I have five brothers—so that he may warn them, lest they also come to this place of torment.'

"But Avraham said, 'They have Moshe and the Nevi'im (Prophets). Let them listen to them.'

"And he said, 'No, father Avraham! But if someone from the dead goes to them, they will repent!'

"But he said to him, 'If they do not listen to Moshe and the Nevi'im, they will not be convinced even if someone rises from the dead.'"

Warnings Against Causing Others to Stumble Luke 17:1–2

Yeshua said to his talmidim (disciples): "It is impossible for the world to be without miksholim (stumbling blocks), but woe to the one through whom they come. It would be better for him if a millstone were hung around his neck and he were thrown into the sea, than that he should cause one of these little ones to stumble."

"Though sin and offense are inevitable in this fallen world. Those who lead the innocent astray—those who corrupt the pure—place themselves in terrible danger before the judgment of Heaven." Yeshua's warning burned like fire his voice carried the weight of divine justice, stirring the hearts of those who heard him.

The Call to Forgive Freely Luke 17:3–4

"Pay attention to yourselves. If your brother sins, rebuke him; and if he makes teshuvah (repentance), forgive him. Even if he sins against you seven times in a day, and seven times returns to you saying, 'I make teshuvah,' you shall forgive him." As he spoke, a hush fell over his talmidim. The demand was not for leniency alone, but for relentless mercy. A spirit that withholds forgiveness is not the spirit of Elohim.

Faith as a Mustard Seed Luke 17:5–6

The shlichim (apostles) said to the Master: "Increase our emunah (faith)!"

Yeshua said to them: "If you had emunah like a mustard seed, you could say to this mulberry tree, 'Be uprooted and be planted in the sea,' and it would obey you." Their request was met with a vision of power hidden in simplicity. The tiniest spark of faith, truly alive, could defy the limits of creation—not by magic, but by trusting in the Creator's power

The Duty of Servants   Luke 17:7–10

Yeshua continued: "Which of you who has an eved (servant) plowing or shepherding will say to him when he comes in from the field, 'Come immediately and recline at the table'? Will he not say to him, 'Prepare something for me to eat, prepare yourself and serve me until I have eaten and drunk; and afterward you may eat and drink'? Does he thank the eved because he did the things that were commanded? I don't think so. So, you also, when you have done all that is commanded of you, say, 'We are unworthy avadim (servants); we have only done what it was our duty to do.'" True humility flowed not from self-hatred, but from recognizing that doing the will of the Master is the highest honor of all.

Ten Metzorim Are Healed   Luke 17:11–19

As Yeshua was traveling on the way to Yerushalayim, he passed between Shomron (Samaria) and the Galil (Galilee). As he entered a certain village, ten metzorim (lepers) met him. They stood at a distance and lifted up their voices in desperation, saying: "Yeshua, Rabbi, have rachamim (mercy) on us!"

When Yeshua saw them, he said: "Go and show yourselves to the kohanim (priests)." And as they went, they were metaherim (cleansed). One of them, when he saw that he was healed, turned back, glorifying Elohim with a loud voice. He fell on his face at Yeshua's feet, giving him thanks—and he was a Shomroni (Samaritan).

Yeshua answered and said: "Were not ten cleansed? But where are the nine? Was no one found who returned to give kavod (glory) to Elohim except this foreigner?" The disappointment was evident in his voice, and he said to him: "Arise and go your way. Your emunah has made you whole."

The grateful Shomroni, though doubly outcast by leprosy and by lineage, became a living example of the true worship Elohim desires—gratitude rooted in faith. In him, the unseen Malchut (Kingdom) shone more brightly than in the outwardly righteous.

The Kingdom of Elohim Is Within You   Luke 17:20–21

When questioned by some Perushim (Pharisees) as to when the Malchut Elohim (Kingdom of God) would come, Yeshua answered: "The Malchut Elohim is not coming with visible signs that can be watched. People will not say, 'Look, here it is!' or 'There it is!' For behold, the Malchut Elohim is b'kerevchem (within you / among you)." His words shattered the hopes of those looking for political upheaval or apocalyptic spectacle.

The Days of the Son of Man   Luke 17:22–25

Then he said to the talmidim (disciples): "The days will come when you will long to see even one of the days of the Son of Man, but you will not see it. People will say to you, 'Look there!' or 'Look here!' Do not go and do not run after them. For as lightning flashes and lights up the sky from one end to the other, so will be the coming of the Ben-Adam (Son of Man). But first, he must suffer many things and be rejected by this generation." They longed for glory, but Yeshua pointed to suffering. The radiant flash of his return would come—but only after the darkness of rejection.

As in the Days of Noach and Lot   Luke 17:26–30

"Just as it was in the days of Noach, so it will be in the days of the Ben-Adam: they were eating and drinking, marrying and being given in marriage, until the day Noach entered the teivah (ark), and the flood came and destroyed them all. Likewise, just as it was in the days of Lot: they were eating and drinking, buying and selling, planting and building, but on the day Lot went out from Sedom (Sodom), fire and sulfur rained from the heavens and destroyed them all. Thus, will it be on the day when the Son of Man is revealed." A warning sounded beneath his voice—a world lost in routine pleasures would not discern the day of divine reckoning until it was too late.

Do Not Turn Back   Luke 17:31–33

Yeshua continued: "On that day, let the one who is on the housetop, with his belongings in the house, not come down to take them away. And likewise, the one who is in the field must not turn back. Remember Lot's wife. Whoever seeks to preserve his soul will lose it, but whoever loses it will keep it alive."

TO CLING TO THE FADING WORLD WAS TO LOSE ETERNITY. THE KINGDOM REQUIRES URGENCY, DETACHMENT, AND TRUST.

One Taken, One Left   Luke 17:34–37

"I tell you, in that night, there will be two lying in one bed—one will be taken and the other left. Two women will be grinding at the same mill—one will be taken and the other left. Two men will be in the field—one will be taken and the other left."

They answered him, saying: "Where, Master?"

And he said to them: "Where the carcass is, there the eagles will gather." In his closing cryptic response, Yeshua hinted that judgment would come where decay already existed—where corruption drew its own destruction.

The Persistent Widow and the Righteous Judge   Luke 18:1–8

Yeshua spoke a mashal (parable) to his talmidim (disciples), to show them that they should always pray and not grow weary, saying: "In a certain city there was a shofet (judge) who neither feared Elohim nor respected any man. And in that city there was a widow, who kept coming to him, saying, 'Grant me justice against my adversary.'

"For a while he refused. But afterward he said to himself, 'Though I neither fear Elohim nor regard people, yet because this widow keeps bothering me, I will give her justice, lest by her continual coming she wear me out.'"

Then the Master said: "Hear what the unrighteous judge says. And shall not Elohim bring about justice for His bechirav (chosen ones), who cry out to Him day and night? Will He delay long over them? I tell you; He will bring about justice for them speedily. Nevertheless, when the Bar Enash (Son of Man) comes, will he find emunah (faith) on the earth?" Even an unjust man yielded to persistence—how much more will the Righteous Judge respond to the ceaseless cries of His faithful ones?

The Parush and the Moches   Luke 18:9–14

Yeshua spoke this mashal (parable) to some who trusted in themselves that they were tzaddikim (righteous) and treated others with contempt: "Two men went up to the Beit HaMikdash (Temple) to pray—one a Parush (Pharisee), and the other a moches (tax collector). The Parush stood by himself and prayed like this: 'Elohim, I thank You that I am not like other men—extortioners, unrighteous, adulterers, or even like this moches. I fast twice a week and I give ma'aser (a tithe) of all I acquire.' But the moches, standing far off, would not even lift up his eyes toward the heavens, but beat upon his chest, saying: 'Elohim, show me rachamim (mercy), for I am a sinner.'"

Yeshua concluded: "I tell you the truth: this man went down to his house declared yashar (upright) before Elohim rather than the other. For everyone who exalts himself will be humbled, but the one who humbles himself will be exalted." Two men entered the Temple—but only one left with heaven's approval. Pride paraded righteousness before men, but humility bowed before the mercy seat of Elohim. It was the broken heart, not the polished prayer, that reached the Throne.

Teaching on Divorce   Matthew 19:1–9 | Mark 10:1–12

Then Yeshua rose up from there and went to the territory of Yehudah and beyond the Yarden (Jordan). Again, large crowds came to him, and as was his custom, he taught them. Some Perushim (Pharisees) came and tested him, asking: "Is it permitted for a man to send away his wife for any reason?"

He answered them: "What did Moshe command you?"

They said: "Moshe permitted us to write a sefer keritut (certificate of divorce) and send her away."

But Yeshua said to them: "Because of the hardness of your hearts, he wrote you this mitzvah. But from the beginning of creation, 'He made them male and female.' And it is written, 'For this cause a man shall leave his father and mother and cleave to his wife, and the two shall become one flesh.' So, they are no longer two, but one flesh. Therefore, what Elohim has joined together, let no man separate."

They said to him: "Then why did Moshe command to give a get (divorce certificate) and send her away?"

He said to them: "Moshe permitted divorce because of your hardness of heart, but from the beginning it was not so. I tell you, whoever sends away his wife—except for zenut (sexual immorality)—and marries another, commits adultery. And he who marries a woman who was sent away also commits adultery. And if a woman sends away her husband and marries another, she also commits adultery."

<u>As the Torah permitted divorce in cases where the covenant was broken, Yeshua revealed that this was a concession—not an ideal. From the first, the will of Elohim was unity, not separation. The sanctity of marriage, forged by divine hands, was not to be unraveled by human will.</u>

The Talmidim Question Yeshua about Divorce and Celibacy   Matthew 19:10–12; Mark 10:10–12

Later, in the house, the talmidim asked him again about this matter. He said to them, "Whoever sends away his wife and marries another commits adultery against her, and he who marries a woman who was sent away also commits adultery. If she sends away her husband and marries another, she commits adultery."

The talmidim said to him: "If this is the case between a man and his wife, it is better not to marry."

And Yeshua said to them: "Not everyone is able to receive this word—only those to whom it has been given. For there are sarisim (eunuchs) who were born that way from their mother's womb; and there are sarisim who were made that way by men; and there are sarisim who have made themselves that way for the sake of the Malchut HaShamayim (Kingdom of Heaven). The one who is able to receive this, let him receive it."

Yeshua Welcomes the Children   Matthew 19:13–15 | Mark 10:13–16 | Luke 18:15–17

Then they were bringing even infants to Yeshua so that he might lay his hands on them and bless them. But when the talmidim (disciples) saw it, they rebuked those who brought them.

But Yeshua, seeing this, was displeased and said to them in an authoritative voice: "Let the yeladim (children) come to me, and do not hinder them." He then knelt down with his arms spread wide. He continued speaking with a smile on his face and soft voice; "For the Malchut Elohim (Kingdom of God) belongs to such as these. Amen, I say to you: whoever does not receive the Malchut Elohim like a child will by no means enter into it." Then he took the yeladim into his arms and laid his hands on them, and blessed them, then he went on from there.

The Rich Young Ruler   Matthew 19:16–30 | Mark 10:17–31 | Luke 18:18–30

As Yeshua was setting out on the road, a young man—a ruler among the people—ran to him, knelt before him, and asked in desperation between breathes: "Rabbi, what good thing must I do to inherit chayei olam (eternal life)?"

Yeshua smiled down at him and helped him to his feet and said to him: "Why do you ask me about what is good? No one is good except One—that is, Elohim. But if you want to enter into life, obey the mitzvot (commandments)."

"Which ones?" He asked, his breathing starting to slow.

Yeshua replied: "You shall not murder, you shall not commit ni'uf (adultery), you shall not steal, you shall not bear false witness, honor your father and mother, and you shall love your neighbor as yourself."

The young man said: "All these I have obeyed from my youth. What do I still lack?"

Yeshua looked at him and loved him and said: "There is one thing you still lack. If you want to be perfect, go and sell what you have and give to the poor—and you will have treasure in the heavens. Then come, follow me." But when the young man heard this, he became exceedingly sorrowful and went away grieving, for he was very rich.

Yeshua looked around and said to his talmidim: "How hard it is for those who have wealth to enter into the Malchut Elohim (Kingdom of God)!" The talmidim were amazed at his words. But Yeshua continued: "Children, how hard it is to enter the Malchut of Elohim! It is easier for a camel to go through the eye of a needle than for a rich man to enter into the Malchut of Elohim."

They were utterly astonished and said to one another: "Who then can be saved?"

Yeshua looked at them and said: "With men this is impossible, but with Elohim all things are possible."

Then Kefa (Peter) said: "Look, we have left everything and followed you. What then will there be for us?"

Yeshua said to them: "Amen, I say to you: in the renewal (techiyah), when the Ben Adam (Son of Man) sits on the throne of his glory, you who have followed me will also sit on twelve thrones, judging the twelve tribes of Yisrael. And everyone who has left houses or brothers or sisters or father or mother or wife or children or fields for my name's sake and for the sake of the Malchut, will receive a hundredfold and will inherit chayei olam (eternal life). But many who are first will be last, and the last will be first."

The Parable of the Laborers in the Vineyard   Matthew 20:1–16

Then Yeshua said: "The Malchut HaShamayim (Kingdom of Heaven) is like a landowner who went out early in the morning to hire laborers for his vineyard. After agreeing with the workers for a denarius for the day, he sent them into his vineyard. Then he went out around the third hour (mid-morning) and saw others standing idle in the marketplace. He said to them, 'You go also into the vineyard, and I will give you whatever is right.' So, they went.

Again, he went out around the sixth and ninth hour and did the same. Around the eleventh hour (late afternoon), he found others still standing and said to them, 'Why have you been standing here all day doing nothing?' They said to him, 'Because no one has hired us.' He said to them, 'You also go into the vineyard.'"

As the sun dipped toward the horizon and the day's labors came to an end, the hush of anticipation settled over the vineyard. The laborers stood in rows, sweat-streaked and weary, waiting for their wages, each calculating what they believed they deserved. But the master's ways were not the ways of men.

"When evening came, the master of the vineyard said to his foreman: 'Call the laborers and pay them their wages, starting with the last and ending with the first.' Those who were hired at the eleventh hour came and each received a denarius. So, when those hired first came, they expected more — but they also received a denarius. When they received it, they grumbled against the landowner, saying: 'These last worked only one hour, and you have made them equal to us, who bore the burden and heat of the day!'

But he answered one of them: 'Chaver (friend), I am doing you no wrong. Did you not agree with me about a denarius? Take what is yours and go. I choose to give this last the same as to you. Am I not permitted to do what I want with what is mine? Or is your eye evil because I am good?' So, the last will be first, and the first last."

Yeshua Foretells His Suffering and Resurrection   Matthew 20:17–19 | Mark 10:32–34 | Luke 18:31–34

They were on the road, going up to Yerushalayim, and Yeshua was walking ahead of them. The talmidim (disciples) were astonished, and those who followed were afraid. Then Yeshua took the twelve aside privately and said to them: "Behold, we are going up to Yerushalayim, and everything that has been written by the nevi'im (prophets) about the Son of Man will be fulfilled. He will be delivered over to the chief kohanim (priests) and the soferim (scribes), and they will condemn him to death and hand him over to the goyim (Gentiles).

"They will mock him, spit upon him, flog him, and kill him. And on the third day, he will be raised." But the talmidim understood none of these things—the saying was hidden from them, and they did not grasp what was spoken. Though his face was set toward Yerushalayim, Yeshua's heart bore the full weight of what awaited him. Yet, with steady steps, he pressed forward—the Lamb ascending toward the altar—while those around him struggled to comprehend the mystery unfolding before their eyes.

Honor in the Kingdom   Matthew 20:20–28 | Mark 10:35–45

Then the mother of the sons of Zavdai (Zebedee) came to Yeshua with her sons, Yaakov (James) and Yochanan (John). She bowed before him and asked something from him. Yeshua said to her: "What do you want?"

Bowing with her face to the ground, She said: "Say that these two sons of mine may sit, one at your right hand and one at your left, in your Malchut (Kingdom)."

Then Yaakov and Yochanan themselves came forward and knelt before him and said: "Rabbi, we want you to do for us whatever we ask."

Yeshua said to them: "What do you want me to do for you?"

They said to him with desire and devotion in their eyes: "Grant that we may sit, one on your right and one on your left, in your glory."

Yeshua said to them: "You do not know what you are asking. Are you able to drink the kos (cup) that I am about to drink, or to be immersed with the immersion I am immersed with?"

They said to him confidently in unison: "We are able."

Yeshua said to them: "You will indeed drink my kos and be immersed with the immersion I am immersed with. But to sit at my right and at my left is not mine to grant, but it is for those for whom it has been prepared by my Father."

When the ten heard about this, they became indignant with Yaakov and Yochanan. Then Yeshua called them all together and said: "You know that the rulers of the nation's exercise dominion over them, and their great ones wield authority over them. But it shall not be so among you. Instead, whoever wishes to become great among you must be your shamash (servant), and whoever wishes to be first among you must be your eved (slave). For even the Son of Man did not come to be served, but to serve, and to give his life as a kofer (ransom) for many.

<u>The ambition of Yaakov and Yochanan revealed a common yearning among men — to be lifted high in the eyes of others. But Yeshua's path led downward: into suffering, into servanthood, into the very heart of redemption. Greatness in the Malchut Elohim is not about thrones, but about pouring out one's life for others.</u>

Yeshua Heals the Blind Men Near Yericho
Matthew 20:29–34 | Mark 10:46–52 | Luke 18:35–43

As Yeshua was approaching Yericho, a blind man named Bar-Timai ("son of Timai") was sitting by the roadside, begging. He was one of two blind men seated there, waiting for help in the dust of the roadside. When he heard the noise of the crowd passing by, he asked what was happening. They told him: "Yeshua haNotzri (Jesus of Nazareth) is passing by."

Then Bar-Timai cried out, saying: "Yeshua, Ben David, have rachamim (mercy) on us!" The cry came from deep within him — raw, desperate, insistent.

But the crowd rebuked him and those with him, telling them harshly to be silent. They scolded him like an unwanted noise in a holy procession.

Yet he cried out all the more: "Ben David, have rachamim on us!" His voice broke through the resistance, louder, bolder — full of hope that refused to be silenced.

Yeshua stopped. At that moment, all movement seemed to halt, the crowd shifting and whispering. He commanded that the blind men be called to him.

They called to Bar-Timai, saying: "Take courage! Rise — he is calling for you."

Throwing off his cloak, Bar-Timai sprang up and went quickly to Yeshua guided by one of the disciples.

Yeshua said to him: "What do you want me to do for you?"

Bar-Timai said plainly, without hesitation: "Rabbi, that I may regain my sight."

Yeshua said to him: "Receive your sight. Your emunah (faith) has made you whole." Immediately, Bar-Timai received his sight — and so did his companion. They followed Yeshua on the way, glorifying Elohim. And when all the people saw this, they gave praise to Elohim as well.

Zakkai the Chief Moches Welcomes the Master
Luke 19:1–10

Yeshua entered Yericho and was passing through the city. Now there was a man there named Zakkai (Zacchaeus). He was a chief moches (chief tax collector), and he was wealthy. Zakkai was trying to see who Yeshua was, but he could not because of the crowd, since he was short in stature.

He jumped and craned his neck, but the sea of people blocked his view at every turn. So, he ran ahead and climbed a sycamore-fig tree in order to see him, because Yeshua was about to pass that way. His heart pounded with each branch he climbed, his hands gripping the rough bark — he would not miss this moment to catch a glimpse of a well-known prophet since one has not been known to work such miracles for hundreds of years. Zakkai knew the importance of this time in history and this prophet Yeshua.

When Yeshua came to the place, he looked up and said to him: "Zakkai, hurry and come down! For today I must stay at your house." His voice was warm and firm, as if he had been waiting for this encounter all along.

So, he hurried down and welcomed him with joy. Zakkai's face beamed with disbelief and delight as he scrambled down from the tree, brushing leaves, bark and dust from his tunic. When the crowd saw this, they all grumbled, saying: "He has gone in to be the guest of a man who is a sinner." Their voices were thick with contempt, murmuring through clenched teeth as they looked upon the despised tax collector.

But Zakkai stood and said to the Master: "Behold, Adoni, I give half of my possessions to the poor, and if I have defrauded anyone of anything, I repay them fourfold." His voice trembled with conviction, arms outstretched, not seeking pity — only justice and mercy.

Yeshua said to him: "Today yeshuah (deliverance) has come to this house, because he too is a son of Avraham. For the Son of Man came to seek and to save that which was lost." And in that moment, the house of a sinner became a dwelling place of divine restoration.

The Parable of the Minas   Luke 19:11–27

As they heard these things, Yeshua went on to speak a mashal (parable), because he was near Yerushalayim, and they supposed that the Malchut Elohim (Kingdom of God) was about to appear immediately. The crowd listened with anticipation, their hearts aflame with expectation — surely now the Kingdom would break forth.

So, he said: "A nobleman went to a distant land to receive for himself kingly authority and then return. He called ten of his avadim (servants), gave them each a mina (a unit of silver worth about three months' wages), and said to them: 'Conduct business until I return.'

But his citizens hated him and sent a delegation after him, saying: 'We do not want this man to reign over us.' After receiving the kingdom and returning, he called the servants to whom he had given the money, so he might know what each had gained by trading. The first came and said: 'Master, your mina has produced ten minas.'

He said to him: 'Well done, good servant! Because you have been faithful in a very little, you shall have authority over ten cities.'

The second came and said: 'Your mina has made five minas.'

He said to him: 'You shall also rule over five cities.'

Another came and said: 'Master, here is your mina, which I kept laid away in a cloth. I was afraid of you, because you are a harsh man. You take what you did not deposit and reap what you did not sow.'

He said to him: 'Out of your own mouth I judge you, wicked servant! You knew that I am a harsh man, taking what I did not deposit and reaping what I did not sow? Then why didn't you put my money in the bank, so that at my coming I might have collected it with interest?'

Then he said to those standing by: 'Take the mina from him and give it to the one who has ten minas.'

They said to him: 'Master, he already has ten minas!'

He replied: 'I tell you, to everyone who has, more will be given. But from the one who does not have, even what he has will be taken away. But as for those enemies of mine who did not want me to reign over them — bring them here and slaughter them before me.''

The Raising of El'azar   John 11:1–44

Now a man named El'azar (Lazarus) was sick. He was from Beit-Anyah (Bethany), the village of Miryam (Mary) and her sister Marta (Martha). It was this Miryam who had anointed the Master with oil and wiped his feet with her hair, and El'azar was her brother. So, the sisters sent word to Yeshua, saying: "Master, the one you love is sick." The message was short, but the weight of sorrow behind it was heavy — spoken between tears and choked hope.

When Yeshua heard this, he said, "This sickness is not unto death, but for the glory of Elohim, so that the Ben Elohim (Son of God) may be glorified through it." Though his tone was calm, there was a spark of something unshakable behind his words — not denial, but certainty.

Yeshua loved Marta and her sister and El'azar. Yet when he heard that El'azar was sick, he remained where he was two more days. Then he said to his talmidim: "Let us go to Yehudah again."

They said to him: "Rabbi, the Yehudim there were just now seeking to stone you — and you are going back?" Their voices rose with anxiety, the danger still fresh in their minds.

Yeshua answered: "Are there not twelve hours in the day? If anyone walks during the day, he does not stumble, because he sees the light of this world. But if one walks in the night, he stumbles, because the light is not in him." Then he said: "Our friend El'azar has fallen asleep, but I go to wake him."

The talmidim said: "Master, if he has fallen asleep, he will recover."

But Yeshua had spoken about his death, while they thought he was talking about natural sleep. So, Yeshua told them plainly: "El'azar has died. And for your sakes I am glad I was not there, so that you may believe. But let us go to him."

Then T'oma (Thomas), called the Twin, said to the others: "Let us also go, that we may die with him." His voice was weary but loyal — resigned to danger, unwilling to leave the Master alone.

When Yeshua arrived, he found that El'azar had already been in the tomb four days. Now Beit-Anyah was near Yerushalayim, about two miles away, and many of the Yehudim had come to Marta and Miryam to comfort them. The house was filled with mourning — the hushed murmur of prayers, the weeping of friends, the weight of finality.

When Marta heard that Yeshua was coming, she went out to meet him, but Miryam stayed seated in the house. Marta said to Yeshua: "Master, if you had been here, my brother would not have died. But even now I know that whatever you ask of Elohim, He will give you." Her voice was filled with pleading grief and tears streamed from her eyes.

Yeshua said to her in a calming tone: "Your brother will rise again."

Marta replied wiping tears from her eyes: "I know that he will rise again in the resurrection on the last day."

Yeshua said to her: "I am the resurrection and the life. The one who believes in me will live, even though he dies. And everyone who lives and believes in me will never die. Do you believe this?"

Her voice quivering slightly, she said: "Yes, Master, I believe that you are the Mashiach, the Ben Elohim, the one coming into the world." After she said this, she went and called her sister Miryam secretly, saying: "The Master is here and is calling for you." When she heard this, she rose quickly and went to him. Now Yeshua had not yet come into the village but was still at the place where Marta met him.

The Yehudim who were with Miryam in the house, consoling her, saw her get up quickly and followed Marta, and they thought: "She is going to the tomb to weep there."

When Miryam came to where Yeshua was, she fell at his feet clinging to them, sobs shaking her body and said: "Master, if you had been here, my brother would not have died."

When Yeshua saw her weeping, and the Yehudim with her also weeping, he was deeply moved in spirit and troubled. The grief of his friends pierced him — their pain became his pain. His soul trembled with compassion and sorrow. He said: "Where have you laid him?"

They said to him: "Master, come and see."

Yeshua wept. So, the Yehudim said: "See how he loved him!"

But some of them said: "Could not he who opened the eyes of the blind have also kept this man from dying?"

Then Yeshua, again deeply moved, came to the tomb. It was a cave, and a stone lay against it. The place was still, the air heavy with grief and expectation. Yeshua said: "Take away the stone."

Marta, the sister of the dead man, said: "Master, by now he stinks, for he has been dead four days." Her voice trembled — caught between faith and the finality of death's stench.

Yeshua said to her: "Did I not tell you that if you believed, you would see the glory of Elohim?"

So, the crowds put cloth to their noises while they took away the stone. The grating sound of the stone echoed against the walls. Yet to their surprise there was no stench that came from the tomb.

Yeshua lifted up his eyes and said: "Father, I thank You that You have heard me. I knew that You always hear me, but I said this for the sake of the crowd standing around so that they may believe that You sent me." Then with a loud voice, Yeshua cried out: "El'azar, come out!" The voice thundered with authority — shaking the stillness of death.

And the man who had died came out — his hands and feet bound with linen strips, and his face wrapped with a cloth. Yeshua said to them: "Unbind him and let him go." And so, the dead walked again — not by the power of men, but by the voice of the Resurrection.

Chapter 15 The Countdown to Passover

The Plot to Kill Yeshua   John 11:45–57

Many of the Yehudim who had come to Miryam and seen what Yeshua did believed in him. But some of them went to the Perushim (Pharisees) and told them what Yeshua had done. Then the chief kohanim and the Perushim gathered a Sanhedrin council and said: "What are we doing? For this man is performing many signs! If we let him go on like this, everyone will believe in him, and the Romans will come and take away both our Mikdash (Temple) and our nation!"

But Kayafa (Caiaphas), who was Kohen Gadol (High Priest) that year, said to them: "You know nothing at all! Nor do you consider that it is better for us that one man should die for the people, rather than the whole nation perish." His voice cut through the chaos cold, strategic, calculated. He did not say this on his own, but being Kohen Gadol that year, he prophesied that Yeshua was about to die for the nation — and not only for that nation, but also to gather together into one the children of Elohim who are scattered abroad. Though he meant it politically, his words bore a truth deeper than he knew — spoken by the Spirit through a man unaware of the weight of his own tongue.

So, from that day on, they plotted to put him to death. The decision was sealed — whispered behind closed doors, sharpened like a blade in the shadows. Therefore, Yeshua no longer walked openly among the Yehudim but withdrew from there to a region near the wilderness, to a town called Efrayim. There he remained with his talmidim.

The Atoning Power of the Righteous
Source: Talmud Bavli – Moed Katan 28a
"**Just as the Red Heifer brings atonement, so too the death of the righteous brings atonement. Just as the priestly garments bring atonement, so too the death of the righteous brings atonement.**"
In this passage, the sages noticed a pattern in the Torah. The death of **Miriam** is placed next to the laws of the **Red Heifer**, and the death of **Aharon** is placed next to the laws of the **priestly garments**. Both the Red Heifer and the garments are described elsewhere in the Torah as means of kapparah — atonement. From this, the rabbis taught that the **death of the righteous** also has an atoning power for the community.
This is not because the tzaddik dies in place of others like a sacrificial offering, but because the passing of the righteous awakens repentance, inspires fear of Heaven, and invokes divine mercy — restoring spiritual balance to the people.
Connection to the Gospel Narrative:
When Kayafa, the Kohen Gadol (High Priest), declared:
"It is better that one man should die on behalf of the people, so that the whole nation does not perish,"
he spoke more than he understood. Though motivated by political strategy, his words reflected a timeless spiritual principle: that the **suffering or death of a tzaddik can bring national redemption**.
In the case of Yeshua, this Talmudic teaching gives a **Jewish context** to his suffering — not as a foreign idea, but as one deeply rooted in the Torah and affirmed by Chazal. Just as the deaths of Miriam and Aharon brought merit to Israel, so too does the death of a righteous one stir heavenly mercy and offer a path of atonement.

Now the Pesach (Passover) of the Yehudim was near, and many went up to Yerushalayim from the countryside to purify themselves before the feast. The city swelled with pilgrims and animals, the scent of livestock and incense thick in the air, the tension mounting unseen beneath the celebrations. They were looking for Yeshua, and as they stood in the Temple, they said to one another: "What do you think? That he won't come to the festival at all?" The whispers passed from mouth to mouth like sparks in dry grass — questions laced with both wonder and dread. Now the chief kohanim and Perushim have given orders: If anyone knew where he was, he should report it, so that they might arrest him.

Nisan 8 – Wednesday night into Thursday, April 18–19, 31 CE

Miryam Anoints Yeshua's Feet   John 12:1–11

Six days before Pesach (Passover), Yeshua came to Beit-Anyah (Bethany), where El'azar (Lazarus) lived—the one whom he had raised from the dead. The memory of the miracle still clung to the village like the scent of incense lingering after a festival. They prepared supper for him there. Marta (Martha) was serving, and El'azar was reclining at the table with him. Then Miryam (Mary) took a pound of very costly nard perfume—pure and fragrant—and anointed the feet of Yeshua, wiping them with her hair. The house was filled with the aroma of the perfume.

But Yehudah Ish-Keriot (Judas Iscariot), one of Yeshua's talmidim—the one who was about to betray him—said exasperatedly: "Why wasn't this perfume sold for three hundred denarii and given to the poor?"

Yeshua in a calm voice said: "Leave her alone. She kept this for the day of my burial. For the poor you always have with you, but me you do not always have."

A large crowd from among the Yehudim (Judeans) heard that Yeshua was there, and they came—not only because of him, but also to see El'azar, whom he had raised from the dead. Curiosity burned in them. Was it true? Had the grave really surrendered a man to this rabbi? So, the chief kohanim (priests) plotted to put El'azar to death also, because on account of him many of the Yehudim were withdrawing and trusting in Yeshua.

Nisan 9 – Friday, April 20, 31 CE The Triumphal Entry

Yeshua Enters Yerushalayim   Matthew 21:1–11 Mark 11:1–10 | Luke 19:29–40 | John 12:12–15

As Yeshua approached Yerushalayim, coming near to Beit-Phageh and Beit-Anyah at the Mount of Olives, he sent two of his talmidim (disciples). Yeshua said to them: "Go into the village ahead of you, and as you enter it, you will find a donkey tied there with her colt beside her. Untie them and bring them to me. If anyone asks you, 'Why are you untying it?' say, 'The Master has need of it and will return it soon.'"

The talmidim went and found everything just as Yeshua had said. As they were untying the colt, its owners asked them: "Why are you untying the colt?"

The talmidim replied: "The Master has need of it."

They brought the donkey and the colt to Yeshua. They laid their cloaks on them, and Yeshua sat upon the colt. This happened to fulfill what was said by the prophet: "Say to Bat Tziyon (Daughter of Zion), Behold, your king comes to you, humble and riding on a donkey, on a colt, the foal of a donkey." (Zechariah 9:9)

As he rode along, many spread their cloaks on the road, and others cut branches from the trees and spread them out. The whole crowd of talmidim began to rejoice and praise Elohim with a loud voice for all the mighty works they had seen, saying: "Hoshana, to the Son of David! Barukh haba b'shem Adonai! (Blessed is he who comes in the name of Adonai!) Blessed is the coming kingdom of our father David! Hoshana in the highest!"

Some of the Prushim (Pharisees) in the crowd said to him: "Rabbi, rebuke your talmidim!"

Yeshua answered: "I tell you, if these were silent, the stones would cry out."

When he entered Yerushalayim, the whole city was stirred, asking: "Who is this?"

And the crowds were saying: "This is the Navi (prophet) Yeshua, from Natzeret in the Galil."

Yeshua Weeps Over Yerushalayim and Enters the Temple   Luke 19:41–44 | Mark 11:11

As Yeshua came near and saw the city of Yerushalayim, he wept over it and said: "If only you had known, even now, the things that would bring you shalom! But now they are hidden from your eyes. For the days will come upon you when your enemies build a siege ramp around you, surround you, and hem you in on every side. They will raze you to the ground—you and your children within your walls—and they will not leave one stone upon another, because you did not recognize the time of your visitation."

Then Yeshua entered Yerushalayim and went into the Beit HaMikdash (Temple). He looked around at everything. His eyes moved slowly across the colonnades and courts — taking in the spiritual state of the House that bore his Father's Name. He saw the merchants preparing their wares. He heard the low murmur of business in the holy place. But since it was already late in the day, he went out with the twelve back to Beit-Anyah.

Nisan 10 – Shabbat, April 21, 31 CE Cleansing the Temple

The Cursed Fig Tree and the Cleansing of the Temple   Matthew 21:18–27 | Mark 11:12–19 | Luke 19:45–48

The next morning, as Yeshua and his talmidim (disciples) were coming from Beit-Anyah, he became hungry. He saw a fig tree in the distance with leaves, and he approached it to see if he might find any fruit on it. But when he reached it, he found nothing but leaves, for it was not the season for figs. Yeshua said to the tree: "May no one ever eat fruit from you again." And his talmidim heard him say it.

Then they came to Yerushalayim, and Yeshua headed straight towards the Temple with determination in his steps and righteous anger in his eyes. He entered the Beit HaMikdash (Temple) and he immediately began to drive out those who were buying and selling there. He overturned the tables of the moneychangers causing the coins to fly across the floor. He overturned the benches of those selling doves causing the doves to fly free. He would not allow anyone to carry merchandise through the Temple courts. Yeshua rebuked them, saying: "It is written, Beiti beit tefillah yikarei l'chol ha'amim (My House shall be called a House of Prayer for all nations), but you have made it a me'arat peritzim (den of robbers)!" (Isaiah 56:7, Jeremiah 7:11)

Nisan 11 – Sunday, April 22, 31 CE The Withered Fig Tree

The Withered Fig Tree and Question of Authority   Matthew 21:18–27 | Luke 20:1–8

The next morning, as they were returning to Yerushalayim from Beit-Anyah, Yeshua and his talmidim (disciples) passed by the fig tree that he had cursed the previous day. They saw that it had withered from the roots up. Kefa (Peter) remembered and said in a shocked voice his eyes wide: "Rabbi, look! The fig tree that you cursed has withered!"

Yeshua answered them nonchalantly: "Have emunah (faith) in Elohim. Amein, I tell you, whoever says to this mountain, 'Be lifted up and thrown into the sea,' and does not doubt in his heart but believes that what he says will happen—it will be done for him. Therefore, I say to you, whatever you ask in tefillah (prayer), believe that you have received it, and it will be yours. And whenever you stand praying, if you hold anything against anyone, forgive him, so that your Father in heaven may forgive you your offenses."

With the Gentile court free of the animals and the merchants, blind and lame people came to him in the Temple, and he healed them. But when the chief priests and Torah scholars saw the wonders he performed and the children shouting in the Temple courts, "Hoshana to Ben-David (Son of David)!" they became indignant. They said to him: "Do you hear what these children are saying?"

Yeshua said to them: "Yes. Have you never read, From the mouth of infants and nursing babies, you have prepared praise for yourself?"— (Psalm 8:2)

They came again to Yerushalayim, and as Yeshua was walking in the Temple courts, the chief kohanim (priests), scribes, and elders came to him and said: "By what authority are you doing these things? Who gave you this authority?"

Yeshua answered them: "I will also ask you one question. If you answer me, then I will tell you by what authority I do these things. The tevilah (immersion) of Yochanan—was it from Shamayim (Heaven) or from men? Answer me."

They reasoned among themselves: "If we say, 'From Shamayim,' he will say, 'Then why didn't you believe him?' But if we say, 'From men,' all the people will stone us, because they are convinced Yochanan was a navi (prophet)." So, they answered: "We do not know."

Yeshua replied: "Then neither will I tell you by what authority I do these things."

The Parable of the Two Sons   Matthew 21:28–32

Yeshua asked: "What do you think? A man had two sons. He went to the first and said, 'Son, go work in the vineyard today.' The son answered, 'I will not,' but later changed his mind and went. Then the man went to the second and said the same. The second son answered, 'I will go, sir,' but did not go. Which of the two did the will of the father?"

They answered: "The first."

Yeshua said to them: "Amen, I tell you: the tax collectors and zonot (prostitutes) are entering the Malchut Elohim (Kingdom of God) before you. For Yochanan came to you in the way of tzedek (righteousness), and you did not believe him. But the tax collectors and prostitutes did. And even after seeing that, you still did not repent and believe him."

The Parable of the Wicked Tenants Matthew 21:33–46 | Mark 12:1–12 | Luke 20:9–19

Yeshua said: "Hear another mashal (parable): A man planted a vineyard, put a fence around it, dug a winepress, and built a tower. Then he rented it to farmers and went away. At harvest time, he sent a servant to collect his share of the fruit. But the tenants beat him and sent him away empty-handed. He sent another servant, and they struck him on the head and treated him shamefully. He sent many others—some they beat, others they killed. Last of all, he sent his beloved son, saying, 'They will respect my son.' But the tenants said to one another, 'This is the heir. Come, let us kill him and seize his inheritance.' So, they seized him, threw him out of the vineyard, and killed him. What then will the owner of the vineyard do?"

They answered: "He will come and destroy those tenants and give the vineyard to others."

Yeshua looked at them and said: "Have you never read this Scripture? The stone the builders rejected has become the cornerstone; This is from Adonai, and it is wondrous in our eyes." (Psalm 118:22–23)

Yeshua continued: "Therefore, I say to you: the Malchut Elohim will be taken away from you and given to a people producing its fruit. Whoever falls on this stone will be broken to pieces, but anyone on whom it falls—it will crush him."

When the chief priests and Prushim heard the mashal, they realized he was speaking about them. They sought to arrest him but feared the crowd, because the people regarded him as a navi (prophet).

The Parable of the Wedding Banquet Matthew 22:1–14

Yeshua gave another mashal: "The Malchut HaShamayim (Kingdom of Heaven) is like a king who prepared a wedding banquet for his son. He sent servants to call those invited to the feast, but they refused to come. He sent other servants, saying, 'Tell those invited: I have prepared my banquet—oxen and fattened cattle have been slaughtered; everything is ready. Come to the feast.' But they ignored the invitation and went away—one to his field, another to his business. Others seized his servants, mistreated them, and killed them.

The king was enraged. He sent his army, destroyed those murderers, and burned their city. Then he said to his servants, 'The banquet is ready, but those invited were not worthy. Go to the street corners and invite everyone you find.' So, the servants went out and gathered all they could find—both bad and good—and the banquet hall was filled with guests.

But when the king came to see the guests, he noticed a man there who was not wearing wedding clothes. He said to him, 'Friend, how did you get in here without wedding garments?' The man was speechless. Then the king said, 'Bind him hand and foot, throw him outside into the outer darkness, where there will be weeping and gnashing of teeth.' For many are called, but few are chosen."

Paying Taxes to Caesar Matthew 22:15–22 | Mark 12:13–17 | Luke 20:20–26

The Prushim (Pharisees) and Herodians plotted together how they might trap Yeshua in his words. So, they sent spies, pretending to be sincere, to catch him in something he said and hand him over to the authority of the governor. The spies asked him: "Rabbi, we know that you speak and teach rightly and show no partiality but teach the way of Elohim in truth. Is it lawful to pay taxes to Caesar, or not?"

But Yeshua perceived their craftiness and said: "Why are you testing me, you hypocrites? Show me the denarius used for the tax." They brought him a denarius. He examined the coin flipping it over in his hand and he asked: "Whose image and inscription is this?"

They said: "Caesar's."

Yeshua said to them: "Then give to Caesar what is Caesar's, and to Elohim what is Elohim's." They marveled at his answer and were silent.

Question About the Resurrection Matthew 22:23–33 | Mark 12:18–27 | Luke 20:27–40

Then some of the Tzedukim (Sadducees), who say there is no resurrection, came to Yeshua with a question: "Rabbi, Moshe wrote for us that if a man dies childless, his brother must marry the widow and raise up offspring for him. There were seven brothers. The first married and died without children. The second did the same, and so on through the seventh. Last of all, the woman died. In the resurrection, whose wife will she be, since all seven were married to her?"

Yeshua shaking his head with a smirk answered them: "You are mistaken, because you do not know the Scriptures or the power of Elohim. For you see, the children of the resurrection neither marry nor are they given in marriage, but they are like the malakhim (angels) in heaven. And concerning the resurrection of the dead have you not read what was spoken to you by Elohim: 'I am the Elohim of Avraham, the Elohim of Yitzchak, and the Elohim of Yaakov?' He is not the Elohim of the dead, but of the living for all live to Him." The crowd was astonished at his teaching.

The Greatest Commandment   Matthew 22:34–40 | Mark 12:28–34

When the P'rushim heard that he had silenced the Sadducees, one of them who was a Torah scholar asked: "Rabbi, which mitzvah is the greatest in the Torah?"

Yeshua said: "Ve'ahavta et Adonai Elohekha — You shall love Adonai your Elohim with all your heart, with all your soul, and with all your mind. This is the first and greatest mitzvah. And the second is like it: Ve'ahavta l're'akha kamokha — You shall love your neighbor as yourself. On these two mitzvot hang all the Torah and the Nevi'im (Prophets)."

The scholar replied nodding his head in acknowledgement: "Well said, Rabbi. You have spoken truthfully, for there is one Elohim, and besides Him there is no other. To love Him with all the heart and to love one's neighbor as oneself is more than all burnt offerings and sacrifices."

Yeshua said to him approvingly with a smile on his face: "You are not far from the Malchut Elohim."

Whose Son Is the Mashiach?   Matthew 22:41–46 | Mark 12:35–37 | Luke 20:41–44

As the P'rushim were gathered, Yeshua decided to test them: "What do you think about the Mashiach? Whose son is he?"

They answered: "Ben-David." (The son of David)

Yeshua said to them: "How is it then that David, by the Ruach HaKodesh (Holy Spirit), calls him 'Adon,' saying: The LORD said to Adoni, Sit at my right hand until I make your enemies your footstool?
If David calls him 'Adon,' how is he his son?"

No one was able to answer him a word, and from that day on no one dared to question him further.

Yeshua Warns Against Hypocrisy   Matthew 23:1–12

Then Yeshua spoke to the crowds and to his talmidim, saying: "The Torah scholars and the P'rushim sit on Mosheh's seat. They have the smicha authority straight from Mosheh just as Elisha had Eliyahu's authority and my Shlichim have mine, so whatever the Prushim tell you to do, do and observe, `but do not act according to their deeds. For they say things but do not do them. They tie up heavy burdens, hard to bear, and lay them on people's shoulders, but they themselves are unwilling to lift a finger to help.

All their works they do to be seen by others: they broaden their tefillin and lengthen the tassels of their garments. They love the place of honor at feasts, the best seats in the synagogues, respectful greetings in the marketplaces, and to be called 'Rabbi' by others.

But you are not to be called 'Rabbi,' for you have one Rabbi, and you are all brothers. Do not call anyone on earth your 'father,' for you have one Father—your Av shebashamayim (Father in heaven). Do not be called instructors either, for you have one Instructor—the Mashiach. The greatest among you will be your servant. Whoever exalts himself will be humbled, and whoever humbles himself will be exalted."

Woes Upon the Torah Scholars and P'rushim　　　　　　　　　Matthew 23:13–36 | Mark 11:18-19

Then Yeshua declared: "Woe (Oy) to you, Torah scholars and P'rushim, hypocrites! You shut the gates of the Malchut HaShamayim (Kingdom of Heaven) in people's faces—you do not enter yourselves, and you prevent others from entering. You travel across sea and land to make a single proselyte, and when you do, you make him twice as much a son of Gehinnom as yourselves. Teaching them the Words of Elohim but then failing to teach them how to keep and obey them.

You say, 'If anyone swears by the Temple, it is nothing, but if anyone swears by the gold of the Temple, he is bound.' Blind fools! Which is greater—the gold or the Temple that sanctifies the gold? You say, 'If anyone swears by the altar, it means nothing, but whoever swears by the gift on it is obligated.' Blind men! Which is greater—the gift or the altar that makes the gift sacred?

You tithe mint, dill, and cumin, but have neglected the weightier matters of the Torah: mishpat (justice), chesed (mercy), and emunah (faithfulness). You should have done this without neglecting the others. Blind guides! Straining out a gnat and swallowing a camel.

You clean the outside of the cup and the dish, but inside they are full of greed and self-indulgence. First clean the inside, so the outside may be clean also. You are like whitewashed tombs—beautiful on the outside but full of dead men's bones and all uncleanness on the inside. You appear righteous to people but inside are full of hypocrisy and lawlessness.

Woe to you! You build tombs for the prophets and adorn the graves of the righteous, saying, 'If we had lived in the days of our ancestors, we would not have taken part in shedding the blood of the prophets.' So, you testify against yourselves—you are sons of those who murdered the prophets. Fill up, then, the measure of your fathers! You serpents, brood of vipers! How will you escape being condemned to Gehinnom?"

The chief kohanim (priests) and the Torah-teachers heard what Yeshua was doing, and they began seeking a way to destroy him. Yet they were afraid of him, because the entire crowd was amazed at his teaching and clung to him, listening intently. After healing the blind and lame in the Temple and responding to the children's praises, Yeshua left them. When evening came, he went out of the city with the twelve and returned to Beit-Anyah.

Lament Over Yerushalayim Matthew 23:37–39

Yeshua cried out: "O Yerushalayim, Yerushalayim, you who kill the prophets and stone those sent to you—how often I longed to gather your children together as a hen gathers her chicks under her wings, but you were not willing! Behold, your house is left to you desolate. For I tell you, you will not see me again until you say, Barukh haba b'shem Adonai (Blessed is he who comes in the name of Adonai)."

Beware the Show of the Torah Scholars Mark 12:38–40 | Luke 20:45–47

Yeshua said to the people: "Beware of the Torah scholars who like to walk around in long robes, who love greetings in the marketplaces, the best seats in the synagogues, and places of honor at banquets. They devour widows' houses and for a show make long prayers. These will receive a harsher judgment."

The Widow's Offering Mark 12:41–44 | Luke 21:1–4

Yeshua sat down opposite the treasury in the Beit HaMikdash (Temple), watching as the people were putting their gifts into the offering boxes. Many rich people came and gave large sums. Then a poor widow came and put in two small copper coins—perutot—worth only a few cents.

Yeshua called his disciples and said to them: "Amen, I tell you, this poor widow has put in more than all the others. For all of them gave from their excess, but she, in her poverty, gave all she had to live on."

Foretelling the Temple's Destruction Mark 13:1–2 | Matthew 24:1–2 | Luke 21:5–6

Later, as they were leaving the Temple, one of Yeshua's talmidim pointed to the massive stones that made up the Temple mount: "Rabbi, look at these magnificent stones and the splendid buildings!"

Yeshua replied: "Do you see all these great buildings? Amen, I tell you: the days will come when not one stone here will be left upon another. Everyone will be thrown down."

The Olivet Discourse: Signs of the End Matthew 24:3–14 | Mark 13:3–13 | Luke 21:7–19

Later that evening, Yeshua sat on the Mount of Olives, overlooking the Temple. His talmidim—Kefa (Peter), Yaakov (James), Yochanan (John), and Andrei (Andrew)—came to him privately wishing for the messianic kingdom to come soon and needing to know when it will happen. So they said to him: "Tell us, when will these things happen? What will be the sign of your coming and of the end of the age?"

Yeshua answered them: "Be careful that no one leads you astray. For many will come in my name, and saying, 'I am the anointed one (HaMashiach),' and they will deceive many. You will hear of wars and rumors of wars. See that you are not alarmed, for these things must happen, but the end is not yet. Nations will rise against nation, and kingdom against kingdom. There will be famines, plagues, and earthquakes in various places. These are only the beginning of birth pains.

Before all this, they will lay hands on you and persecute you, delivering you up to synagogues and prisons, bringing you before kings and governors for my name's sake. This will be a time for you to bear witness. Settle it in your heart not to prepare beforehand what to say, for I will give you a mouth and wisdom which none of your adversaries will be able to contradict.

You will be betrayed even by parents, brothers, relatives, and friends. Some of you will be put to death. You will be hated by all for my name's sake, but not a single hair of your head will perish. By your endurance, you will gain your souls."

The Fall of Yerushalayim　　　　　　　Luke 21:20–24 | Matthew 24:15–22 | Mark 13:14–20

Yeshua continued: "When you see Yerushalayim surrounded by armies, know that its desolation has drawn near. Then let those in Yehudah flee to the mountains; let those in the city get out and don't let those in the countryside enter. These are the days of vengeance, to fulfill all that has been written.

Woe to those who are pregnant or nursing in those days! Pray that your flight will not be in winter or on a Shabbat. For there will be great distress upon the land and wrath upon these people. They will fall by the edge of the sword and be led captive among the nations. Yerushalayim will be trampled by the Gentiles until the times of the Gentiles are fulfilled.

Then there will be great tribulation, such as has not been from the beginning of the world until now—nor ever will be. Unless those days were shortened, no flesh would be saved; but for the sake of the chosen (bechirim), those days will be shortened."

Warnings Against False Messiahs　　　　　　　Matthew 24:23–28 | Mark 13:21–23

Yeshua said: "If anyone says to you, 'Look! Here is the Mashiach!' or 'There he is!'—do not believe it.
For false messiahs and false prophets will arise, performing great signs and wonders, so as to deceive—even the elect, if possible.

Behold, I have told you beforehand. If they say, 'He is in the wilderness!' do not go out. Or 'He is in the inner rooms!'—do not believe it. For just as lightning flashes from the east and is seen even to the west, so will be the coming of the Son of Man (Ben Enosh). Wherever the carcass is, there the eagles will gather."

The Coming of the Son of Man   Matthew 24:29–31 | Mark 13:24–27 | Luke 21:25–28

Yeshua concluded: "Immediately after the tribulation of those days: The sun will be darkened, The moon will not give its light, The stars will fall from the sky, And the powers of the heavens will be shaken.

Then the sign of the Son of Man will appear in the heavens, and all the tribes of the earth will mourn.
They will see the Son of Man (Ben Enosh) coming on the clouds of the heavens with power and great glory.
And he will send his malakhim (messengers) with a great shofar blast, and they will gather his chosen ones from the four winds—from one end of the heavens to the other."

Yeshua added: "When these things begin to happen, stand up and lift your heads, because your geulah (redemption) draws near."

The Plot and the Betrayal of Yehudah   Matthew 26:1–5, 14–16 | Mark 14:1–2, 10–11 | Luke 22:1–6

When Yeshua had finished all these words, his tone changed and became somber and he said to his talmidim (disciples), "You know that after two days the Pesach (Passover) comes, and the Son of Man will be handed over to be executed."

Now the Chag hamotzi (Feast of Unleavened Bread), called the Pesach, was approaching. And the chief kohanim (priests) and the scribes and the elders of the people gathered together in the courtyard of the Kohen Gadol (High Priest), whose name was Kayafa (Caiaphas).
They were seeking a way to seize Yeshua by trickery and to kill him, but they were saying, "Not during the Moed (Festival), lest there be an uproar among the people."

Meanwhile, the Satan entered into Yehudah called Ish-Keriot (Judas Iscariot), who was numbered among the Twelve. He went and discussed with the chief kohanim and Temple officers how he might deliver Yeshua over to them. When they heard this, they were glad and rejoiced, and they agreed to give him silver—thirty pieces. From that moment on, Yehudah began seeking an opportunity to deliver Yeshua to them at a time when the crowd would not be present.

Monday Nisan 12 April 23, 31 CE The Plot to Kill Yeshua

The Anointing at Beit-Anyah Matthew 26:6–13 | Mark 14:3–9

While Yeshua was in Beit-Anyah (Bethany), in the house of Shimon the leper, as he was reclining at the table, a woman came to him with an alabaster jar of very expensive perfume made of pure nard. She broke the jar and poured it over his head as he reclined.

When the talmidim (disciples) saw this, they became indignant, saying, "Why this waste? This perfume could have been sold for more than three hundred denarii and given as tzedakah (charity) to the poor." And they began to scold her. For Yeshua had already been anointed once by Mariyam.

But Yeshua said, "Leave her alone. Why do you trouble her? She has done a beautiful thing for me. You always have the poor with you, and whenever you wish you can do good to them, but you will not always have me. She has done what she could. She has anointed my body beforehand for burial. Amen, I tell you: Wherever this besorah (good news) is proclaimed in the whole world, what she has done will also be told in memory of her."

Tuesday Nisan 13 April 24, 31 CE Yeshua's Final Public Sermon

The Son of Man Must Be Lifted Up John 12:20–50

Now there were some Greeks among those going up to worship at the feast. They came to Philip, who was from Beit-Tzaidah (Bethsaida) in Galil, and said, "Adon, we want to see Yeshua." Philip went and told Andrai (Andrew), and Andrew and Philip went and told Yeshua.

Yeshua answered them, saying: "The hour has come for the Son of Man to be glorified. Amen, amen I say to you: unless a grain of wheat falls to the ground and dies, it remains alone. But if it dies, it bears much fruit. Whoever loves his life will lose it, and whoever hates his life in this world will preserve it for eternal life. If anyone serves me, let him follow me—and where I am, there my servant will also be. Now my soul has become troubled. What shall I say—'Abba, save me from this hour'? But it was for this purpose I came to this hour. Abba, glorify Your Name."

Then a bat kol (heavenly voice) came from the heavens, saying, "I have glorified it, and will glorify it again."

The crowd standing there heard it and said it thundered; others said, "An angel has spoken to him."

Yeshua answered: "This voice came not for my sake but for yours. Now is the judgment of this world; now the ruler of this world will be thrown out. And I, when I am lifted up from the earth, will draw all people to myself." He said this to indicate the kind of death he was about to die.

The crowd responded: "We have heard from the Torah that the Mashiach (Messiah) remains forever. How can you say the Son of Man must be lifted up? Who is this Son of Man?"

Yeshua replied: "The light is with you a little while longer. Walk while you have the light, so that darkness will not overtake you. While you have the light, believe in the light, so that you may become bnei ha'or (children of light)."

After saying these things, Yeshua departed and hid himself from them. Even though Yeshua had performed so many signs, the people still did not believe in him. This fulfilled the word of Yeshayahu (Isaiah): "Adonai, who has believed our report?" (Isaiah 53:1) "He has blinded their eyes and hardened their hearts…" (Isaiah 6:10)

Yet many among the rulers believed in him, but because of the Perushim (Pharisees), they would not confess it, for fear of being put out of the synagogue. They loved the kavod (honor) of men more than the kavod of Elohim.

Yeshua cried out and said: "Whoever believes in me does not believe in me alone, but in the One who sent me. And whoever sees me sees the One who sent me. I have come as or le'olam (light into the world), so that no one who believes in me should remain in darkness.

I did not come to judge the world, but to save it. The one who rejects me and does not receive my words has a judge—the word I have spoken will judge him on the last day. For I did not speak on my own, but the Father who sent me has commanded me what to say and speak. And I know that His mitzvah (command) is eternal life. What I speak, therefore, I speak just as the Father has told me."

CHAPTER 16 Yeshua Spends Time with His Disciples

Preparing the Pesach   Matthew 26:17–19 | Mark 14:12–16 | Luke 22:7–13

Then came the day of matzot (unleavened bread), on which the Pesach lamb was to be slaughtered. The talmidim (disciples) came to Yeshua and said: "Where do you want us to go and prepare for you to eat the Pesach (Passover)?"

So, he sent Kefa (Peter) and Yochanan (John) and said to them: "Go into the city, and a man carrying a jar of water will meet you. Follow him into the house that he enters. Say to the owner of the house, 'The Rav (Teacher) says: My time is near. Where is the guest room where I may eat the Pesach with my talmidim?' He will show you a large upper room, furnished and ready. Prepare it there for us." The talmidim did as Yeshua instructed them and went into the city. They found it just as he had told them, and they prepared the Pesach.

Yeshua Washes His Disciples' Feet   Matthew 26:20 | Mark 14:17 | Luke 22:14–18, 24–27 | John 13:1–17

When evening came, Yeshua reclined at the table with the Twelve. He said to them, "I have earnestly desired to eat this Pesach with you before I suffer. For I say to you, I will not eat it again until it is fulfilled in the Malchut Elohim (Kingdom of God)."

A dispute arose among them about who was the greatest. Yeshua said, "The kings of the nation's dominate them, and those who have authority are called benefactors. But it shall not be so among you. Rather, the greatest among you must become like the youngest, and the one who leads like the one who serves. I am among you as one who serves." Then Yeshua rose from the meal, laid aside his outer garment, and took a towel. He poured water into a basin and began to wash the feet of his talmidim and dry them. Each of them watched in shock but remained silent as Yeshua washed their feet.

Kefa watched in shock as Yeshua washed each of their feet. When he came to Kefa (Peter), Kefa said, "Adon, are you going to wash my feet?"

Yeshua answered, "You do not understand now, but you will understand later."

Kefa said, "You will never wash my feet!"

Yeshua replied, "If I do not wash you, you have no part with me."

Kefa said, "Then not only my feet but also my hands and head!"

Yeshua said, "One who has bathed is completely clean. And you are clean—but not all of you." (For he knew who would betray him.)

After washing their feet, he reclined again and said: "Do you understand what I have done for you? You call me Rabbi and Adon, and rightly so. If I, your Rabbi and Adon, have washed your feet, you also ought to wash one another's feet. I have given you an example—that you should do as I have done for you."

The Betrayer is Revealed Matthew 26:20–25 | Mark 14:17–21 | Luke 22:14, 21–23 | John 13:21–35

As evening fell, Yeshua reclined with the twelve at the table. While they were eating, Yeshua became troubled in spirit, and he proclaimed in a somber tone, "Amen, amen, I say to you: one of you who is eating with me will betray me."

The talmidim (disciples) were deeply distressed, and they began to look at one another, uncertain of whom he spoke. One after another asked him: "Is it I, Adon?" They began to discuss among themselves which of them could be the one who would do this. Suspicion began to grow among the twelve they began to look at each other with distrust in their hearts.

One of the talmidim, the one whom Yeshua loved, was reclining at the table close to his side. Shimon Kefa (Simon Peter) needed clarity, so he looked to the one disciple who could never betray Yeshua—knowing the deep devotion he had for the Master. Kefa nodded to him to ask Yeshua who he meant.

So the beloved talmid leaned back against Yeshua's chest and asked: "Adon, who is it?"

Yeshua answered: "The hand of the one who is betraying me is with mine on the table. It is the one to whom I will give the morsel after I have dipped it. The Son of Man (Bar Enash) will go as it has been decreed—but woe to that man by whom he is betrayed! It would have been better for that man if he had never been born."

Then Yehudah, who would betray him, also asked: "Rabbi, is it I?"

Yeshua said: "You have said it." He dipped the morsel and gave it to Yehudah, son of Shim'on—the one called Ish Kriot (Judas Iscariot). Then Yeshua said to him: "What you are about to do—do quickly." After receiving the morsel, Satan entered into him. Yehudah immediately got up and went out into the night.

None of the others at the table understood why he said this. Since Yehudah had the money bag, some thought Yeshua was telling him to buy what was needed for the festival, or to give tzedakah (charity) to the poor. Still unaware of his intentions, they watched as he departed into the night.

Once he had gone out, Yeshua said: "Now the Son of Man is glorified, and Elohim is glorified in him.
Little children, I am with you only a little longer. You will seek me, and as I said to the Yehudim, so now I also say to you: 'Where I am going, you cannot come.' A new mitzvah I give you: love one another. Just as I have loved you, so you also must love one another. By this, all people will know that you are my talmidim—if you have love for one another."

The Covenant Meal Matthew 26:26–29 | Mark 14:22–25 | Luke 22:19–20

During the meal, Yeshua took matzah (unleavened bread), made a berakhah, broke it, and gave it to them, saying: "Take and eat; this is my body, broken and given for you. Eat and do this in memory of me."

Then he took the cup after the meal, made a berakhah, and gave it to them, saying: "Drink from it, all of you. This cup is the berit chadashah (new covenant) in my blood, which is poured out for many for the forgiveness of sins. I say to you, I will not drink again of the fruit of the vine until that day when I drink it new with you in my Father's Malchut (Kingdom)."

The Prediction of Betrayal Matthew 26:31–35 | Mark 14:27–31

Yeshua then said: "This night, all of you will fall away because of me. For it is written: 'I will strike the shepherd, and the sheep of the flock will be scattered.' But after I have been raised, I will go ahead of you into the Galil (Galilee)."

Kefa (Peter) declared: "Even if all fall away, I will never fall away!"

Yeshua replied: "Amen, I say to you: this very night, before the rooster crows, you will deny me three times."

Kefa insisted: "Even if I must die with you, I will never deny you." And all the talmidim said the same.

Comfort and the Way to the Father John 14:1–12

Yeshua said to them: "Let not your hearts be troubled. You have emunah (faith) in Elohim—have emunah also in me. In my Father's Beit (house) are many mishkenot (dwelling places). If it were not so, would I have told you that I am going to prepare a place for you? And if I go and prepare a place for you, I will come again and take you to myself, so that where I am, there you may be also. And you know the way to the place where I am going."

T'oma (Thomas) said to him: "Adon, we do not know where you are going. How can we know the way?"

Yeshua said: "I am the derekh (way), the emet (truth), and the chayim (life). No one comes to the Father except through me. If you have known me, you will also know my Father. From now on, you do know Him—and have seen Him."

Ha'Derekh	Ha'Emet	Ha'Chayim
*Deuteronomy 5:33 – "You shall walk in all the way (derekh) which Adonai your Elohim has commanded you, that you may live and that it may be well with you…" *Isaiah 30:21 – "This is the way (derekh), walk in it…"	*Psalm 119:142 – "Your righteousness is an everlasting righteousness, and Your Torah is truth (emet)." *Malachi 2:6 – "The Torah of truth (Torat emet) was in his mouth…" — referring	*Deuteronomy 30:15–16, 19–20 – "See, I have set before you today life (chayim) and good, death and evil… therefore choose life, that you and your seed may live, by loving Adonai your Elohim, by obeying His voice, and by clinging to Him…"

*Proverbs 6:23 – "The commandment is a lamp, and the Torah is light, and reproofs of discipline are the way (derekh) of life." Yeshua, as the living embodiment of Torah, walked this Derekh perfectly—halakhically, morally, spiritually. To follow him is to follow the Torah.	to the ideal priest who walks with Elohim. Yeshua's claim to be "the Emet" is a direct claim of being filled with, and faithful to, Torat Emet—the true instruction of Elohim.	*Proverbs 3:1–2 – "My son, do not forget my Torah… for length of days and years of life and peace they will add to you." Yeshua, in perfect Torah observance, embodied Chayim—the life that results from walking in covenantal obedience.

*Jeremiah 22:15–16 – "He judged the cause of the poor and needy… was not this to know Me? says Adonai."

*Hosea 4:6 – "My people are destroyed for lack of knowledge; because you have rejected knowledge, I reject you… seeing you have forgotten the Torah of your Elohim."

*Proverbs 2:5–6 – "Then you will understand the fear of Adonai and find the knowledge of Elohim. For Adonai gives wisdom; from His mouth come knowledge and understanding."

*Psalm 119:1–2 – "Blessed are those whose way is blameless, who walk in the Torah of Adonai… who seek Him with the whole heart."

In these passages, knowing Torah is equated with knowing Adonai—just as rejecting Torah is rejecting knowledge of Him. When Yeshua said: "I am the Derekh (Way), the Emet (Truth), and the Chayim (Life)… If you have known me, you will also know my Father."
He was not speaking apart from Torah, but directly within its framework. His listeners, familiar with the TaNaKh, would have understood this as a profound claim of perfect Torah embodiment. To know Yeshua is to know the Torah lived out in full covenantal obedience. And to know the Torah is to know the will and nature of the Father.

Philippos (Philip) said: "Adon, show us the Father—and that will be enough for us."

Yeshua replied: "Have I been with you so long, and you still do not know me, Philip? Whoever has seen me has seen the Father. How can you say, 'Show us the Father'? Don't you believe that I am in the Father, and the Father is in me? The words I say to you are not from myself, but the Father who dwells in me does His works. Believe me: I am in the Father and the Father is in me. Or at least believe it because of the works themselves. Amen, amen I tell you: whoever trusts me will also do the works I do. And greater than these he will do—because I go to the Father."

The Promise of the Advocate   John 14:13–24

Then Yeshua said: "Whatever you ask in my name, this I will do—so that the Father may be glorified in the Son. If you ask anything in my name, I will do it. If you love me, you will obey my mitzvot (commandments). And I will ask the Father, and He will give you another Melitz (Advocate)—the Ruach haEmet (Spirit of Truth)—to be with you forever. The world cannot receive Him because it neither sees nor knows Him. But you know Him, for He dwells with you and will be in you.

I will not leave you as orphans—I will come to you. In a little while, the world will see me no more, but you will see me. Because I live, you will also live. On that day, you will know that I am in my Father, and you in me, and I in you. The one who has my mitzvot and keeps them, he is the one who loves me. And the one who loves me will be loved by my Father, and I will love him and reveal myself to him."

Yehudah (not Ish-Keriot) said to him: "Adon, why is it that you will reveal yourself to us and not to the world?"

Yeshua answered: "If anyone loves me, he will obey my word, and my Father will love him, and we will come to him and make our dwelling with him. The one who does not love me does not keep my words. And the word you hear is not mine, but the Father's who sent me."

The Promise of Peace and the Coming Departure — John 14:25–31

Yeshua continued: "These things I have spoken to you while still with you. But the Melitz haKodesh (Holy Advocate), the Ruach haKodesh, whom the Father will send in my name, will teach you all things and remind you of everything I have said to you. Shalom I leave with you — my shalom I give to you. I do not give as the world gives. Let your heart not be troubled, and do not be afraid.

You heard me say, 'I am going away, and I am coming to you.' If you loved me, you would rejoice that I am going to the Father, for the Father is greater than I. I have told you now before it happens, so that when it does happen, you may believe. I will not speak with you much longer, for the ruler of this world is coming. He has no claim on me, but I do as the Father has commanded me, so that the world may know that I love the Father."

The Hallel and Departure from the Upper Room — Matthew 26:30 | Mark 14:26

After they had completed the meal, Yeshua and his talmidim recited the final blessings of the Hallel. With voices still echoing the words of Tehillim (Psalms): "Give thanks to Adonai, for He is good; His chesed (loving-kindness) endures forever."

The Vine and the Branches — John 14:31b; 15:1–8

Then Yeshua said: "Rise, we should leave from here."

They rose together and departed from the house into the cool night air of Yerushalayim. As they made their way through the narrow streets, descending from the Upper City toward the Kidron Valley, Yeshua spoke to them, saying: "I am the true geffen (vine), and Avi (my Father) is the gardener. Every branch in me that bears no fruit, He removes. But every branch that bears fruit, He prunes so that it may bear even more."

The talmidim listened intently as the Master, walking by moonlight — possibly near the Temple gates adorned with vine carvings — continued: "You are already clean because of the words I have spoken to you. Remain in me, and I will remain in you. Just as a branch cannot bear fruit by itself unless it remains on the vine, so neither can you unless you remain in me. I am the vine; you are the branches. The one who remains in me, and I in him, will bear much fruit — for apart from me, you can do nothing. If anyone does not remain in me, he is thrown away like a branch and dries up. Such branches are gathered and thrown into the fire and are burned. If you remain in me, and my words remain in you, ask whatever you will, and it will be done for you.

By this my Father is glorified — that you bear much fruit and prove to be my talmidim."

The Command to Love and the World's Hatred John 15:9–27

Yeshua slowed his pace as he turned toward them. "Just as Abba has loved me, so I have loved you. Remain in my ahavah (love). If you obey my mitzvot (commandments), you will remain in my love, just as I have obeyed my Father's mitzvot and remain in His love. I have told you these things so that my simchah (joy) may be in you, and your joy may be made full."

Looking each one of them in the eyes, he said: "This is my commandment — that you love one another as I have loved you. Greater ahavah has no one than this: that one should lay down his life for his friends. You are my friends, if you do what I command you. I no longer call you avadim (servants), for a servant does not know what his master is doing. But I have called you chaverim (friends), because everything I heard from Avi I have made known to you.

You did not choose me, but I chose you and appointed you to go and bear fruit — fruit that will last — so that whatever you ask from Avi in my Name, He may give it to you. These things I command you, so that you may love one another."

And with that, they continued walking — Yeshua, the living vine, leading his branches toward the place of pressing: Gat Shemanim. As they continued their walk under the moonlit sky, Yeshua's voice turned somber: "If the world hates you, know that it hated me before it hated you. If you belonged to the world, the world would love its own. But because you are not of the world — because I chose you out of the world — the world hates you."

He paused, then reminded them of something he had said before: "Remember the word I spoke to you: A servant is not greater than his master. If they persecuted me, they will also persecute you. If they kept my word, they will also keep yours. But all these things they will do to you for the sake of my Name, because they do not know the One who sent me.

If I had not come and spoken to them, they would not be guilty of sin. But now they have no excuse. The one who hates me also hates Abba. If I had not done the work no one else did among them, they would not be guilty of sin. But now they have both seen and hated both me and my Father — to fulfill what is written in their Torah: 'They hated me without cause.'" (Tehillim/Psalm 35:19)

Then he said: "When the Melitz (Advocate) comes — the Ruach ha'Emet (Spirit of Truth) who goes out from the Father — He will testify about me. And you also will testify, because you have been with me from the beginning."

The Spirit Will Convict the World John 16:1–11

Yeshua turned his face toward the Mount of Olives and said: "I have spoken these things to you so that you will not stumble. They will put you out of the synagogues. Indeed, a time is coming when whoever kills you will think he is offering service to Elohim. They will do these things because they have not known the Father or me. But I have told you these things so that when their time comes, you may remember that I told you.

I did not tell you about these things at the beginning because I was with you. But now I am going to the One who sent me — and none of you asks me, 'Where are you going?' Yet because I have said these things, sorrow has filled your heart."

He continued: "But I tell you the truth — it is better for you that I go away. For if I do not go, the Melitz (Helper/Advocate) will not come to you. But if I go, I will send him to you. When he comes, he will convict the world concerning chet (sin), tzedek (righteousness), and mishpat (judgment): concerning sin, because they do not believe in me; concerning righteousness, because I go to the Father and you will no longer see me; and concerning judgment, because the ruler of this world is judged."

Your Grief Will Turn to Joy John 16:12–24

"I still have many things to tell you, but you cannot bear them now. But when the Ruach ha'Emet (Spirit of Truth) comes, he will guide you into all truth. For he will not speak on his own, but whatever he hears, he will speak. And he will declare to you what is going to come. He will glorify me, because he will take from what is mine and declare it to you. All things that belong to Abba are mine. That is why I said he will take from what is mine and declare it to you."

Yeshua looked ahead quietly, then turned to his talmidim and said: "A little while, and you will no longer see me — and again a little while, and you will see me."

His words puzzled them. Among themselves they asked: "What does he mean by, 'A little while and you will not see me,' and 'again a little while and you will see me'? And what is this he says, 'because I go to the Father'?"

They said: "What is this 'little while'? We don't understand what he's talking about."

Yeshua, knowing their thoughts, said to them: "Are you asking one another about what I said: 'A little while and you will not see me, and again a little while and you will see me'? Amein, amein, I tell you: You will weep and lament, while the world rejoices. You will be filled with grief — but your grief will turn into simchah (joy)."

He gave them a mashal (parable): "When a woman is in labor, she has pain because her hour has come. But when the child is born, she no longer remembers the anguish — because of the joy that a human being has come into the world.

"So also, you have grief now. But I will see you again — and your hearts will rejoice, and no one will take your simchah from you. On that day, you will ask me nothing. Amein, amein, I tell you: Whatever you ask of Avi in my Name, He will give you. Until now you have not asked for anything in my Name — ask, and you will receive, so that your simchah may be full."

Take Heart, I Have Overcome the World — John 16:25–33

"I have spoken these things to you in riddles (mashalim), but a time is coming when I will no longer speak in riddles but will speak plainly to you about the Father. On that day you will ask in my Name — and I do not say that I will ask the Father on your behalf, for the Father Himself loves you, because you have loved me and believed that I came forth from Elohim. I came forth from the Father and have come into the world. Now I am leaving the world and returning to the Father."

His talmidim said: "Look — now you're speaking plainly, not using riddles! Now we know that you know everything and don't need anyone to ask you questions. By this we believe that you came from Elohim."

Yeshua answered: "Do you now believe? Look — an hour is coming, and has already come, when each of you will be scattered to his own place, and you will leave me alone. Yet I am not alone, because the Father is with me. I have spoken these things to you so that in me you may have shalom. In the world, you will have tribulation — but take heart: I have overcome the world."

Yeshua's Prayer for His Disciples — John 17:1–19

Yeshua lifted his eyes toward the heavens and began to pray: "Avi (Father), the hour has come. Glorify your Son, so that the Son may glorify You — just as You gave him authority over all flesh, so that he might give chayei olam (eternal life) to all You have given him. And this is chayei olam: to know You — the only true Elohim — and the one You sent, Yeshua the Mashiach."

"I have glorified You on the earth, having finished the work You gave me to do. So now, Avi, glorify me together with Yourself, with the kavod (glory) I had with You before the world existed. I have revealed Your Name to the men You gave me out of the world. They were Yours — You gave them to me, and they have kept Your word. Now they know that everything You have given me is from You. The words You gave me; I have given to them. They received them, and truly understood that I came forth from You, and they believed that You sent me."

"I ask on their behalf — not for the world, but for those You have given me, for they are Yours. All that is mine is Yours, and Yours are mine — and I have been glorified in them. I am no longer in the world, but they are in the world, and I am coming to You. Abba Kadosh (Holy Father), protect them by Your Name, which You have given me, so that they may be echad (one), just as we are echad. While I was with them, I protected them by the Name You gave me. I guarded them, and not one of them was lost — except the son of destruction — so that the Scripture would be fulfilled."

"Now I am coming to You, and I say these things while I am in the world, so that they may have my simchah (joy) made full in them. I have given them Your word, and the world has hated them — for they are not of the world, just as I am not of the world. I do not ask that You take them out of the world, but that You protect them from the evil one. They are not of the world, just as I am not of the world. Set them apart in the truth — Your word is truth. Just as You sent me into the world, I also have sent them into the world. For their sake, I sanctify myself, so that they too may be set apart in truth."

Yeshua's Prayer for All Believers John 17:20–26

"I do not ask for these only, but also for those who will trust in me through their word — that they all may be echad (one), just as You, Avi, are in me, and I am in You — so that they also may be in us, so that the world may believe that You sent me. The kavod (glory) You have given me, I have given to them — that they may be one just as we are one — I in them and You in me — that they may be perfected in unity, so that the world may know that You sent me, and that You loved them just as You loved me."

"Avi, I desire that those You have given me may also be with me where I am — so, they may behold my kavod — the glory You have given me because You loved me before the foundation of the world. Tzaddik Avi (Righteous Father), though the world did not know You, I knew You, and these knew that You sent me. I made Your Name known to them and will continue to make it known — so that the love with which You loved me may be in them, and I in them."

And with that, Yeshua completed his final words of teaching and prayer. The night was now well advanced as he and the eleven talmidim approached the olive grove at Gat Shemanim, where his final test would begin.

Yeshua Prays in Gat Shemanim Matthew 26:36–46 | Mark 14:32–42 | Luke 22:39–46 | John 18:1

After Yeshua had finished praying for his talmidim, he and the eleven crossed over the Kidron Valley. There, on the lower slopes of Har HaZeitim (Mount of Olives), lay a garden called Gat Shemanim (Olive Press). Yeshua often went there with his disciples. Yehudah, the one who would deliver him, also knew the place — for Yeshua had met there with his talmidim many times.

He said to them, "Sit here while I go over there and pray." He took Kefa (Peter), Yaakov (James), and Yochanan (John) with him, and he began to be deeply grieved and distressed. Yeshua said to them: "My nefesh (soul) is overwhelmed with sorrow, even to the point of death. Remain here and stay awake with me."

He walked a little farther — about a stone's throw — fell on his face, and prayed: "Avi (Father), if it is possible, let this kos (cup) pass from me — yet not as I will, but as You will."

Returning to the three, he found them sleeping. He said to Kefa: "Couldn't you stay awake with me one hour? Stay awake and pray, so that you won't enter into nisayon (trial). The spirit is willing, but the flesh is weak."

Again, he went away and prayed: "Avi, if this cannot pass unless I drink it, may Your will be done." Returning again, he found them sleeping, for their eyes were heavy. They didn't know how to answer him.

A third time, he went and prayed the same words. Then an angel from the heavens appeared to him and strengthened him. And being in agony, he prayed more fervently, and his sweat became like drops of blood falling to the ground. Then he returned to the talmidim and said: "Are you still sleeping and resting? Look — the hour is near, and the Son of Man is handed over into the hands of chata'im (sinners). Get up, let's go. See — the one who delivers me is drawing near."

Yeshua Is Betrayed and Arrested Matthew 26:47–56 | Mark 14:43–52 | Luke 22:47–53 | John 18:2–12

While he was still speaking, Yehudah approached — one of the Twelve — accompanied by a troop of soldiers and officers from the ruling kohanim (priests) and Perushim (Pharisees). They came with torches, swords, and clubs. Yehudah had given them a signal: "The one I kiss — he is the man. Arrest him and lead him away securely." He drew near to Yeshua and said, "Shalom, Rabbi!" and kissed him.

But Yeshua said to him: "Yehudah — are you delivering up the Son of Man with a kiss?"

Yeshua stepped forward and asked the crowd: "Whom are you seeking?"

They answered: "Yeshua haNotzri (the Nazarene)."

He said: "I am he."

At these words, they drew back and fell to the ground. He asked again: "Whom are you seeking?"

They repeated: "Yeshua haNotzri."

Yeshua answered: "I told you; I am he. So, if you're seeking me, let these others go." (This fulfilled his earlier words: "Of those You have given me, I have lost none.")

When those with Yeshua saw what was happening, they said: "Adon, shall we strike with the sword?" Then Shimon Kefa, having a sword, drew it and struck the servant of the Kohen Gadol (High Priest), cutting off his right ear. The servant's name was Malchus.

But Yeshua said: "Put your sword back in its place! All who take up the sword will perish by the sword. Do you think I cannot call on my Father, and He would send more than twelve legions of malachim (angels)? But how then would the Scriptures be fulfilled that it must happen this way?"

He touched the servant's ear and healed him.

Then Yeshua turned to the crowd and said: "Have you come out with swords and clubs to seize me, as if I were a robber? Each day I was with you in the Beit HaMikdash (Temple), and you didn't seize me. But this is your hour — and the power of darkness."

Then they seized Yeshua and arrested him. At that moment, all the talmidim abandoned him and fled. But a certain young man was following, clothed only with a linen cloth over his naked body. They grabbed him — but he left the cloth behind and fled naked.

CHAPTER 17 Yeshua's Trial and Crucifixion

3:00 AM Nisan 13, Wednesday, April 25, 31 CE Interrogation Before Chanan

Yeshua Before Chanan, and Kefa's First Two Denials
John 18:12–24 | Matthew 26:58, 69–72 | Mark 14:54, 66–68 | Luke 22:54–58

Yeshua was first led by the group of soldiers and the Temple officers to Chanan (Annas), the father-in-law of Kayafa (Caiaphas), the Kohen Gadol (High Priest) that year. Kayafa was the one who had advised the Yehudim that it was better for one man to die on behalf of the people.

Shimon Kefa and another talmid followed Yeshua at a distance. That other disciple was known to the Kohen Gadol and went with Yeshua into the courtyard, but Kefa remained outside at the gate. Then the other disciple went out and spoke to the servant girl guarding the gate and brought Kefa in.

The servant girl at the door said to Kefa, "You're not also one of this man's talmidim, are you?"

He replied, "I am not."

Inside, Chanan questioned Yeshua about his talmidim and his teachings. Yeshua answered: "I have spoken openly to the world. I always taught in the synagogue and in the Beit HaMikdash (Temple), where all the Yehudim come together. I have said nothing secretly. Why do you question me? Ask those who heard what I said to them — they know what I said."

When he said this, one of the officers standing nearby struck Yeshua, saying, "Is that how you answer the Kohen Gadol?"

Yeshua replied: "If I spoke wrongly, bear witness to the wrong. But if I spoke rightly, why do you strike me?"

Then Chanan sent him, still bound, to Kayafa the Kohen Gadol.

Now Kefa was standing with the servants and officers, warming himself by the fire in the courtyard. As they gathered around him, another servant girl saw him and said to those nearby, "This man was with Yeshua of Natzaret."

Again, he denied it with an oath: "I do not know the man!"

Yeshua Before Kayafa and the False Witnesses   Matthew 26:57–68 | Mark 14:53–65

They brought Yeshua to the house of Kayafa, where the chief priests, elders, and Torah scholars had gathered. The whole Sanhedrin was seeking false testimony against Yeshua to put him to death — but they found none. Many false witnesses came forward, but their testimonies did not agree. At last, two came forward and said: "This man said, 'I am able to destroy the Temple of Elohim and rebuild it in three days.'"

The Kohen Gadol stood up and said: "Do you answer nothing? What is this that these men testify against you?" But Yeshua remained silent.

Then the Kohen Gadol said to him: "I adjure you by the living Elohim: tell us if you are the Mashiach, the Son of the Blessed One."

Yeshua said: "You have said it. But I tell you: from now on, you will see the Son of Man (Bar Enash) sitting at the right hand of the Power and coming with the clouds of heaven."

Then the Kohen Gadol tore his garments and said: "He has spoken blasphemy! What further need do we have of witnesses? You have now heard the blasphemy. What do you think?"

They answered, "He is guilty and deserves death."

Then they spat in his face and struck him. Others blindfolded him and mocked him, saying: "Prophesy to us, Mashiach! Who is the one who hit you?" And the men who were guarding Yeshua continued to mock him, beat him, and speak many other blasphemous things against him.

Kefa's Third Denial   Matthew 26:73–75 | Mark 14:70–72 | Luke 22:59–62 | John 18:26–27

A little while later, one of the bystanders came up to Kefa and said, "Surely you are one of them. Your accent gives you away."

Then Kefa began to curse and swear, saying: "I do not know the man!"

At that very moment, while he was still speaking, a rooster crowed. Then Adon turned and looked straight at Kefa. And Kefa remembered the word that Yeshua had spoken: "Before the rooster crows, you will deny me three times." And he went out and wept bitterly.

4:40 am Nisan 13, Wednesday, April 25, 31 CE

The Morning Verdict Before the Sanhedrin   Matthew 27:1 | Mark 15:1 | Luke 22:66–71 | John 18:28

As daylight began to break, the ziknei ha'am (elders of the people), along with the rosh ha-kohanim (chief priests) and soferim (scribes) — that is, the full Sanhedrin — convened for a formal verdict. Yeshua was brought from the house of Kayafa to their council chamber.

They said, "If you are the Mashiach (Anointed One), tell us."

But Yeshua said, "If I tell you, you will not believe. And if I ask you, you will not answer. But from now on, the Bar Enash (Son of Man) will be seated at the right hand of the Gevurat Elohim (Power of Elohim)."

Then they all said, "Are you then the Son of Elohim?"

Yeshua responded, "You yourselves are saying that I am."

Then they said, "What further need do we have of testimony? For we have heard it ourselves from his own mouth!"

At this point, they formally reached the verdict that he was guilty of blasphemy — though, notably, blasphemy for claiming to be the Son of Man seated at Elohim's right hand, not for claiming to be Elohim Himself. They bound him again and prepared to bring him to Pilate, the Roman governor.

5:52 am Nisan 13, 31 CE

Transferred to the Romans   Matthew 27:1–2 | Mark 15:1 | Luke 23:1 | John 18:28

At dawn, the Sanhedrin formally bound Yeshua and led him away from the home of Kayafa to the Roman governor's residence to stand before Pontius Pilatus (Pilate). The whole assembly arose and brought him from Kayafa's house to the Praetorium.

But they did not enter the Praetorium themselves, so they would not become ritually defiled and thus be unable to eat the Pesach (Passover) offering.

Before Pilate: First Interrogation   John 18:29–38 | Luke 23:2–5 | Matthew 27:11–14 | Mark 15:2–5

So, being woken up in the early hours Pilate came out to them and asked making his annoyance clear, "What accusation do you bring against this man?"

They answered, "If he were not doing evil, we wouldn't have handed him over to you. He is subverting our nation, forbidding the payment of taxes to Caesar, and claiming to be Mashiach, a king!"

So Pilate went back inside, summoned Yeshua, and asked, "Are you the King of the Jews?"

Yeshua replied, "Do you say this of your own accord, or did others tell you about me?"

Pilate his annoyance growing answered, "Am I a Jew? Your own nation and chief priests handed you over to me. What have you done?"

Yeshua answered, "My kingdom is not of this world. If it were, my servants would be fighting to prevent my arrest. But now my kingdom is not from here."

Pilate said, "So then, you are a king?"

Yeshua answered, "You say that I am a king. For this I was born, and for this I came into the world—to testify to the truth. Everyone who belongs to the truth hears my voice."

Pilate replied mockingly, "What is truth?"

He went out again to the crowd and declared, "I find no fault in this man. Take him yourselves and judge him according to your own Laws."

They replied, "It is not permitted for us to put anyone to death." This happened so that the word Yeshua had spoken would be fulfilled—indicating what kind of death he was going to die.

But the chief priests and zekenim (elders) began to accuse Yeshua of many things.

Yeshua gave no answer to their accusations. Then Pilate asked him, "Do you hear how many things they testify against you?" But Yeshua still gave no reply, not even to a single charge. Pilate was amazed.

They kept insisting and said, "He stirs up the people, teaching throughout all Judea, beginning in Galilee and even to this place."

Sent to Herod Luke 23:6–12

When Pilate heard that Yeshua was a Galilean, he asked whether he belonged to Herod Antipas's jurisdiction. When he learned that he did, he sent him to Herod, who was also in Jerusalem for the festival.

Herod was very glad to see Yeshua, for he had long desired to meet him. When Yeshua arrived, he questioned him at length, but Yeshua gave no answer. The chief priests and soferim (scribes) stood by, accusing him vehemently. Herod and his soldiers, after mocking him, dressed him in a royal robe, and sent him back to Pilate. That day, Herod and Pilate, who had previously been enemies, became friends.

The Remorse and Death of Yehudah Ish Kriot Matthew 27:3–10

Now when Yehudah Ish Kriot (Judas Iscariot), who had betrayed him, saw that Yeshua had been condemned, he was seized with regret. He brought back the thirty pieces of silver to the rosh ha-kohanim (chief priests) and zekenim (elders), saying: "I have sinned by betraying innocent blood!"

They said: "What is that to us? You see to it yourself!"

Throwing the silver into the Heikhal (Temple sanctuary), he departed and went out. Then he went and hanged himself.

The chief priests said: "It is not lawful to put this into the Temple treasury, since it is blood money."

So, they conferred and used the silver to buy the field of the potter as a burial place for strangers. Therefore, that field has been called to this day: S'deh HaDam (Field of Blood). This fulfilled what had been spoken by the prophet, saying: "They took the thirty silver pieces, the price set on him by the sons of Israel, and gave them for the potter's field, as Adonai commanded."

Yeshua Is Rejected and Mocked by the Crowd

Matthew 27:15–31| Mark 15:6–20 | Luke 23:13–25 | John 18:38–40, 19:1–3

Pilate called together the rosh ha-kohanim (chief priests), rulers, and the people, and said to them: "You brought this man to me as one who incites the people. Look, I have examined him in your presence and found no basis for your charges. Neither has Herod, for he sent him back to us. Behold, he has done nothing deserving death. I will therefore punish him and release him."

Now it was Pilate's custom at the festival to release for the people one prisoner of their choice. At that time, there was a notorious prisoner named Bar-Abba (Barabbas), who had been imprisoned for insurrection and murder.

The crowd began to shout and demand that Pilate keep the custom. So, Pilate asked: "Do you want me to release to you the King of the Yehudim?" For he knew it was out of kinah (envy) that the chief priests had delivered Yeshua.

As Pilate sat on the judgment seat (bema), his wife sent a message to him, saying: "Do not have anything to do with that tzaddik (righteous man), for I suffered greatly today in a dream because of him."

But the chief priests and zekenim (elders) stirred up the crowd to ask for Bar-Abba instead.

Then, wishing to release Yeshua, Pilate again addressed them: "Which of the two do you want me to release for you?"

They cried out: "Not this man, but Bar-Abba! Release Bar-Abba!"

Pilate then asked: "Then what shall I do with the one you call the King of the Yehudim?"

They shouted again: "Crucify him!"

Pilate said to them a third time: "Why? What evil has he done? I have found in him no guilt deserving death. I will therefore have him flogged and release him."

But they kept shouting all the more: "Crucify him! Let him be crucified!"

They were urgent, shouting loudly and demanding his crucifixion. And their voices prevailed.

So, Pilate, wishing to appease the crowd, released Bar-Abba to them—the one imprisoned for insurrection and murder. Then he ordered Yeshua to be scourged and handed him over to be crucified.

Then the soldiers of the governor took Yeshua into the Praetorium (governor's headquarters). The entire cohort (speira — about 600 soldiers) was gathered around him. They stripped him and put a scarlet robe on him. Then, twisting together a crown of thorns, they placed it on his head, and put a reed (staff) in his right hand.

They mocked him, kneeling before him and saying: "Hail, King of the Yehudim!" They spat on him and took the reed and struck him on the head repeatedly. They also struck him with their hands and continued mocking him.

Pilate Delivers Yeshua to Be Crucified

John 19:4–17 | Matthew 27:24–34 | Mark 15:20–23 | Luke 23:26–31

Then, Pilatus stepped outside again and addressed the crowd: "Look, I bring him out to you, that you may know I find no fault in him."

Yeshua emerged, still wearing the crown of thorns and the mocking robe. His form marred beyond human likeness. Beaten bloody, swollen face, bruises all over his face and body. Deep gashes along his back and sides from the torment the guards put him through. Pilatus announced: "Behold the man!"

But when the chief priests and their officers saw him, they shouted: "Crucify! Crucify him!"

Pilatus replied: "Take him yourselves and crucify him, for I find no charge against him."

The Judean leaders answered: "We have a Torah, and by that Torah he must die, for he claimed to be the Son of Elohim."

When Pilatus heard this, he became even more afraid. He returned to the inner chamber and asked Yeshua: "Where are you from?"

Yeshua gave no answer. So, Pilatus said: "Do you not speak to me? Don't you know I have the authority to release you and the authority to crucify you?"

Yeshua answered him: "You would have no authority over me unless it had been given to you from above. Therefore, the one who handed me over to you bears the greater guilt."

From then on, Pilatus tried to release him, but the crowd cried out: "If you release this man, you are no friend of Caesar! Everyone who claims to be a king sets himself against Caesar!"

So, Pilatus brought Yeshua out once more and sat on the judgment seat, at a place called Gabbatha (The Stone Pavement). It was about the sixth hour by Roman reckoning. He said to them: "Behold your King!"

But they shouted: "Away with him! Away with him! Crucify him!"

He asked: "Shall I crucify your King?"

The chief priests answered: "We have no king but Caesar."

Seeing that he was gaining nothing and that a riot was beginning, Pilatus took water and washed his hands before the crowd: "I am innocent of this man's blood—see to it yourselves."

And all the people shouted back: "His blood be on us and on our children!"

Finally, after the final sentence was declared Pilatus handed him over to the Roman soldiers to be crucified. They, took Yeshua and removed the robe, then clothed him again in his own garments, and led him away carrying his own crossbeam to be crucified on "Gulgolta" (Golgotha) — which means "Place of the Skull."

As they were leading him out he was having a hard time carrying his crossbeam due to his injuries and loss of blood, so they seized a man named Shim'on (Simon) of Cyrene, who was coming in from the countryside. He was the father of Alexander and Rufus. They laid the crossbeam on him and forced him to carry it behind Yeshua, assisting him on the way.

A large crowd of the people followed him, including women mourning and lamenting for him. Yeshua turned and said to them: "Daughters of Yerushalayim, do not weep for me. Weep for yourselves and for your children. For the days are coming when they will say, 'Blessed are the barren, the wombs that never bore, and the breasts that never nursed.' Then they will begin to say to the mountains, 'Fall on us,' and to the hills, 'Cover us.' For if they do these things when the tree is green, what will happen when it is dry?"

They brought Yeshua to Gulgolta and there were two other criminals, who were also led out to be executed with him. Upon arrival, they offered Yeshua wine mixed with gall (or myrrh), a bitter sedative — but he refused to drink it.

9:00 AM, Wednesday – Nisan 13, April 25, 31 CE

Yeshua is Crucified Matthew 27:33–38 | Mark 15:25–28 | Luke 23:32–33 | John 19:18

Then they crucified him, at the third hour (9:00 AM), fulfilling the prophecy of the Righteous One being numbered with the wicked. And with him, they crucified two transgressors—one on his right and one on his left. Thus was fulfilled the Scripture: "He was counted among the transgressors."

Yeshua's First Words from the Stake Luke 23:34

While Yeshua was being lifted up, he said: "Abba, forgive them — they do not know what they are doing."

The Soldiers Divide His Garments   Matthew 27:35 | Mark 15:24 | Luke 23:34b | John 19:23–24

The soldiers then divided his garments, casting lots to determine who would take each piece, fulfilling the Scripture: "They divided my garments among them, and for my clothing they cast lots." (Tehillim/Psalm 22:18)

They took his outer garments and made four parts, one for each soldier. However, his tunic was seamless, woven in one piece from top to bottom. So, they said to one another: "Let us not tear it, but cast lots for it, to see whose it shall be." The soldiers sat down and kept watch over him.

The Inscription on the Stake   Matthew 27:37 | Mark 15:26 | Luke 23:38 | John 19:19–22

Above his head, they placed the written charge against him. It read: "Yeshua HaNotzri, Melech HaYehudim" — "Yeshua the Nazarene, King of the Jews." It was written in Hebrew, Latin, and Greek so all could read it.

The chief priests protested: "Don't write 'King of the Jews,' but 'He said he was King of the Jews!'"

Pilatus replied: "What I have written, I have written."

Mocking and Insults from Onlookers   Matthew 27:39–44 | Mark 15:29–32 | Luke 23:35–37 | John 19:29

As he hung on the stake, those who passed by hurled insults and shook their heads, saying: "You who would destroy the Beit HaMikdash and rebuild it in three days — save yourself! If you are the Son of Elohim, come down from the stake!"

The chief priests, scribes, and elders also mocked him: "He saved others, but he cannot save himself! He is the King of Israel — let him come down now from the stake and we will believe in him. He trusts in Elohim — let Elohim rescue him now if He wants him, for he said, 'I am the Son of Elohim.'"

Even the two criminals crucified with him reviled him in the same way at first. And the soldiers also mocked him, coming to offer him sour wine, saying: "If you are the King of the Jews — save yourself!"

The Repentant Criminal   Luke 23:39–43

One of the criminals hanging there railed at Yeshua, saying: "Aren't you the Mashiach? Save yourself and us!"

But the other rebuked him and said: "Don't you even fear Elohim, seeing that you are under the same sentence? We are getting what we deserve for our actions — but this man has done nothing wrong!"

Then he turned and said: "Yeshua, remember me when you come into your malchut (kingdom)."

And Yeshua said to him: "Amein, I tell you today — you will be with me in Gan-Eden (Paradise)."

Yeshua Entrusts His Mother to the Beloved Talmid　　　　　　　　　　　John 19:25–27

Meanwhile, Yeshua's mother Miriam, and Miriam of Magdala, and Miriam the wife of Clopas, and the beloved talmid Yochanan stood nearby. Seeing them, Yeshua said to his mother: "Woman, behold your son."
Then to the talmid: "Behold your mother." From that moment, the talmid took her into his own home.

Darkness Falls　　　　　　　　　　　Matthew 27:45 | Mark 15:33 | Luke 23:44

It was now about the sixth hour (noon), and darkness came over all the land until the ninth hour. The sun was darkened, and the heavens mourned with the earth.

> A pagan named Thallus in 52 CE wrote about the darkness. We have lost his writings, but we have Julius Africanus who quotes him in a fragment preserved by George Syncellus, Chronology, 18.1 that says "Thallus, in the third book of his histories, explains away this darkness as an eclipse of the sun – unreasonably, as it seems to me because a solar eclipse cannot occur at the time of the full moon."

Yeshua Cries Out in Fulfillment of Psalm 22　　　　　　　　　　　Matthew 27:46–47 | Mark 15:34–36

At about the ninth hour, Yeshua cried out with a loud voice: "Eli, Eli, lamah sabachthani?" ("My God, my God, why have You forsaken me?" / Psalm 22:1)

Some of the bystanders, hearing it, said: "Look, he is calling for Eliyahu!

Yeshua Declares His Thirst　　　　　　　　　　　John 19:28–29

After this, Yeshua, knowing that everything had now been accomplished, and so that the Scripture might be fulfilled, said: "I thirst." Immediately, one of them ran and took a sponge, filled it with sour wine (vinegar), put it on a reed of ezov (hyssop), and offered it to him to drink.

But others said: "Wait! Let's see if Eliyahu comes to save him."

3:00pm, Wednesday – Nisan 13, April 25, 31 CE

Yeshua Yields Up His Spirit　　　　　　John 19:30 | Luke 23:46 | Matthew 27:50 | Mark 15:37

When Yeshua had received the sour wine, he said: "It is finished." And then, Yeshua cried out again with a loud voice, saying: "Abba, into Your hands I commit my ruach (spirit)!" And with that, he bowed his head and yielded up his spirit.

Signs Accompany His Death   Matthew 27:51–53

Immediately after Yeshua breathed his last, the veil (parokhet) of the Beit HaMikdash (Holy Temple) — the curtain separating the Kodesh (Holy Place) from the Kodesh HaKodashim (Most Holy Place) — was torn in two from top to bottom.

Talmud Bavli, Yoma 39b "Our Rabbis taught: During the last forty years before the destruction of the Temple:			
The lot for the Lord did not come up in the right hand.	The crimson strap did not turn white.	The westernmost lamp of the menorah refused to stay lit.	And the doors of the Temple would open by themselves…"
On Yom Kippur, the Kohen Gadol would draw two lots—one for Adonai and one for Azazel (Leviticus 16:8). Tradition held that the lot for Adonai would normally come up in the right hand (a sign of divine favor). From around 30 CE on, it never did again. Suggests a rejection of Israel's atonement system at that point — possibly indicating a divine shift in the means of atonement.	Traditionally, a scarlet thread was tied to the scapegoat or the Temple doorpost on Yom Kippur. When the offering was accepted by Heaven, the thread would turn white, symbolizing Isaiah 1:18: "Though your sins are like scarlet, they shall be white as snow." For the last 40 years, it remained scarlet — implying sins were no longer being forgiven through the Yom Kippur service.	The Ner Ma'aravi (Western Lamp) of the Temple Menorah was known to miraculously stay lit continuously, even when the others were extinguished. It symbolized the Shekhinah (Divine Presence). From 30–31 CE on, it refused to stay lit, despite priestly efforts. Could symbolize the withdrawal of the Shekhinah from the Holy Place.	The great doors of the Heikhal (Temple sanctuary) began to open by themselves, unprovoked. This was interpreted as a bad omen, as if the Temple was saying, "Enter and destroy me." Rabbi Yohanan ben Zakkai interpreted this as a sign of the Temple's coming destruction (Yoma 39b, and Midrash Shir HaShirim Rabbah 6:4).

There was a great earthquake, and rocks split apart. Tombs were opened, and many bodies of the righteous ones who had died were raised. They came out of the tombs after his resurrection and entered the holy city, and many saw them.

Geologists Karcz & Williams, 2012 studied sediment layers near the dead sea, and they found evidence of two earthquakes: 1. One Major one in 31 BCE (well known) 2. One smaller, localized event: dated between 26 CE and 36 CE They suggested this smaller quake could correlate with the crucifixion of Yeshua. The Dead Sea sediment evidence makes this a strong candidate

Testimony of the Roman Centurion   Mark 15:39 | Matthew 27:54 | Luke 23:47

When the centurion who stood facing him saw how Yeshua died, and witnessed all that had happened, he said: "Truly, this man was righteous! Truly, this man was the Son of Elohim!"

Mourning and Witnesses Among the Women   Luke 23:48–49 | Matthew 27:55–56 | Mark 15:40–41

When all the people who had gathered to witness his death, they returned home beating their breasts.
Many women were standing at a distance, watching these things. They had followed Yeshua from the Galil and had served him. Among them were Miryam of Magdala, Miryam the mother of Yaakov (James) and Yosef, and the mother of the sons of Zavdai (Zebedee).

The Piercing of Yeshua's Side   John 19:31–37

Because it was the Day of Preparation, and the next day was a high Shabbat (the first day of Chag HaMatzot), the Yehudim asked Pilate to have the legs of the executed men broken and the bodies removed — so they wouldn't remain on the cross into the holy day.

The soldiers came and broke the legs of the first man who had been crucified with Yeshua, and then those of the second. But when they came to Yeshua and saw that he was already dead, they did not break his legs. Instead, one of the soldiers pierced his side with a spear, and immediately blood and water flowed out.

The one who saw it has testified — and his testimony is true. He knows that he speaks the truth, so that you also may believe. These things happened in order that the Scripture would be fulfilled: "Not one of his bones will be broken." (cf. Exodus 12:46; Psalm 34:20)

And again, another passage says: "They will look upon the one whom they have pierced." (Zechariah 12:10)

Yosef of Ramatayim Requests Yeshua's Body   Mark 15:42–45 | Luke 23:50–52 | John 19:38

Now when evening approached, since it was the Day of Preparation, and the next day was a High Shabbat, a respected council member named Yosef of Ramatayim (Arimathea) — a good and righteous man who had not consented to the council's verdict — came forward. He was a disciple of Yeshua, though secretly for fear of the Judean leaders. Yosef went boldly to Pilatus (Pilate) and asked for the body of Yeshua. Pilate was surprised to hear that Yeshua was already dead. He summoned the centurion and confirmed it. Then he granted the body to Yosef.

The Burial of Yeshua   Mark 15:46 | John 19:39–42 | Matthew 27:59–60

Yosef bought fine linen, took Yeshua's body down, and wrapped it in the linen cloth. At the same time, Nakdimon (Nicodemus) — the one who had earlier visited Yeshua at night — came with about a hundred Roman pounds of myrrh and aloes, a mixture of spices for burial. Together, they wrapped Yeshua's body with the spices, according to the Judean burial customs.

Now there was a garden near the place where Yeshua had been crucified, and in that garden was a new tomb, carved out of the rock, where no one had ever been laid. Because it was the Day of Preparation and the tomb was nearby, they laid Yeshua there quickly before sunset. Yosef rolled a large stone against the entrance of the tomb and departed.

The Women Witness the Burial   Matthew 27:61 | Luke 23:55–56

Miryam of Magdala and Miryam the mother of Yosef (also called the "other Miryam") were sitting opposite the tomb, watching where he was laid. The women from Galil who had followed him saw the tomb and how his body was laid. Then they returned and prepared spices and ointments. And they rested on the Shabbat according to the mitzvah (commandment).

The Guard at the Tomb   Matthew 27:62–66

On the next day — that is, the day after the Preparation (meaning the High Sabbath, Nisan 14) — the rosh ha-kohanim (chief priests) and the Perushim (Pharisees) gathered before Pilatus (Pilate).

They said: "Sir, we remember that when that deceiver was still alive, he said, 'After three days I will rise again.' Therefore, command that the tomb be made secure until the third day, so his disciples cannot come, steal the body, and say to the people, 'He has been raised from the dead.' The last deception will be worse than the first."

Pilate said to them: "You have a guard. Go, make it as secure as you know how." So, they went and secured the tomb, placing a seal on the stone and setting a guard.

Source	Date	Extra Biblical Sources for the Crucifixion of Yeshua Mentions Crucifixion?	Notes
Tacitus (Annals)	~115 CE	"Christus, from whom the name [Christian] had its origin, **suffered the extreme penalty** during the reign of Tiberius at the hands of one of our procurators, Pontius Pilatus… and a most mischievous superstition, thus checked for the moment, again broke out…"	Strong Roman confirmation
Josephus (Antiquities)	~93 CE	"Now there was about this time Yeshua, a wise man… Pilate, at the suggestion of the principal men among us, **condemned him to the cross**, and those that loved him at the first did not forsake him…"	Jewish record, partly interpolated
Lucian of Samosata	~165 CE	"The Christians… worship a man to this day—the distinguished personage who introduced their novel rites, and was **crucified** on that account… their first lawgiver persuaded them that they are all brothers and should live under his laws."	Satirical but independent
Mara bar Serapion	1st–2nd century	"What advantage did the Jews gain from executing their wise king? It was just after that their kingdom was abolished… Nor did the wise king die altogether, for the new teaching he had given lived on…"	Philosophical reflection
Talmud (Sanhedrin 43a)	Oral tradition compiled ~200 CE	"On the eve of Passover they hanged Yeshu. A herald went out for forty days beforehand, saying: 'He is going to be stoned, because he practiced sorcery and enticed Israel to apostasy.' But no one came forward in his defense, so they hanged him on the eve of Passover."	Polemical, but confirms timeline

Chapter 18 The Resurrection and Ascension

The Earthquake and the Angel Matthew 28:1–4

Just before dawn on the first day of the week, there was a great earthquake. A messenger of Adonai descended from heaven, rolled away the stone, and sat on it. His appearance was like lightning, and his garments white as snow. The guards trembled and became like dead men. As soon as they recovered, the guards fled the scene.

Miryam of Magdala Sees the Stone Rolled Away John 20:1–2

While it was still dark, Miryam of Magdala arrived alone and saw the stone had already rolled away. She did not enter the tomb. Instead, she ran to tell Shim'on Kefa and the beloved disciple: "They have taken the Master out of the tomb, and we don't know where they have laid him."

Other Women Arrive and See Angels Mark 16:1–8 | Luke 24:1–8 | Matthew 28:5–7

After Miryam of Magdala had run to find the disciples, other women — Miryam the mother of Yaakov, Shlomit, and others — arrived at the tomb just as the sun had risen, bringing spices. They saw that the stone had already been rolled away. They entered and did not find the body of the Master Yeshua.

Suddenly, two messengers in dazzling garments appeared to them. The women were terrified, but the angel said: "Do not fear! I know you seek Yeshua who was crucified. He is not here — He has risen! Come, see the place where He lay. Remember how He told you in the Galil that the Son of Man (Bar Enash) must be delivered into the hands of sinful men, crucified, and rise on the third day. Now go quickly and tell His disciples that He has risen from the dead. He is going ahead of you to the Galil — there you will see Him."

They fled from the tomb trembling and astonished. They were afraid and initially said nothing to anyone.

Kefa and the Beloved Disciple Visit the Tomb John 20:3–10 | Luke 24:12

Meanwhile, Shim'on Kefa and the beloved disciple ran to the tomb after hearing from Miryam of Magdala. The other disciple arrived first but didn't go in. Kefa arrived and entered, seeing the linen strips and the face cloth folded by itself. Then the other disciple entered, saw, and believed. They still did not understand the Scripture that Yeshua must rise. They returned to their homes.

Yeshua Appears to Miryam of Magdala   Mark 16:9 | John 20:11–17

Now Yeshua, having risen early on the first day of the week, appeared first to Miryam of Magdala, from whom He had cast out seven shedim (demons). Miryam of Magdala, having returned to the tomb, stood outside weeping. She looked inside and saw two Malakhim (Angels) in white, one at the head and one at the feet where Yeshua's body had been. They asked: "Woman, why are you weeping?"

She answered: "They have taken my Master, and I don't know where they've laid Him."

She turned and saw Yeshua standing there, but didn't recognize Him. Yeshua said: "Woman, why are you weeping? Whom are you seeking?"

She replied, thinking He was the gardener: "Sir, if you've carried Him away, tell me where, and I'll take Him."

Yeshua said: "Miryam."

She turned and exclaimed: "Rabboni!" (Hebrew: My Teacher) She went to grab hold of him being overcome with joy at seeing him again and alive she wanted to hug him.

Yeshua stopping her said: "Do not cling to Me, for I have not yet ascended to the Father. But go to My brothers and tell them: 'I ascend to My Father and your Father, to My Elohim and your Elohim.'"

Yeshua Appears to the Other Women   Matthew 28:9–10

On their way to tell the disciples, Yeshua appeared to the other women, saying: "Shalom!"

They came to Him, took hold of His feet, and worshiped Him. He said: "Do not be afraid. Go and tell My brothers to go to the Galil — there they will see Me."

The Guards Report to the Chief Priest   Matthew 28:11–15

While the women were still on their way to tell the talmidim (disciples), some of the Roman guards went into the city and reported to the rosh ha-kohanim (chief priests) everything that had happened. After gathering with the zekenim (elders), they took counsel and agreed to bribe the soldiers with a large sum of silver, saying: "You are to say: 'His disciples came by night and stole him while we were sleeping.' If this reaches the ears of the governor, we will satisfy him and keep you out of trouble." So, the guards took the silver and did as they were instructed. And this story has been circulated among the Yehudim (Jews) until this day.

The Disciples Disbelieve the Women's Report   Mark 16:10–11 | Luke 24:9–12 | John 20:18

Meanwhile, Miryam of Magdala went and told the disciples: "I have seen the Master!"

But when she told them — while they were still mourning and weeping — they did not believe that He was alive and had appeared to her. After the other women had encountered the malakhim (angels) at the tomb — and after Yeshua had appeared to Miryam of Magdala and then to the other women — they returned quickly from the tomb to report everything to the eleven and the rest of the talmidim (disciples).

Those women included Miryam of Magdala, Yochanah, and Miryam the mother of Yaakov, along with other women who were with them. They relayed all these things to the shlichim (apostles), but their words seemed like nonsense to them, and they did not believe them. However, Kefa rose and ran back to the tomb. Stooping down, he saw only the linen strips lying there. He went away, wondering to himself what had taken place.

The Road to Amma'us (Emmaus)　　　　　　　　　　　　　　　　　　　　　　Luke 24:13–35

That same day, two of Yeshua's talmidim (disciples) were walking to a village called Amma'us (Emmaus), about sixty stadia from Yerushalayim — roughly seven miles. As they talked with each other about all the things that had just happened, Yeshua himself approached and began walking with them. But their eyes were kept from recognizing him.

He said to them, "What are you discussing as you walk along, looking so distressed?"

One of them, named Klefah (Cleopas), answered, "Are you the only visitor in Yerushalayim who doesn't know what has happened there in these days?"

Yeshua said, "What things?"

They replied, "About Yeshua haNotzri — the man who was a navi (prophet), powerful in word and deed before Elohim and all the people. Our chief priests and zekenim (elders) handed him over to be condemned to death, and they crucified him. But we were hoping that he was the one who would redeem Yisrael. And now, it is the third day since these things took place.

Also, some women among us amazed us. They went to the tomb early this morning and didn't find his body. They came saying they had seen a vision of malakhim (angels), who said he is alive. Some of our group went to the tomb — and found it just as the women had said — but they did not see him."

Yeshua said to them, "Oh, foolish ones — slow of heart to trust all that the nevi'im (prophets) have spoken! Was it not necessary for HaMashiach to suffer these things and enter into his kavod (glory)?" Then beginning with Mosheh and all the Nevi'im, he explained to them everything in the Ketuvim (Writings) concerning himself.

The Breaking of the Bread　　　　　　　　　　　　　　　　　　　　　　　　Luke 24:28–35

As they approached the village, he acted as though he were going farther. But they urged him strongly, saying: "Stay with us, for it is almost evening, and the day is nearly over." So, he went in to stay with them. And as he reclined at the table with them, he took the bread, said the berakhah (blessing), broke it, and gave it to them.

Then their eyes were opened — and they recognized him — but he vanished from their sight. They said to one another, "Were not our hearts burning within us while he was speaking with us on the way, and while he opened the Scriptures to us?"

They got up that very hour and returned to Yerushalayim. There they found the eleven and those with them gathered together, saying: "It is true! Adoneinu (our lord) has risen and has appeared to Shimon (Peter)!" Then they told them what had happened on the road, and how he was made known to them in the breaking of the bread.

Yeshua Appears to the Disciples Luke 24:36–49 | John 20:19–23

That evening, while the talmidim (disciples) were gathered together, the doors were locked out of fear of the Perushim (Pharisees) and Judean authorities.

While they were still talking about these things — the report of the women, of Klefah and his companion from Amma'us — Yeshua himself suddenly stood among them and said: "Shalom aleichem (Peace be upon you)."

They were startled and frightened, thinking they were seeing a ruach (spirit). But he said to them: "Why are you troubled? And why do doubts arise in your hearts? Look at my hands and my feet — it is I myself. Touch me and see; a ruach does not have flesh and bones as you see I have."

He showed them his hands and his feet — and his side. Yet they still struggled to believe because of joy and amazement. So, he asked them: "Do you have something here to eat?" They gave him a piece of broiled fish, and he took it and ate it in their presence.

Then Yeshua said to them: "These are the words I spoke to you while I was still with you: that everything written about me in the Torah of Moshe, the Nevi'im (Prophets), and the Tehillim (Psalms) must be fulfilled."

Then he opened their minds to understand the Scriptures. He said: "Thus it is written: the Mashiach must suffer and rise from the dead on the third day, and teshuvah (repentance) and the forgiveness of sins must be proclaimed in his name to all the nations — beginning from Yerushalayim. You are my eidim (witnesses) of these things. And behold — I am sending upon you what my Father promised. But you must stay in the city until you are clothed with power from on high."

Then Yeshua breathed on them and said: "Receive the Ruach HaKodesh (Holy Spirit). If you forgive anyone's sins, they are forgiven. If you retain them, they are retained."

The Doubt of T'oma (Thomas)   John 20:24–29

At this time, T'oma (Thomas), called Didymus, was not with them. So later that evening, the other talmidim kept telling him: "We have seen the Master!"

But he replied: "Unless I see the nail marks in his hands and put my finger into the mark of the nails and put my hand into his side — I will never believe."

Eight days after Yeshua's first appearance to the other talmidim, they were again gathered together — and T'oma was with them. Though the doors were locked, Yeshua came and stood among them and said: "Shalom aleichem (Peace be upon you)."

Then he turned to T'oma and said: "Put your finger here and see my hands. Reach out your hand and put it into my side. Stop doubting and believe."

T'oma answered: "Adoni (my Master) and Elohai (my God)!"

Yeshua said to him: "Because you have seen me, you have believed. Blessed are those who have not seen and yet have believed."

The Disciples Return to the Galil   Matthew 28:16 | John 21:1–14

After Yeshua had appeared multiple times in Yerushalayim, the eleven talmidim (disciples) traveled north to the Galil, just as Yeshua had told them earlier. They came to a mountain Yeshua had designated beforehand.

Sometime during this Galilean period, seven of the disciples — Kefa (Peter), T'oma (Thomas), Netan'el (Nathanael), the sons of Zavdai (Zebedee), and two others — went out fishing on the Sea of Galil (Tiberias). They caught nothing that night.

At daybreak, a man stood on the shore and told them to cast the net on the right side. They did — and caught 153 large fish. Yochanan (John) said: "It is the Master!"

Kefa threw on his outer garment and swam to shore. Yeshua had a fire ready with fish and bread and said: "Bring some of the fish you've just caught... Come and eat."

None dared ask, "Who are you?" — they knew it was Yeshua. When they saw him, they bowed before him — though some still struggled with inner doubt.

Yeshua Restores Kefa   John 21:15–19

After they had finished eating, Yeshua turned his eyes to Shim'on Kefa, the one who had once boldly promised loyalty but had denied him three times.

He asked, gently but firmly: "Shim'on Bar Yonah, do you love me more than these?"

Kefa, startled but sincere, replied: "Yes, Master — you know that I am your friend."

Yeshua said: "Feed my lambs."

A pause lingered. Then again, Yeshua looked at him and asked: "Shim'on Bar Yonah, do you love me?"

Kefa's voice was steady, though his heart was stirring: "Yes, Master — you know I have affection for you."

Yeshua responded: "Be shepherd for my sheep."

Then, a third time — Yeshua asked: "Shim'on Bar Yonah, do you consider me a friend?"

This pierced Kefa. It echoed the shame of that terrible night. Grieved, but broken and honest, he said: "Master, you know everything. You know that I care for you."

Yeshua answered: "Feed my sheep. Amen, amen I tell you — when you were young, you dressed yourself and walked where you wished. But when you are old, you will stretch out your hands, and another will dress you and lead you where you do not wish to go."

With these words, he alluded to the kind of death by which Kefa would glorify Elohim. Then, Yeshua said simply: "Follow me."

Kefa's Question About Yochanan   John 21:20–23

Kefa turned and saw Yochanan (the disciple whom Yeshua loved) walking behind them. He asked, "Master, what about him?"

Yeshua replied: "If I want him to remain until I return, what is that to you? You — follow me."

The Great Commission   Matthew 28:18–20 | Mark 16:15–18

Then Yeshua came near and said to his talmidim (disciples): "All authority in the heavens and on the earth has been given to me. Go into all the world and proclaim the Good News to all creation. The one who believes and is immersed will be saved, but the one who does not believe will be condemned.

And these signs will accompany those who believe: In my Name they will drive out shedim (unclean spirits), they will speak in new tongues, they will pick up serpents, and if they drink anything deadly, it will not harm them. They will lay hands on the sick, and they will recover."

He also said: "Therefore, go and make talmidim (disciples) of all the nations, immersing them in the Name of the Father, and of the Son, and of the Ruach HaKodesh (Holy Spirit), teaching them to obey everything that I have commanded you. And behold — I am with you always, even to the end of the age."

Final Appearances and Teaching   Acts 1:1–5 | John 21:25

In the forty days after Yeshua's resurrection, he appeared to his talmidim many times, speaking with them about the Malchut Elohim (Kingdom of God). He gave them many convincing proofs that he was alive and taught them all that would be fulfilled.

There were many more things that Yeshua did that the world would not be able to fully record in a book. On one of those days, while eating with them, he commanded: "Do not leave Yerushalayim. Wait for the promise of the Father, which you have heard from me: For Yochanan immersed in water, but you will be immersed in the Ruach HaKodesh (Holy Spirit) not many days from now."

The Final Question and Ascension   Acts 1:6–12 | Luke 24:50–53 | Mark 16:19–20

So, they gathered and asked him: "Master, is it at this time that you are restoring the kingdom to Yisrael?"

He replied: "It is not for you to know the times or seasons that the Father has set by His own authority. But you will receive power when the Ruach HaKodesh comes upon you, and you will be my witnesses in Yerushalayim, in all Yehudah and Shomron, and to the ends of the earth."

Then Yeshua led them out of the city, up the Mount of Olives, as far as Beit-Anyah. He lifted up his hands and blessed them. And while he was blessing them, he was taken up — and a cloud received him out of their sight. He ascended into the heavens and sat down at the right hand of Elohim.

As they stood there gazing into the sky, suddenly two men in white clothing stood beside them and said: "Men of Galil, why are you standing here looking into the heavens? This same Yeshua, who has been taken from you into heaven, will come in the same way you have seen him go."

Then the talmidim bowed in worship and returned to Yerushalayim with great joy — a Sabbath day's journey from the Mount of Olives. They stayed continually in the Beit HaMikdash (Temple), praising and blessing Elohim, and went out proclaiming the Good News everywhere. And Adonai worked with them, confirming the message by the signs that accompanied them.

Witness the life of the Son of God unfold in new detail. Experience the Gospel like never before!

The Biography of the Son of God is a reverent, richly detailed harmony of the four Gospels—faithfully combined in chronological order by author and Torah teacher Moreh J. I. Roe. With every verse included, this Gospel Harmony brings the life of Yeshua of Natzeret into focus, restored to his Jewish context, voice, and mission. Through Hebraic phrasing, TaNaKh parallels, rabbinic insight, and Chassidic reflections, Moreh Roe unveils the Torah-observant teacher in the light of Scripture and tradition. Whether you are a disciple, a truth-seeker, or a student of the Bible, this harmony will take you deeper into the world of Yeshua and the faith he lived and taught.

Features

- **Full Gospel chronology from birth to resurrection**
- **Integrated TaNaKh and Talmudic references**
- **Historic context and commentary**
- **Hebraic-English phrasing with transliterated names**
- **Clear subheadings and thematic structure**

Moreh J. I. Roe is an ordained Moreh through the United Messianic Jewish Assemblies, and the founder of Beit Talmidim Ha'Derech as well as the faith-based fitness movement Faith Forged Fitness. A devoted student of Torah and Jewish tradition, Moreh Roe is passionate about restoring the Jewish identity of Yeshua and grounding his teachings in their original cultural and religious context. A follower of Yeshua since the age of five, he was raised in a Baptist home and later attended Fairwood Bible Institute in Dublin, New Hampshire, continuing his studies independently with a deep commitment to Scripture and discipleship.

www.ingramcontent.com/pod-product-compliance
Lightning Source LLC
Chambersburg PA
CBHW080411230426
43662CB00016B/2377